# UNLIKELY ALLIES IN THE ACADEMY

*Unlikely Allies in the Academy* brings the voices of women of Color and White women together for much-overdue conversations about race. These well-known contributors use narrative to expose their stories, which are at times messy and always candid. However, the contributors work through the discomfort, confusion, and frustration in order to have honest conversations about race and racism.

The narratives from Chicanas, Indigenous, Asian American, African American, and White women academicians explore our past, present, and future, what separates us, and how to communicate honestly in an effort to become allies. Chapters discuss the need to interrupt and disrupt the norms of interaction and engagement by allowing for the messiness of discomfort in frank discussion. The dialogues model how to engage in difficult dialogues about race and begin to illuminate the unspoken misunderstandings about how White women and women of Color engage one another. This valuable book offers strategies, ideas, and the hope for moving toward true alliances in the academy and for improving race relations. This important resource is for higher education administrators, faculty, and scholars grappling with the intersectionality of race and gender as they work to understand, study, and create more inclusive climates.

**Karen L. Dace** is Deputy Chancellor for Diversity, Access and Equity at the University of Missouri–Kansas City, USA.

# UNLIKELY ALLIES IN THE ACADEMY

Women of Color and
White Women in Conversation

*Edited by*
*Karen L. Dace*

 Routledge
Taylor & Francis Group

NEW YORK AND LONDON

First published 2012
by Routledge
711 Third Avenue, New York, NY 10017

Simultaneously published in the UK
by Routledge
2 Park Square, Milton Park, Abingdon, Oxon OX14 4RN

*Routledge is an imprint of the Taylor & Francis Group, an informa
business*

*Library of Congress Cataloging in Publication Data*
Unlikely allies in the academy : women of color and white women
in conversation / [edited by] Karen L. Dace.
p. cm.
Includes bibliographical references and index.
1. Women in higher education—United States. 2. Discrimination in
higher education—United States. 3. Sex differences in education—
United States. 4. Intercultural communication—United States.
5. Cultural pluralism—United States. I. Dace, Karen L.
LC1568.U55 2012
378.19822—dc23
2011044262

ISBN: 978-0-415-80903-0 (hbk)
ISBN: 978-0-415-80905-4 (pbk)
ISBN: 978-0-203-13669-0 (ebk)

Typeset in Sabon
by HWA Text and Data Management, London

# CONTENTS

*Foreword*                                                                     vii

*Preface*                                                                        x

**PART I**

**Origins, Problems, and the Need for Conversation**                             1

1   What Makes Cross-Race Alliances Unlikely?                                     3
    ANGELINA E. CASTAGNO, MARQUITA T. CHAMBLEE,
    PAMELA HUANG CHAO, KAREN L. DACE, LOUANN GERKEN,
    LIZ LECKIE, KRISTI RYUJIN, THERESA L. TORRES, MALIA VILLEGAS
    AND RACHELLE WINKLE-WAGNER

2   A White Woman Talks to White Women                                          15
    FRANCES E. KENDALL

**PART II**

**Women of Color Talk**                                                         25

3   On Friendship, Kinship, and Skinship: Healing Relationships
    between Indigenous and White Women Scholars                                 27
    MALIA VILLEGAS AND ADREANNE ORMOND

4   The Whiteness of Truth and the Presumption of Innocence                     42
    KAREN L. DACE

5   On Becoming Allies: Opportunities and Challenges in Creating
    Alliances Between White Women and Women of Color in the
    Academy                                                                     54
    MARQUITA T. CHAMBLEE

6   A Latina *Testimonio:* Challenges as an Academic, Issues of
    Difference, and a Call for Solidarity with White Female Academics           65
    THERESA L. TORRES

CONTENTS

7  What Do I Do With All of Your Tears?                                    76
   KAREN L. DACE

**PART III**
**White Women Talk**                                                      **89**

8  Too Much History Between Us                                            91
   PEGGY MCINTOSH

9  Friends in Deed, Friendship *Indeed*?                                  101
   LIZ LECKIE

10 Moments of Suspension and Other Instances of Whiteness
   in the Academy                                                         112
   ANGELINA E. CASTAGNO

11 Using Tenure as a White Woman: Speaking Truth to Power                 124
   MARYBETH GASMAN

**PART IV**
**Women of Color and White Women in Conversation**                       **135**

12 Are We There Yet? Trust, Faith, and the Power of a Common Goal         137
   KRISTI RYUJIN AND MARTHA SONNTAG BRADLEY

13 Twins Separated at Birth? Critical Moments in Cross-Race
   Mentoring Relationships                                                149
   STEPHANIE A. FRYBERG AND LOUANN GERKEN

14 Play on White: The Intimate Politics of (Be)Longing                    160
   KAREN LEE ASHCRAFT AND LISA A. FLORES

15 What's Love Got to Do with It?                                         171
   PAMELA HUANG CHAO AND ELIZABETH CASSANOS

16 Race at First Sight: The Funding of Racial Scripts Between
   Black and White Women                                                  181
   LORI D. PATTON AND RACHELLE WINKLE-WAGNER

   *Contributors*                                                         192
   *Index*                                                                194

# FOREWORD

Popular culture, especially in the area of motion pictures, is full of examples of characters saying to each other, "You don't want to hurt me" or "I don't want to hurt you" and "We just need to talk." Later, as the process becomes more problematic, the language shifts from a need to talk it out to how one "just needs to talk some sense," into the other who does not clearly understand a problem. At this point in the interaction emotions are high, hurt feelings and dissonance override the process, resulting in, as best articulated in the late 1960s motion picture *Cool Hand Luke*, "What we got here is ... failure to communicate."

This breakdown or failure to communicate, especially between women of Color and White women, has spread and can be seen throughout society, particularly within the walls of higher education. Within the academy there have been calls for forums, conventions, seminars, summits and all matter of discussions and dialogue to address the divide between White women and women of Color with little progress. What is clear is that the problem has particularly deep roots in America—articulated through evidently held truths about the equality of *all* men accompanied by the exclusion of everyone who is not white and male. What has not yet successfully occurred is, at least until now, the taking up of the challenge raised by Gloria Anzaldúa (1990) and Audre Lorde (1984) for a real dialogue about what separates White women and women of Color, and prevents honest communication and alliance building.

Communication and dialogue are confounded because our histories and role in the system have remained invisible and the very nature of the act, conversation, is driven by the rules of a system not designed to foster a sense of inclusion or connection to each other. As a quick example, how do we decide tenure? Is it based on each individual's merit or some previously constructed standard that each individual is forced to follow and measure up to, called the norm? Is the process as open as we would like to claim or are our systematic histories invisibly working through us during the process, which, later, all can deny?

What makes conversation, real conversation, important and significant is the potential for individual connection on issues and topics of mutual concern, and the life-long bonding that occurs. The conversations that come to mind here are not those guarded, intellectually sterile, theoretically bound, perspective taking, ego and professional status affirming conversations that occur across the country on a daily basis at academic gatherings or conventions on and off the public and private campuses of America. The conversation referred to here is the kind of deep exploration of real issues and their impact on the individual, community and even sometimes the immediate world. These conversations can only be heard around tables or circles of women who share a common history and experience. These real conversations, for outsiders or those who do not recognize the ground rules and group dynamic, could be described as simplistic, dysfunctional or easy exchanges. Such evaluations miss the raw passion, philosophical and intellectual depth, life affirmation, and spiritual feeding present during these dialogues. Traditionally, these conversations are restricted to segregated gatherings—communities of majority or non-majority women. Anyone who has been blessed or privileged to be present as an observer of one of these circles learns lessons that last a lifetime. More than wisdom and intellect are exchanged. The dialogue includes the sharing of experiences and history, the "living it," "fighting the good fight" and coming out with one's sanity and soul intact. It is this showing and telling, the fleshing out of words, lives, experiences that connect the speakers. For those willing to "hear," this book will be profoundly significant. The "conversations" presented have a raw side and include questions and comments, the vulnerabilities associated with sharing personal tales that lead to painful disclosures and private revelations, or flat-out disagreements that put the timid to flight. Yet, in the end bitter challenge and confrontation become sweet (perhaps bittersweet) resolution. A deep personal connection between people who may not agree but who see, share, hear and understand, and most importantly, do not judge, emerges.

In many ways *Unlikely Allies in the Academy: Women of Color and White Women in Conversation* is one of these talking circles. Although it is not an immediate and direct response to the call for a dialogue or conversation raised by Lorde and Anzaldúa it was born out of those calls and the failure of the dialogue to take hold. In fact, the text grew out of a series of discussions about the challenges associated with creating alliances between women of Color and White women. The first chapter, "What Makes Cross-Race Alliances Unlikely," is an ongoing conversation. Still, the reader is able to grasp the complexity and depth of the problem because, like each chapter of this text, one is taken inside the conversation to a place where history and experience inform, rather than hinder understanding. We are afforded an opportunity to see, hear, feel and thus comprehend what has kept us separate for so long. From the position of one seated in the circle, a White woman, Frances Kendall, instructs other White women to pay attention to the preceding and following essays for their own benefit and growth. As others in the text point out, one problem, for White women, is their unwillingness to honestly acknowledge their privilege while simultaneously acting upon it freely. Another concern is their participation in sterile dialogues about race when anything more challenging appears too difficult.

With the foundation laid in Part I, we are prepared to listen, learn and engage as women of Color and White women "talk" about their experiences in Parts II and III, respectively. Both groups come together in the final section offering us the opportunity to "hear" about successful, if hard-fought and painfully created, alliances and friendships across race. Here the conversations come full circle and the power of dialogue becomes clear. Authors directly exhibit not only the required courage for dialogue, they show and develop ways to embrace and learn from the past, providing examples of engaging challenging, risky and frightening discussions and relationships across race.

Ideally one might define dialogue as an exchange of ideas or opinions on a particular issue, especially a political or religious issue, with a view to reaching an amicable agreement or settlement. This project, however, is not about ideal dialogues, or about being nice, safe or amicable, it is about the very real and the difficult. As this text shows, effective communication on issues of this magnitude requires us to look at the past and current state of affairs—the challenges associated with cross-race alliances between women of Color and White women. The brave contributors to this project expose what separates women of Color and White women in the academy. They take this discussion a step further, doing the heavy lifting of communicating honestly and directly with the goals of, at least, mutual understanding. Women of Color and White women are provided an opportunity and may, following the lead provided here, move from unlikely to probable allies working together to make the system inclusive. Whether this will happen remains to be seen.

Ronald B. Scott
*Associate Professor in the Department of Communication*
*Associate Vice President for Institutional Diversity*
*Miami University*

## References

Anzaldúa, G. (1990). La conciencia de la mestiza / Towards a new consciousness. In G. Anzaldúa (Ed.), *Making Face, Making Soul* (pp. 377–389). San Francisco: Aunt Lute Books.

Lorde, A. (1984). *Sister Outsider*. Freedom, CA: The Crossing Press.

# PREFACE

This letter has been delayed because of my grave reluctance to reach out to you, for what I want us to chew upon here is neither easy nor simple.

(Audre Lorde, *Sister Outsider*, 1984, p. 66)

This letter attempts to break a silence which I had imposed upon myself ... I had decided never again to speak to white women about racism. I felt it was wasted energy because of destructive guilt and defensiveness, and because whatever I had to say might better be said by white women to one another at far less emotional cost to the speaker, and probably with a better hearing. But I would like not to destroy you in my consciousness, not to have to.

(Audre Lorde, *Sister Outsider*, 1984, pp. 70–71)[1]

Audre Lorde's open letter to Mary Daly resonates throughout the essays that follow. Women of Color and White women have much to "chew upon" as we continue a discussion about race and gender that has had many starts (some of them false), a number of interruptions, delays, postponements and, for many, remains incomplete and inadequate. *Unlikely Allies in the Academy* is an "attempt to break a silence" many of us have imposed upon ourselves or have had imposed upon us by others. For a number of years, perhaps as many as 20, I have been making notes, saving messages, letters, thoughts and memories of encounters and engaging in conversations with other women of Color and progressive White women about the status of cross-race relationships. Often, at the end of a particularly painful tale of the treatment suffered at the hands of White women, some women of Color I know utter the statement "that's why we can't be friends." It is not that we are pining away on predominantly white campuses in hopes of becoming friends with White women. Most of us do indeed enjoy such relationships. Rather, this statement has served as an empowering affirmation about the ability of women of Color to choose our friends in an environment in which we may not be able to select our co-workers, colleagues, bosses and officemates.

My early imaginations of this book gave it the title "Why We Can't Be Friends." After a conversation with Peggy McIntosh, I agreed the title "Why

We Can't 'Just' Be Friends" better portrayed the intent. Further discussion revealed an even more appropriate title. Bringing together the voices of women of Color and progressive White women, revealed a reality for some and possibilities for others—alliances across race. For there are cross-race alliances between White women and women of Color on some college campuses. And there are women who desire a better understanding of the obstacles that prevent them, others who have managed to break down those barriers and many occupying the spaces somewhere in between. This book is for all of those who want to move beyond the "we can't just be friends" to "how do I make this cross-race alliance work for all of us?" To that end, we open with a dialogue between women of Color and White women about the barriers to creating these alliances and their hopes for this project and what could be called "an open letter to White women" written by a White woman about the importance of this work and their attention to it. That sets the stage for essays written by women of Color about the many challenges they face in their day-to-day interactions with White women in Part II. In Part III, White women discuss their own experiences in creating cross-race alliances—the successes, failures, challenges and frustrations with themselves, other Whites and, sometimes, people of Color. Finally, in Part IV the cross-race alliance is addressed in four very different essays co-authored by women of Color and White women who have successfully navigated these waters, moved from adversaries to advocates and allies, are questioning the apparent "ease" of their relationship or are involved in the study of such interactions.

I acknowledge White women like Peggy and Francie Kendall for their encouragement. Although the idea of the book was ever present, it was not until Francie invited me to participate on a panel during her one-day workshop on the role of White women in supporting racism on university campuses at the 2009 National Conference on Race and Ethnicity in Higher Education in San Diego that I finally decided to move forward. In fact, all of the panelists from that session contributed to this project—Marquita Chamblee, Pamela Chao, Liz Leckie and Ron Scott. Francie is here too, along with Peggy McIntosh who, from her front row seat, made some valuable contributions to our discussion. During that session, I read what I called "An Open Letter to White Women" in which I listed with vivid description an assortment of "crimes" perpetrated by White women against people of Color. I wasn't sure how that letter would be received as I "held no punches." Add to that the fact that I had to literally run from the room to catch a plane, I felt I missed the post-discussion processing. However, I ran in to two White women at the airport who thanked me for the letter and encouraged me to publish what I shared during the meeting. This project is an attempt to do just that. Like Audre Lorde, "I would like not to destroy" White women "in my consciousness, not to have to." There are, after all, examples of courageous White women who believe in and are willing to add their voices (and pens) to the struggle for social justice for everyone. Some of them are represented in this book. They join forces with women of Color who, once again, openly share their disappointments and successes in working with White women—the progressive, not so progressive, and those occupying the spaces in between. Working across race with other women requires all of the attributes Papusa Molina[2] identifies, with "our rebellious spirits and sense of justice" leading the way.

## Notes

1 Taken from Audre Lorde's "An Open Letter to Mary Daly" in *Sister Outsider* (pp. 66–71). Freedom, CA: The Crossing Press.
2 Papusa Molina's essay "Recognizing, Accepting and Celebrating Our Differences" appears in Gloria Anzaldúa's (1990) *Making Face, Making Soul* (pp. 326–321). San Francisco: Aunt Lute Books.

# Part I

# ORIGINS, PROBLEMS, AND THE NEED FOR CONVERSATION

# 1

# WHAT MAKES CROSS-RACE ALLIANCES UNLIKELY?

*Angelina E. Castagno*
*Marquita T. Chamblee*
*Pamela Huang Chao*
*Karen L. Dace*
*LouAnn Gerken*
*Liz Leckie*
*Kristi Ryujin*
*Theresa L. Torres*
*Malia Villegas*
*Rachelle Winkle-Wagner*

This project grew out of a number of discussions, some heated, others humorous, many frustrating, about the challenges associated with cross-race alliances between women of Color and White women. What follows is a discussion between five women of Color (two Asian Americans, Pamela Chao and Kristi Ryujin; an African American, Marquita Chamblee; an Indigenous woman, Malia Villegas, and a Latina/Chicana, Theresa Torres) and four White women (Angelina Castagno, LouAnn Gerken, Liz Leckie and Rachelle Winkle-Wagner) in conversation about the status of cross-race relations between women, challenges associated with creating alliances across race and their hopes for this project.

**Decades ago Audre Lorde and Gloria Anzaldúa called for women of Color and White women to gather the courage required to have a real dialogue in an effort to become allies. How have women in the academy responded to this call? How do you characterize the relationships between women of Color and White women in the academy?**

**Pamela Chao:** As women in the academy, we have been trained to value our intellect. Yet intellect is insufficient and we too often remain stymied, frustrated and puzzled in our efforts to have conversations about difference and understand the nature of alliances. In addition, the academic information and knowledge our intellect is honed upon is often incomplete and biased toward dominant group superiority. Successful dialogue and alliances occur when we bring emotion and heart with honest knowledge of ourselves and of the systemic nature of oppression–which includes the exploration of the oppressions we embrace and internalize to become part of the academy. I do believe that there are small committed groups who have carved space outside of the day-to-day routine of the academy to have sustained, difficult conversations that are the foundation for seeding institutional change. More commonly, we might come together to build programs or discuss papers or put on a conference, but I have not seen most of our attempts to be longitudinally or radically successful.

**Theresa Torres:** As a Latina/Chicana, I have to admit the distance between women of Color and White women remains significant. While I am a junior scholar ready to complete the tenure process to become an associate professor, I am older than the majority of junior scholars since I changed careers in my forties. My experiences with making allies with White women inside and outside of the academy have not been very promising. My main allies have been other women of Color.

**Pamela Chao:** I think it is difficult to generalize across all women of Color and White women in the academy. As I think about my own experiences and those with which I'm familiar, I see a range of relationships. I think some of us have taken Lorde's and Anzaldúa's call seriously and are engaged in the kind of dialogue they envision, and I think some of us have not.

**Angelina Castagno:** I am somewhat conflicted by this notion of dialogue. On the one hand, I understand the need for it. On the other hand, I am perhaps more concerned about the *work* that needs to be done within the academy by women in the academy. I realize work cannot be engaged without dialogue, but I feel too often we stop at the dialogue, or get stuck in the dialogue, so that we never get to the real work. I also believe dialogue is a safe space for many White women. We have gotten to a place where we can talk with our colleagues, allies and sisters; but we do not push beyond that dialogue to actually *do* things with our hands, our heads, our writing, our teaching, our committee work—things that will make an actual difference for women, people of Color, students, staff, faculty, people both inside and outside the academy.

**Are alliances between women of Color and White women important in the academy? Why?**

**LouAnn Gerken:** These alliances are important, because they potentially give women from both groups perspective on their particular experiences. Both White women and women of Color are relatively new to the academy, both have been admitted in part due to social justice campaigns of the 1960s, and both continue to have uneasy relations with White men, who are the original inhabitants of the academy. Nevertheless, White women and women of Color have different relations with White men, at least outside of the academy, and these differences, coupled with other social and cultural differences, cause White women and women of Color to experience their minority status differently. Working to understand these differences as both groups of women ally to solidify their place in the academy can be enlightening.

**Pamela Chao:** Alliances between women of Color and White women are critical if we accept that the academy is an institution that generates knowledge to empower and enrich the lives of all people in our societies and should include those who have historically been excluded from education. These alliances are core to the notion that we live in a world that includes people who are different. It is in a conscious and principled cooperation that individuals can unite and create enough leverage to change an institution. If we don't have alliances in the academy, where can we truly interact with each other to test the ways in which the institutionalized "isms" are internalized in us as well as operating in the organization?

**Angelina Castagno:** Absolutely. Alliances between all kinds of groups of people are important because there are just too many opportunities for the institution to suck people in. However, like dialogue, I think alliances are not enough. I fear sometimes that White women become satisfied and comfortable with friendships and alliances with women of Color. If we tell ourselves that alliances are the goal, we may never put those alliances to work to create the kind of change that we need to see in the academy.

**What makes these alliances unlikely?**

**LouAnn Gerken:** The differences (relations to White men, social and cultural background) that potentially provide perspective are hard to overcome, partly because they are hard to identify without having been trained to look for them, and partly because they are hard to talk about once they've been identified. In addition, in many academic departments, White women are much less of a minority than women of Color. This asymmetry might make the need for cross-racial allies among women of Color stronger than the same need for most White women. The asymmetry in need for allies can feel unfair.

**Pamela Chao:** Regardless of the commitment and intent of the women in the academy who may engage in conversations about social justice, creation of knowledge or educating our students, given the social structure in which we operate, it becomes very difficult to break free of the hierarchical values and rewards. We are not separate from the academy and society, we are a part of them and they are part of who we are.

**Angelina Castagno:** Building alliances is hard work; it takes time, energy and commitment. Everyone is spread thin and the current context in higher education of shrinking budgets, increased bureaucracy and an exploding market mentality only intensify the workload and anxiety about our jobs. In this climate, it is even more difficult to carve out the space needed to build and nurture relationships.

I think many White women are unable, unwilling and perhaps unknowledgeable about how to build and nurture alliances with women of Color. Some of us may be nervous about what our role is, anxious about entering new and unfamiliar spaces, or fearful of saying and doing the "wrong" thing. It is easier to stay where we are comfortable and assume that we aren't needed or wanted and that someone else will do the work that needs to be done.

I also think many women of Color have become weary of alliances across race and gender. Unfortunately, those of us in privileged positions sometimes engage alliances when it is convenient for us or somehow advantageous for us; and when the convenience and advantage wanes, so too does our commitment to the alliance.

**Theresa Torres:** I believe that women on both sides of the color line need to change. For women of Color, we need to be resilient and give White women opportunities for change and not to hold on to past wounds and experiences that have separated us. We must be willing to heal, open to the new opportunities for alliances, and patient as we challenge White women and have the creative imaginations that allow us to move forward together. I believe the burden of the alliance has always tended to fall on women of Color and that is tiring. I believe some women of Color, those of us who are aware of these challenges, decide that this burden is too exhausting since we have so many other challenges like tenure requirements that generally are not the same for women of Color, few mentors so we have to create support systems for ourselves within the university, being mentors for others, particularly students of Color, greater community service requirements since we have a responsibility to give back to those who have helped us. Some of us are just too tired to deal with the hard work of forging alliances.

**Rachelle Winkle-Wagner:** These conversations are sometimes painful for both White women and women of Color. Sometimes the dialogue is embarrassing and downright troubling, particularly for White women as we face some of the troubled racial history in the country and our own lives. In my experience, women of Color have not had the privilege of ignoring this in the way White women have.

There are also social forces that make it more difficult to create alliances. As we forge friendships and collegial relationships, do people in our own racialized groups support it? That is, as women of Color and White women make meaningful relationships, it seems that sometimes they risk losing the support of those in their own racial group. Additionally, I believe there are times when we have experiences that reinforce our separation. For instance, if a relationship is risked and it does not go well, it makes it that much harder the next time. So, we all carry the baggage of our past relationships-gone-wrong with us and we bring this into our new interactions.

**Do the responsibilities for creating a meaningful dialogue differ for women of Color and White women?**

**Pamela Chao:** I believe the responsibilities of those who are dominant and those who are subordinate are different because, structurally, those who are dominant gain their advantages from the disadvantages experienced by other groups. Those who are dominant are responsible for acknowledging that they systemically benefit from their dominance. At the same time, it is important that they do not seek personal forgiveness/approval from women of Color. The historical, economic, political and legal advantages attached to whiteness in the United States, and the ability to stand racially with White men belong uniquely to White women and thus White women also need to take the initiative to gather with and learn from other White women and men and to carry other White people along with them in the process.

Women of Color are responsible to examine their sources of empowerment and places of accountability. We must also challenge ourselves to heal and find ways to interact across boundaries when we have been hurt by this interaction and it triggers inexplicable emotions and reactions for us to do so.

**LouAnn Gerken:** I'm not sure if the responsibilities of women of Color and White women are different in such discussions. But the two groups probably need to be prepared for different kinds of pain in sharing their assumptions about the foundations of the academy. White women may need to be prepared to feel more racist than they thought they were. Women of Color may need to be prepared to question the possibility of any cross-racial allies and thereby feel more isolated. Both groups of women need to be responsible to talk about and talk through the pain and to agree how the discussion should continue or if it should end.

**Marquita Chamblee:** Women of Color and White women bear different responsibilities for engaging in these conversations. White women have to be willing to really engage the issues and be prepared to do some hard, painful excavation of race and class privilege. They have to be willing to move from cerebral analyses of the issues to heart-rending, gut-wrenching, messy emotional experiences. They need to be prepared to hear some hard, unpleasant truths and be willing to sit with discomfort and pain.

Women of Color also need to come prepared to work on some of "our stuff" about White women and about ourselves as women of Color. We need to explore the extent to which we've internalized and bought into the systems that separate and pit us against one another. We also have to be willing to, once again, take on some teaching roles in helping White women come to a clearer understanding of how the systems of oppression work and the roles they (and we) play in keeping them in place.

**When many of our colleagues learned about this project they called it important, necessary and brave. Some even referred to it as potentially daring and risky. How do you make sense of these statements?**

**Pamela Chao:** In working on this project, the conversations I have had with friends about this book were not much different than the conversations I would normally have with my friends if I weren't working on this book. So in many ways, it doesn't feel brave or daring or risky. However, sharing these thoughts with strangers and people who may not see the link between institutional structures, culture, and individual behavior changes the emotion attached. It does feel vulnerable.

It is important to have a space to talk, read, think about racism and how women of Color and White women can come together. I worry that others do not understand the history and the institutional underpinnings of all of our individual and psychological responses to race and gender. I am concerned that when I talk about racism as a system of advantage based on whiteness in the United States, many readers will not understand its far-reaching historical, political and legal foundations and reduce it to an individual experience of racial identity. If people are not able to understand or hear the institutional nature of the inequality and hierarchy imbedded in our society then I fear they will turn off and stop considering the issues involved. Historically, the consequences for women of Color who talk about racism have included loss of friends and relationships, jobs, homes, dignity, and even their lives. Society sanctions those who challenge the norms. Rather than worry about the risks, I want be hopeful about the conversations and alliances that may grow because of this project.

**Liz Leckie:** My initial reaction is that this project is not as risky or daring for White women. I believe this because in my experiences as a White woman who speaks about race, I am often congratulated or condoned for my efforts when my female colleagues of Color who speak about race are condemned. Occasionally, I have felt alienation and heard the mean things that my colleagues have said about me behind my back or sometimes to my face. Still, part of me has learned to wear these honorable badges as proof of my efforts that I am doing "the right thing." I have never lost a job, been written up for insubordination, called into my boss' office and told to "play nice" or had my integrity questioned—all things that I know have happened to my female friends of Color in the academy.

But when I think about this further, it is a lie to say that I do not feel this project is risky. The fact is that I have hidden it from a number of people in my life. I have not discussed it with my boss, I have not told most of my work colleagues, and I did not share it with my mother before her passing. When I think about the number of people that I have actually talked to about this project outside of the women who are working on it, the list is quite small. Unlike other projects that I work on in the academy that I share openly and listen to others' opinions about, I have not invited the same feedback about this work.

When I get honest, I do fear some of the reactions that I may hear if I share this work. I do not want to argue with people about "how far we have come" or try to answer questions about if I think this book is really relevant today. I am not interested in receiving White women's unsolicited histories about their relationships with women of Color or White women's accounts about the ways that women of Color make it too difficult to be friends. I did not want to risk having the recurring fight with my mom about my choices to study and write about white supremacy and racism. I have taken the less courageous road and, for the most part, kept quiet. So, I am not sure what others are referring to as daring or risky but for this White woman this work has a level of personal risk of which I am cautious—perhaps too cautious.

**What do you hope women of Color will take from this book?**

**Malia Villegas:** My hope is that women of Color will come to know that so many of the painful and frustrating experiences they have with their White women colleagues are not about them—that women of Color will no longer question their brilliance, capabilities, insights, instincts or power when confronted with the interests of White women who have not dealt with their privilege or responsibilities. While I hope this book will help us as women of Color recognize that we are not alone in these experiences, the goal is not merely "misery loves company." Instead, we aim to work towards theorizing our experiences in order to become more active agents in our relationships with White women colleagues rather than objects of their professional development. I also hope that this work can help us heal our relationships with each other by exposing the institutional contexts and interpersonal dynamics that shape how we understand ourselves as scholars, as women and as people of Color. These contexts and dynamics impact our relationships with White women, but they also impact our relationships with each other. This project provides an opportunity to explore the nature of race relationships, friendship and collegiality in ways that may guide us in reflecting on what *we* want in our professional relationships with other women, including other women of Color. In this vein, I hope that women of Color readers appreciate the range of ways we experience our relationships with White women and the various approaches to dealing with them as reflective of a broad sisterhood with a deep sense of responsibility to one another on this journey. In the same way that when you are feeling daunted by an overwhelming task, all it takes is a sister to come along rolling up her sleeves, turning on your favorite radio station and jamming with you until it is done, we offer this volume to our sisters around the world as a way of saying, we have been there, we will be there again, but we will be there together until it is done.

**Rachelle Winkle-Wagner:** Hope. I wish for this project that women of Color may see some glimmers of hope that there *are* White women who care about creating alliances so that we all can become allies. There are White women who have committed their research, work and lives to working for racial justice. There are White women who are willing to begin the process of doing the hard work to confront the difficult history that separates us. And there are ways that we can become allies together.

**Pamela Chao:** I hope that women of Color will look at our very complex identities and find places where we can embrace our "intersections" or "borderlands" in ways that are not the traditional binaries. I also hope that women of Color will take away increased awareness of internalized oppression, how we participate in the oppression of other people of Color and how it drives who we are and what we choose to do. Emotionally, I hope women of Color take away more insight into our own empathy and capacity to receive and give love. Structurally, I hope women of Color take away a more complete story of our history that will give more meaning and explanation to the experiences of today. And, I hope more connections are forged through conversation and interaction between women of Color.

**Marquita Chamblee:** I hope that women of Color will see themselves and their struggles in this book, but also gain insights and tools for understanding how we (as well as White women) function in a system that is not set up for us. I want us to understand that the system of white male supremacy can deeply affect our relationships with one another as women of Color. I believe the system can pit women of Color against one another, as well as put us in opposition to White women. My hope is that in looking at how to create meaningful relationships with White women, we are also continuing to explore how to strengthen relationships among women of Color both across and within our various racial/ethnic identities.

**Theresa Torres:** I hope that women of Color will still be hopeful and willing to try one more time …

**What do you hope White women will take from this book?**

**Marquita Chamblee:** I hope White women will come away from this wanting to engage in meaningful conversation and action in building alliances with women of Color and other White women who are doing this work. I hope they can put down any defensiveness or denial ("They're not talking about me") that comes up and take an honest look at where they contribute to the system of white supremacy that is rife in the academy. I hope they can see potential benefits of building alliances with women of Color, not *against* White men, but *for* the advancement and support of women across academia.

I hope White women will begin to ask questions of themselves and then begin to challenge one another with the idea that doing this work is valuable, important and right. And I further hope that White women who are already doing this work can put aside any competitive instincts they might have with other White women and work with one another for the good of us all. Sometimes I think White antiracist activists spend time either talking amongst themselves or competing with one another and miss opportunities to genuinely connect with people of Color around issues that matter. I want the White women reading this book to be able not just to learn how to collaborate and ally with women of Color, but also to learn to work effectively with other White women.

**Malia Villegas:** I hope this book serves as a mirror to White women, enabling them to see themselves as they are experienced by women of Color. Healing our relationships requires that White women engage in deep self-reflection about their racialization, privilege and ontology in the academy. In saying this, there are two key points I want to be sure to emphasize here. First, the work that needs to be done here is not that of women of Color, it is White women's responsibility. Second, there is not a checklist of "things to do" as so much of what is needed is a willingness to engage in a process of self-discovery with themselves and with one another. It is not important for me that White women feel guilt about any of this; instead, I want them to identify the strengths and limitations that being a White woman scholar

11

brings to professional relationships with women of Color and to the work they do in the academy. As such, I want to say to White women: there is importance in simultaneously acknowledging your power and de-centering yourself because it is not always about you and your interests. While there has been a lot of respect lost for you through time and experience, it does not behoove us to disrespect you in turn. As such there is anger, pain, disappointment and a lot of sadness in these pages; but I hope that you know that there is also a great deal of love, humor, truth and a deep abiding faith in the power of women to see each other through this place in a way that will make it better for those who come behind us.

**Rachelle Winkle-Wagner:** Hope. Beyond a history that separates us, I wish for White women to see the way that all of us are connected. One group cannot be kept down without all of us being disparaged. There is hope for the future that White women will stop competing with women of Color for attention or for equality. While we must understand our differences and the history that has separated us, there is hope that White women can be part of the solution, part of the process.

**Theresa Torres:** I hope that White women will do the hard work of listening and challenging themselves and others to acknowledge and address the racism and uneven playing fields that exist within the academy and society.

**Liz Leckie:** My hope is that White women learn some useful and practical ways to remedy the ways white supremacy manifests in our lives and in particular in our relationships with women of Color in the academy. Also, I hope White women will realize how they have participated to keep women of Color marginalized and excluded. They may read stories that remind them of their own failings. My hope is that when these realizations happen, they keep reading not only the pages of this book but others that will help them learn. I hope that they consider how we are all important to the process of change. As White women, if we do not listen, learn and educate, we can become barriers in the process.

**Kristi Ryujin:** I fluctuate in my answer to this question depending on the day. On days when I experience the common White woman, unaware of her privilege and dependency on a system that oppresses us all, I have no hope that White women will take anything away from this book. On those days, I am certain White women will not be reading anything that I believe is essential to my survival or their own.

But then I have an uncommon day, a day when a White woman will "show up," do and say the right thing—not because she thinks she is *helping* us, but because she has a real understanding of the issues operating in the academy.

I hope these White women read this book looking for opportunities to build more relationships and I don't mean friendships. If it comes to that, great, but I don't need friends—I need allies. I need White women who are really committed to issues of equity—fundamentally committed, get it to the core, have done their own work and are ready to challenge the status quo. Lastly, I think this book is full of stories, experiences, theories where White women have figured it out, where ideas have been shared, where theory has been explained. Like a good cook, I hope you see these "recipes" not as something to be copied, but explored, deconstructed, reconstructed and made to fit your own work toward social justice.

## Where Do We Go From Here?

The women of Color and White women who have agreed to contribute to the proposed book are not intimidated by the potential for challenge, discomfort, confusion, hurt feelings and "messiness" (Uttal, 1990) that results from conversations about race and racism:

> Our shared efforts to figure out the differences make us feel closer to women whom we each initially perceived as "others." There is a genuine commitment to work through the confusion no matter how much time it takes. It comes in the form of questions, hurt feelings, taking sides, feeling frustrated, and "aha, so that's what you mean. Okay" expressions. It doesn't always work out. Sometimes we stop with hurt feelings. But just as frequently we plow through the confusion as a group, putting ideas in order and creating a shared picture which we can all see. And all of this is possible because disagreements and confusion are not received as invalidation of our individual ideas. (p. 319)

As the discussants note, creating alliances and dialogue across race can be intimidating, time consuming, emotionally draining and potentially risky. Each of the following chapters is written by women who have counted the costs—of either working through the messiness to arrive at an "expected end" or remaining on the sidelines, avoiding difficult conversations. The latter option is described well in Kathryn Stockett's (2009) novel *The Help*. One of the African American characters, Aibileen, describes a conversation with her boss, a White woman, Mrs. Leefolt:

> My face goes hot, my tongue twitchy. I don't know what to say to her. All I know is, I ain't saying it. And I know she ain't saying what she want [to] say either and it's a strange thing happening here cause nobody saying nothing and we still managing to have us a conversation. (p. 35)

For far too long, women of Color and White women have participated in conversations where both have volumes to convey yet, for a number of reasons, what needs to be said remains unspoken. *Unlikely Allies in the Academy: Women of Color and White Women in Conversation* is an attempt to have those conversations in which women muster the courage to communicate clearly and honestly in hope that alliances between them will not be as unlikely as they have been in the past.

## References

Stockett, K. (2009). *The Help*. New York: Penguin.
Uttal, L. (1990). Nods that silence. In G. Anzaldúa (Ed.), *Making Face, Making Soul* (pp. 317–320). San Francisco: Aunt Lute Books.

# 2

# A WHITE WOMAN TALKS
# TO WHITE WOMEN[1]

## *Frances E. Kendall*

For the past 40 years I have consulted with predominantly white colleges and universities that were attempting to create hospitable climates for the faculty and students of Color they were bringing into the schools. Some schools have made changes in obvious ways: creating racially-based student clubs, beginning to serve ethnic foods in the dining halls, setting up ethnic studies programs and developing more inclusive curriculums. Yet those of us who are attempting to bring about institutional and interpersonal change continue to run up against unyielding resistance in every area of the institution and across all groups of stakeholders. To offer another way of moving ahead, this book shows genuine conversations about and across racial experiences.

Like all the authors included in *Unlikely Allies in the Academy: Women of Color and White Women in Conversation*, I am clear that we White women are swimming upstream. What causes White women to close their eyes to the experiences of women of Color? Do we not want to lose our image of ourselves as good people? Is it that seeing the treatment that many women of Color face would require us to act? Are we comfortable with our lives and do we know that speaking up to the White men in charge would not only jeopardize our jobs but also our relationships with them?

We are in frightening financial times; many people and institutions are dealing with fewer resources than they ever imagined. In fear of scarcity we contract our hearts and hunker down. "Work is hard enough without being involved in more staff development on diversity," I can hear a White woman say. "My personal and emotional resources are stretched to the limit." "I don't want to feel anything more and particularly not guilt!" "Why should I invest myself in other people? I can barely take care of myself."

Expecting that only some of us will survive, and so pitting ourselves against and undercutting one another, means that work becomes more stressful. People draw hard circles around themselves to try to protect their own. Racism and bigotry are rampant; there are new or pending laws in several states aimed at Latinos who have been dubbed "illegal aliens," thus removing them from humanity and from due process. One of the

15

main issues—their access to post-secondary education—is played out on college and university campuses, seriously injuring the climate of those institutions.

As one way to deal with this fear and contraction, I invite White women to listen to the voices in this book. We have an opportunity that we are not frequently offered: to witness the experiences of women of Color as they interact with White women in the academy. The words, feelings and experiences may be painful or shocking. However, the stories are told in the hope that things will change, that White women will hear how what we do affects the lives of women of Color, will reflect on what they learn, and will act to change both their thinking and behavior. Speaking about similar experiences of hearing truth from women of Color, my colleague Leslie Setlock said recently, "[I] have had many similar bubble-popping conversations. In my opinion, while they certainly aren't pleasant, they are necessary. We need to put on our big-girl panties and work through it."

I believe that most of us want to do the right thing, but we don't know what that is. Without crucibles—"transformative experience[s] through which an individual comes to a new or altered sense of identity"[2] (Bennis & Thomas, 2002, p. 40)—we maintain our distance. We often feel that race doesn't pertain to us: "We're all part of the same race, the human race." We don't see ourselves as part of the problem, and therefore we don't feel responsibility to be part of the solution. The stories in this book provide potential crucibles.

In order to use the following chapters to help build real interactions based on more complete awareness of our racialized lives, we must recognize that women of Color and White women experience largely different realities. For example, an August 2003 Bureau of Justice Statistics study predicts that 32 percent of African American boys born in 2001 can expect to spend some time in prison during their lifetimes as opposed to 5.9 percent of White boys born in the same year. To deal with this, most mothers of African American boys train their sons when they are in public—stores, on the street, driving a car, on the subway—always to keep their hands visible. White mothers don't have to do that.

We all exist in institutionalized systems of the supremacy of whiteness. These systems were built and are maintained to benefit those of us who are White. Thus it is essential that we know ourselves and how being White affects our lives; know our histories and how they affect our present-day behavior; identify ways in which we collude with the systems of the supremacy of whiteness; and change our behavior, remembering that we do it *for ourselves*, not to look good to others.

What does it mean to know ourselves? In the context of creating alliances with women of Color and with other White people regarding the issues of race, knowing ourselves requires us first to identify ourselves as White.

Over the years many women of Color, particularly African Americans and Latinas, have told me that White women are their greatest barrier to success. That's because in most schools and universities White women have a high percentage of middle management jobs—assistant professors, assistant vice presidents, vice chancellors, assistant deans and so on. While White men hold the ultimate power, women of Color have to move through the White women to get to the senior positions, and, most often, White women hire other White women or White men to fill mid-level positions, rather than promoting the women of Color. In many instances, the women of Color are the ones who trained the White woman or man who eventually gets the job. Here's an example I heard from one of my colleagues. "A Black woman with a master's degree who has served as an organizational development consultant and management coach has been overlooked for promotions and awards. This has gone on for years despite the recognition her group received as a result of her work and the praise her management clients have given her. Meanwhile, a White woman with less education, who has played a role with no visibility or interaction with client groups, was given a promotion, a raise and recognition for outstanding work by the Black woman's White female boss."

Because we are White we are able to do thoughtless or foolish things that negatively affect women of Color, and we are not held accountable for them. If the woman complains, she is seen as a whiner or "too sensitive." The women of Color describe invasive and infantilizing behavior like asking a Black woman if it's okay to touch her hair. The White woman probably thinks she is being friendly, getting to know the other woman. "That's how you learn about differences, right?" There is no way a Black woman can object that wouldn't come back to haunt her.

Generally White women in academic settings think of themselves as collegial and welcoming. And some tell stories about how standoffish women of Color have been to them and how they are obsessed with issues of race. "They seem so angry. I really don't know what to do." Others work to make women of Color feel comfortable, but they make thoughtless comments like "the manager works us like slaves here" or "I don't know what to call you because you're always changing it. Are you an Hispanic or a Latino or a Mexican?"

Women from all groups of Color describe unrelenting micro-aggressions by many White women such as questioning whether a given incident was *really* about race rather than simply accepting their perceptions; introducing a woman of Color only by her name and the White woman standing next to her by her name and title; dismissing the comments or even the presence of women of Color: "Oh, Juana, I forgot you're here." Repeatedly I hear about patterns of behavior like planning a meeting, changing the time, and "forgetting" to inform the woman of Color so that she either arrives late for the meeting or misses it altogether. This reinforces the stereotype of Black and Latino people always being late. If the stereotype were not so widely known, I might not be so sure that this "forgetting" is actually passive-aggressive. As more staff and faculty of Color join an institution, the frequency and mean-spiritedness of these comments and actions increase; perhaps some White people are threatened by having to accept growing numbers of people of Color as their equals.

Most White women are shocked when I tell them that many women of Color see us as the enemy. This reaction is particularly true of women who pride themselves on being liberal and well-meaning. They become defensive, even resentful. "I've done my best. I've bent over backwards. There's nothing else I can do." Clearly built in to that response is the feeling that the White woman is being welcoming out of the goodness of her heart to "help" this person of Color. Still other White women are determined to act differently, to build real alliances, because they know it benefits them to see and deeply understand a breadth of experiences and realities. It is frightening to hear that what you may have done was painful for others. It is also necessary if we are to move forward together.

Here are stories I have been told in the last six months about dealing with "the enemy."

- From an African American woman diversity officer: "Our provost, a White woman, wants to 'move past' race and gender. She wants us to be 'inclusive' of everyone and not focus on specific identity issues. 'What we need to know,' the provost said, 'is how to recruit and hire in an *unbiased* way.' Yet our faculty remains 94 percent White while our undergraduate student body is 30 percent of Color. The people of Color we do hire leave or don't make it through the tenure process."
- From a Latina faculty member: "I was told by my department chair [a White woman] that my students complained that they can't understand my English. My first language is English! My chair told me that if my student evaluations don't improve my tenure will be in jeopardy."
- From an African American woman faculty member: "Our department chair [a White woman] does not see race as relevant. She explained to me that she and her colleagues see diversity in a 'more nuanced way.'"
- From a White staff person: "There are two problematic groups of faculty and staff on campus: the Hispanic faculty and staff group and the Diversity Council. The Diversity Council is just an angry group of people who meet with each other to complain."

What messages do women of Color hear from the White women? First, you're putting too much emphasis on race; second, my white race is "not relevant" and your race shouldn't be, either; third, people of Color are "problematic" and not qualified to teach at this school; furthermore, you're whining, making a big deal out of nothing, and you don't fit in. At each of these schools, the faculty is overwhelmingly White and there are a significant number of students of Color.

I have heard the comment about seeing diversity in a "more nuanced way" several times recently. In every instance, the White professors see themselves as too sophisticated to have such "mundane" conversations. What is not stated but lies underneath these non-conversations about diversity is something like "We have an African American president. We've moved beyond color." These White women are refusing to see how race has shaped their lives and that they are colluding with others to keep things as they are, to keep systemic white supremacy in place.

Before we move on to a conversation about the role our histories play in separating us, here are some questions to ask yourself. Do you perceive yourself simply as a human being or as a human being who is also a member of larger groups based on sexual orientation, religion, socioeconomic class, physical ability, race and so on? How do these various identities change the ways that you and others see you? How do you reassure yourself every day that your picture of yourself is accurate? At work, with whom do you interact? With whom do you *not* interact, consciously or unconsciously?

Socially, what activities and what people do you surround yourself with to affirm the stories you have told yourself about who you are and to keep yourself from having to be uncomfortable? How do you confirm the rightness of your choices regarding activities you involve yourself in and the people with whom you surround yourself? What do you gain from these choices? Who might you exclude because of the choices you make? By doing so, what experiences and possible learning do you miss?

What does it mean to know our histories, both personal and national? What keeps us from seeing how inextricably our pasts, and therefore our presents and futures, are woven together? We were all presented with White history as though it were the complete story. People of Color are relatively non-existent in schoolbooks, and there is rarely a hint that there are other perspectives about what we are told occurred. This distortion of our nation's history over-privileges some and under-privileges others.

Speaking personally, to know that my history and work to be a genuine and reliable ally on issues of race meant that I was forced to face the reality of what it means to be a White person from the South. I spent a long time looking at my family's history in Mississippi and Texas as cotton growers, a history which continues to play out in our lives today. My journey forced me to look at my family's values and beliefs and decide if those were ones I wanted for myself. I had to choose what sorts of conversations I was willing to enter into with my relatives and what kinds of relationships I wanted to have. This has been a long, profound, and intentional road, filled with ups and downs, finding out things I didn't really want to know, grieving family history, and building life-long relationships with racial justice activists, both of Color and White. I wouldn't give it up for anything. As Leslie Setlock said, "A future built on a lie just won't work."

A complex example of the fabricated national history we have been taught is that of slavery because, as James Loewen (1995) says in his book *Lies My Teacher Told Me*, "Textbooks have trouble acknowledging anything that might be wrong with white Americans, or with the United States as a whole" (pp. 142–143). Few of us were taught, for instance, that most of the Founding Fathers—George Washington, Thomas Jefferson, Benjamin Franklin, and others—were slave owners. We learned in junior high about the Three-Fifths Compromise in Article One, Section 2, of the U.S. Constitution—counting each slave as 3/5ths of a person—as if that were not a barbaric way to view human beings.

"More Americans have learned the story of the South during the years of the Civil War and Reconstruction from Margaret Mitchell's *Gone with the Wind* than from all of the learned volumes on this period."[3] Many of us are oblivious to how the "peculiar institution," the Southern euphemism for slavery, continues to be reflected every day in 21st-century America. As Loewen (1995) says:

> Although textbook authors no longer sugarcoat how slavery affected African Americans, they minimize white complicity in it. They present slavery virtually as uncaused, a tragedy, rather than a wrong perpetrated by some people on others … The very essence of what we have inherited from slavery is the idea that it is appropriate, even "natural," for whites to be on top, blacks on the bottom. (pp. 144–145)

Maintaining the system of the supremacy of whiteness demands that White people be largely oblivious to others' realities, perspectives, and stories. Examples of this are shown in the recent book and movie *The Help*. Set in Jackson, Mississippi, in 1963, the story is about a White woman named Skeeter who writes a book about how the Black maids feel about the White women for whom they work. She bases her writing on interviews with the Black women. One of Skeeter's childhood friends, Hilly, is a White woman so enmeshed in the prejudices of her culture that she won't let her Black maid use the family toilet; instead she has a separate one installed in the garage. Regardless of the many responses about how demeaning *The Help* is and how ahistorical, many people love the book and the film. Feelings in both Black and White audiences run the gamut. How do we understand one another's perspectives and how do we discover why we each feel the way we do?

*The Help* seems to me to encourage insight into how we see ourselves as racial and gendered beings. A few questions for White women who have read

*The Help* or seen the movie: How did you feel about the characters? Who did you care about and who didn't you care about? What emotions came up as you read? Was the history of Civil Rights era Mississippi something you were familiar with or were you learning about it for the first time? Did you see the story as about the daily struggles of the African American women or about a White woman's facing the facts of her culture? With whom did you identify?

My hunch is that most of us who are White identified with Skeeter, the White woman who was writing the book. I doubt that most of us saw ourselves in Hilly. White women, particularly those who see ourselves as "well-meaning," would find that difficult to accept; we see our own good traits and intentions. Yet I am fairly sure that many of the women of Color with whom we come in contact would talk about how much like Hilly we are. One African American woman said to me, "we have twelve Hillys in our department."

Like Hilly, we all receive messages from our culture about a person of Color's lack of worth. Then we frequently collude with what we've been taught, unconsciously figuring out ways to make that person unsuccessful, to undercut her and spread doubt about her competence. It is easy to deny that part of ourselves, but women of Color see through our self-delusion. They have to. Their survival—promotion, tenure, continued employment—depends on it.

Rather than getting defensive or downplaying the connections between our histories and our current experience, it is important to untangle the roots of some of our behavior. In my Southern family, for example, lots of racial jokes and stories were told. Most of them had to do with how dangerous Black men are, a stereotype deeply rooted in our nation's history of slavery, and how stupid, lazy and drunken Latino men are (another nationally held stereotype). Black women were always in the kitchen, like Aunt Jemima. In the Southwest, Latinas played a similar role.

So, when I read about a crime committed by an African American man, I'm not surprised. Often I don't realize I have registered the reinforcement of the stereotype, but of course I have. When I hear about the laws currently being passed in many states that legalize the profiling, arrest, imprisonment and deportation of Latinos, without any proof that they are here without papers or have committed a crime, I don't stop to think about what I'm hearing. If I don't know the long history of the United States' abusive treatment of people who have roots in Mexico, I respond with the prejudices based in the many jokes and stories I took in long ago, without necessarily being conscious of what I am doing. Black men and Latinos become more stereotyped and less human to me.

Then I go to work, taking with me in the recesses of my mind all of the unprocessed and unexamined information I have been exposed to. I sit on a hiring or tenure or promotion committee and a person of Color is a candidate. Unless I am extremely self-aware, chances are good that I will unconsciously judge the candidate based on the stereotypes I hold rather than on that individual's personal strengths and academic achievements. On the other hand, with White women and men whom I know personally, I judge them as individuals, rather than as the expected representations of a group that has been defined negatively.

Part of maintaining and colluding with any system is going along with the status quo, not putting our necks out to call attention to what is taking place. We help maintain the supremacy of whiteness or maleness by our silence. To act as an ally across lines of privilege requires the privileged person—the White person—to make our thoughts known, to "have the backs" of the people who don't have the unearned privilege we do. Here are examples of colluding with white supremacy: regularly aligning with the White men and women in discussions; working to build relationships with White colleagues, particularly those with formal or informal power; sitting quietly by when a White person in a group makes a stereotypic comment, tells a belittling joke, or silences a person of Color; continuing to teach a basically white curriculum; not advocating for candidates of Color because you're worried about how other White people will see you or what that support might cost you; letting stereotypes shape your perceptions and direct your actions.

You could instead choose behavior that makes it clear you believe it is important to have a richly diverse organization. Build honest and open relationships with White men so that you are able to tell them when their attitudes and behavior are off-base. Take an active role in creating new opportunities for women of Color. Co-teach a class with a woman of Color, being sure that you don't take over and squeeze her out. Change your curriculum so that it reflects the racial composition you would like to see in your school. Intentionally build mentoring relationships with people who are racially different from you, paying real attention to how *they* want to be mentored rather than how you were mentored or would like to be mentored.

In all this, it is vital to remember that you are changing your behavior because it is in your own interest. You are making choices based on what you think is right, rather than what seems politically correct. This is not about saving someone or showing that you are a good liberal. It is about creating real conversations with women of Color, and, in so doing, taking steps to change the organization.

Mainly what is missing in us is the *will* to step out and step up. The will to speak and act in ways that promote racial equity and justice requires courage. The payoff is, admittedly, mixed. Potential loss of friendships and ease of connection with family members are possible with any major change we make in ourselves. However, for me, those losses have been greatly outweighed by being able to live in integrity with what I believe is racially just and to develop relationships with others, of Color and White, who are working toward the same end. The hope of the writers in this book is that you, as readers, will open your minds and hearts and increase your will to listen to their words, believe them and take action based on what you have learned.

When we give in to competition our fear is that we will lose some or all of what we have. We can continue to guard our resources, both material and emotional. Or we can choose to do something different. Imagine going to work in a cooperative environment in which everyone is welcome and valued, in which you can breathe with others instead of holding your breath all day. Think about what it would be like to create racially diverse communities in which power is shared, in which you can learn with and from each other, not giving in to the feeling of fear even if conversations get passionate and hard.

It wouldn't be easy at first; hearing people speak their truths that they've finally been invited to express isn't always pretty. In fact, it is often really messy. But it could change your perspective and understanding, yours and others', if you are willing to believe that change is possible. "My belief selects and shapes my evidence, not the other way around."[4]

In their new book *Walk Out Walk On,* Margaret Wheatley and Deborah Frieze (2011) talk about people who "courageously step forward to discover new capacities," who, rather than "wait[ing] passively for help to come from the outside," have "the good sense not to buy into the paralyzing beliefs about themselves and how change happens" (pp. 4–5). It would affect the experience of being in your school if there were connected groups of people who have decided together "how to create healthy and resilient communities where all people matter, all people can contribute," where people are willing to have authentic conversations and take action together.

It's not our fault we were born White or at any particular time in history. Our responsibility comes when we make the choice of how to deal with the race and the time we were born into, the choice of moving to a just world, a world good for everyone. "Historical responsibility has to do with action," said Adrienne Rich (1986), "where we place the weight of our existences on the line, cast our lot with others, move from an individual consciousness to a collective one" (p. 145). We can make those choices.

## Notes

1 A lengthier version of this essay can be found in the second edition of *Understanding White Privilege: Creating Pathways to Authentic Relationships Across Race* (forthcoming). New York: Routledge.
2 Bennis, Warren G., and Robert I. Thomas. "Crucibles of Leadership." *Harvard Business Review* 80, 9 (2002): 40.
3 Beck, Warren and Myles Clowers (as cited in Loewen, p. 138).
4 Crafton, B. (9/2/11). The Almost Daily eMo from GeraniumFarm.org.

# References

Bennis, W.G., & Thomas, R. I. (2002). Crucibles of leadership. *Harvard Business Review, 80*, 39–45.

Crafton, B. (2011). The Almost Daily eMo from GeraniumFarm.org, September, 2.

Loewen, J. (1995). *Lies My Teacher Told Me: Everything your American history textbook got wrong*. New York: Touchstone Simon & Schuster.

Rich, A. (1986). *Blood, Bread, and Poetry: Selected Prose, 1979–1985*. New York: Norton.

Wheatley, M., & Frieze, D. (2011). *Walk Out Walk On*. San Francisco: Berrett-Koehler.

# Part II

# WOMEN OF COLOR TALK

# 3

# ON FRIENDSHIP, KINSHIP, AND SKINSHIP

## Healing Relationships between Indigenous and White Women Scholars

*Malia Villegas and Adreanne Ormond*

## Introduction

> But these [wo]men are your [sisters] ... And if the word integration means anything, this is what it means: that we, with love, shall force our [sisters] to see themselves as they are, to cease fleeing from reality and begin to change it. For this is your home, my friend, do not be driven from it ... We cannot be free until they are free.
>
> (Baldwin, 1963, p. 10)[1]

Existing research documents the challenges facing women scholars of Color at the intersection of patriarchy, racism, colonialism and hegemony in academic institutions (see for example, Williams, 1994; Grande, 2000, 2003; and Hill Collins, 1990). But few researchers deal with questions about how *to be in relationship* in the academy. In other words, research takes up what it means for women scholars of Color to *get through* but not to *be* in the academy. Reflecting with our Elders and mentors on our experiences with White women academics, we began to consider not only the nature of our relationships but also why we *should* be in relationship with White women scholars. When asked why he mentors White women, one senior, Indigenous scholar responded:

> I don't believe I'll see a time when White women are not employed as teachers of Indigenous kids—until that time, I have a responsibility to work with White women in this faculty to extend their understanding of Indigenous cultures and communities.

Others reminded us that we have a responsibility to acknowledge and honor White women's knowledge because to disregard it, as they have so often done to our knowledge, would mean we become complicit in our own colonization. Echoing the sentiment expressed by James Baldwin above, our Elders and mentors explained that our liberation is linked to theirs because being human means treating White women scholars with respect and learning to live in the right relationship with them as our sisters.

Endeavoring to live up to this goal, we also acknowledge the paradox that we feel a responsibility to treat White women scholars with respect in a context that too often rewards those who are disrespectful. We often have different ideas about what it means "to be" in the academy, which can constrain meaningful relationships. Making such a statement is politically dangerous for us as emerging scholars working in Whitestream (Denis, 1997; Grande, 2003) institutions of higher education. However, it is worth the risk because healing our relationships with White women scholars is the right thing to do. Our aim is not to remain oppositional to White women but to create opportunities to speak and engage with our colleagues. It is in this way that we can share our Indigenous values and knowledge systems safely and begin to change the colonial gaze and history of objectification in our relationships with White women academics (Fredericks, in press).

It is important to state that while we share some common perspectives and experiences with other Indigenous women academics, no two of us are the same, and we each must walk our own way. We also know that no two White women academics are the same; so we can only speak from our experiences. As we discuss later, the academy has too often determined the rules by which we work, speak and live as scholars; and the ways we call ourselves—Indigenous/White women academics—are partly the result of identity politics and essential notions of who can claim the right to speak as authentic. Thus, we write this chapter as an invitation to discuss who we are and what our relationships might be with each other in and beyond the academy. Again, James Baldwin is instructive when he notes that loving one another across our differences requires that we simultaneously force ourselves to see one another for what we are *and* that we embrace a sense of home in this place.

## "Mirror, Mirror on the Wall": Friendship in the Academy

The purpose of this section is to hold up a mirror for our White women colleagues so that they can see how we experience them, while wrangling with some of what they have reflected about how they experience us. By doing so, we hope to discuss sites of struggle and possibility in our relationships. We ask that the reader foreground the question of what it means to be a friend in the academy.

For years now, there has been an email circulating that describes three types of friendships—"friends for a reason, friends for a season, and friends for a lifetime." The author of the email encourages us to acknowledge and appreciate the different kinds of friends we have, while recognizing that "friendship" is not a singular experience. The circumstances that give rise to and shape a friendship, as well as who we are in the friendship, may shift across time and place. As humans, we need different kinds of relationships at different points in our lives *and* relationships are both complex and fluid. Yet, we are increasingly concerned that when it comes to relationships between White women and Indigenous women in the academy, it may always be "friends for a reason." This is most apparent in the three stances we have found White women academics often take in relationships with us, which we refer to as the Victim, the Voyeur and/or the Expert.

The Victim competes in the "Oppression Olympics" for the "Most Oppressed" gold medal (Martinez, 1993), reminding her Indigenous colleagues that she too has been oppressed due to her gender, class, marital status, age, ability, sexual orientation and/or field of study *as much* or *more so* than any Indigenous scholar. Re-dubbed the "oppression sweepstakes," these dynamics played out most recently in the U.S. presidential election when White female candidate Hillary Clinton campaigned against African American candidate, Barack Obama (Reed, 2008). Unfortunately, this positioning serves not to foster solidarity with people of Color but to silence and delegitimize our experiences of oppression—again asserting White-female authority.

Māori scholar Kathie Irwin (1992), argues that White academics are in the privileged position of being able to define the cultural and structural aspects which make up the university, which can constrain Indigenous academics' influence over their context. Irwin provides insight from her own experience as an emerging academic trying to balance personal and professional responsibilities. While many White women academics have no doubt had to manage home and career responsibilities, Irwin reports that many of her White female colleagues had the institutional capital to negotiate lighter teaching loads and more office space though they often only reflected on their status as under-paid and under-resourced victims.

Australian Aboriginal scholar, Aileen Moreton-Robinson (2002), acknowledges the institutional racism favoring White, female ontologies in describing how the "myth of commensurable differences" operates, such that it:

> [A]llows white women to position themselves as gendered, classed, sexualized, aged and abled rather than white. However, the myth of commensurable difference does not work the same way for Indigenous women who perceive whiteness to be overwhelmingly and disproportionately predominant. White women occupy the key roles,

they constitute the norm and the ordinary and they represent the standard of womanhood in Australia. (p. 185)

By pointing out the systemic racism and marginalization that can place many Indigenous women academics in tenuous employment positions such as short or fixed-term contracts or even dual appointments, for example, we are not trying to compete for "the gold." Instead we aim to make racism visible and to compel our colleagues to subvert this racism in intentional ways. Ultimately, the Victim plays into the age-old, imperial war tactic of "divide and conquer," preventing women from acknowledging difference as a valuable asset and a distinct synergistic platform from which we can form friendships and scholarly collaboration.

The Voyeur is intrigued by Indigenous difference and exoticness, typically seeking out access to Indigenous communities by leveraging her relationships with Indigenous colleagues. Seemingly harmless, the Voyeur does damage by virtue of never moving past her naïve curiosity in Indigenous cultures— appearing kind yet never challenging the status quo. We have seen the damage the "anthropologist" can have in our lands, homes and countries; and we are aware they often have a conflicting understanding of what it means to be in relationship:

> To know an Indigenous constructed social world you must experience it from within; to know about such a world means you are imposing a conceptual framework from outside.
>
> (emphasis in original, Moreton-Robinson, 2002, p. 185)

> The massive volume of useless knowledge produced by anthropologists attempting to capture real Indians in a network of theories has contributed substantially to the invisibility of Indian people today … Many anthros spare no expense to reinforce this sense of inadequacy in order to further support their influence over Indian people.
>
> (Deloria, 1969, pp. 81–82)

> It is a commonplace for those who consider the story to be just a story to believe that, in order to appropriate the "traditional" storytellers' powers and to produce the same effects as theirs, it suffices to "look for the structure of their narratives." See them as they see each other, so goes the (anthropological) creed. "Tell it the way they tell it instead of imposing our structure," they repeat with the best of intentions and a conscience so clear that they pride themselves on it … The anthropologist, as we already know, does not find things; s/he makes them. And makes them up.
>
> (emphasis in original, Minh-ha, 1989, p. 141)

These three noted Indigenous scholars explain that the problem with the Voyeur is that she does not relate to Indigenous people as real human beings but as relics of the past—or in the worst case scenario as "puppets" or "pets" that she may command and control (Deloria, 2004, p. 29). The Voyeur tends to objectify Indigenous peoples and cultures and can become a danger to healthy Indigenous identity development.

While the metaphor of the "anthropologist" may seem outdated, we use it to characterize the "objective observer" stance of the Voyeur and to demonstrate how easily "looking in from the outside" can turn into a desire to appropriate and exploit the spiritual, intellectual and tangible resources of a people. This does not only do damage to Indigenous people, but may play into the notion that White people have no cultural knowledge to offer and responsibility in relationships. We also use the term to reference the genealogy of research in Indigenous communities that has sought to objectify and commodify our cultures for the benefit of others. While the Victim stance is more commonly adopted by White women, the Voyeur stance is a feature of White colonialism that is adopted by both White men and White women. However, White women academics may play on gendered stereotypes about the harmlessness and collaborative characteristics of women in order to gain access to Indigenous communities.

The Expert claims personal or professional relationships with Indigenous people and tends to speak on behalf of Indigenous peoples, particularly in forums where there is little to no Indigenous representation. The Expert guards her authority to speak for Indigenous peoples and may do so in order to "help," "advocate for," or "inform" others. At the extreme, the Expert may even position herself as telling Indigenous peoples about themselves. We present a brief vignette that demonstrates how the Expert manifests. The exchange took place when one of the authors was working on Indigenous issues as a visiting scholar in another country:

> One week after arriving in this new country, I met the Expert. As an Indigenous visitor to another land I know to always be aware that I am in someone else's country and acknowledge my relationships to the first peoples. Yet my presence clearly unsettled one of my White female colleagues. In my first, full team meeting my boss asked me to share some resources from my home country related to the concept of Indigenous identity. Before I had even finished talking, my White female colleague pointed aggressively across the table at me announcing that "in this country, Indigenous identity is community business; not the domain of the school" when I had said nothing about community or school roles and repeatedly exclaimed that "you have a lot to learn about Indigenous identity in this country!" Later, I reflected that while I will always be learning about Indigenous identity here, I intend to

learn from Indigenous peoples. Yet, my colleague did not offer to broker these relationships or to acknowledge me as an Indigenous person with insights into Indigenous identity anywhere. She told me that I should make an appointment with her so that she could explain the ins-and-outs of Indigenous identity—a meeting that would take "no longer than a half an hour" she assured me.

The Expert is not interested in collaborating with Indigenous scholars, rather she thrives in situations where she can claim authority and will not be challenged. Like the Voyeur, the Expert stance is not solely the domain of White women. However, as Moreton-Robinson (2002) indicates, White women's appropriation of patriarchal forms of *power over* threatens opportunities to connect and build solidarity with Indigenous women:

> White women's conditions and acceptance of their pioneering role precluded friendship with Indigenous women and some displayed a maternalism that allowed them to maintain a position of superiority (Jolly 1993) ... The deployment of the subject position middle-class white woman requires an ideology of true womanhood which positions Indigenous women as less feminine, less human and less spiritual than themselves. (p. 180)

By claiming their "superiority" and truth, White women seek to other Indigenous women and assert their authority. They do so by subverting any sense of connection or relationship so that they can be more than those who are "less." It is this separation that Indigenous women academics are called to heal:

> Indigenous women seek to transform cultural and educational institutions so that our ways of knowing will be taught and respected ... Indigenous women continue to demand and struggle for the return of our lands, the right to our intellectual property, cultural heritage, religion and spirituality, and the right to learn and pass on our morality, attitudes and worldview.
>
> (Moreton-Robinson, 2002, p. 164)

> The world's earliest archives or libraries were the memories of women. Patiently transmitted from mouth to ear, body to body, hand to hand ... Every woman partakes in the chain of guardianship and of transmission ... my story carries with it their stories, their history, and our story repeats itself endlessly ... My story, no doubt, is me, but it is also, no doubt, older than me.
>
> (Minh-ha, 1989, pp. 121–123)

In asserting the White-female ontology, the Expert does not allow for the manifestation of the unique place of Indigenous women, our cultures or our ways of being.

There are some distinct triggers that lead to White women academics taking on these stances. One common trigger is when Indigenous academics make claims about culturally-based knowledge or experiences that seemingly exclude the expertise of anyone who is not Indigenous. For example, a claim that Indigenous teachers may be better suited to work with Indigenous youth may appear threatening to non-Indigenous educators if they feel excluded by such a claim. Another trigger is when Indigenous academics discuss the impacts of colonization and oppression they experience in institutions of higher education, which is often interpreted as a guilt-inducing exercise. A third trigger is when Indigenous academics discuss their cultural beliefs in professional settings. Importantly, all three triggers are those that center the knowledges, experiences and beliefs of Indigenous academics. The Victim, Voyeur and Expert emerge to vigilantly protect and affirm White women's authority and power.

Though different in their manifestations, these stances each seek to constrain the voices of Indigenous women academics *and* to objectify our lived experiences in order to maintain the authority of the White-female academic and exert power over us. They play into and on Indigenous victim narratives and center White normativity. By doing so, they limit the formation of reciprocal relationships between Indigenous and White women academics. Importantly, however, they usually emerge when a White female academic takes liberties in her personal relationships with Indigenous female colleagues. The Victim comes to "know" her Indigenous colleague well enough to assert her own oppression; the Voyeur enough to ask for access; and the Expert enough to claim her own expertise. Knowledge shared in a personal domain becomes categorical knowledge about Indigenous peoples and cultures, which then gets leveraged in professional settings for the benefit of the White female academic. Personal relationships with White women scholars become yet another site of co-optation and colonization.

We present the following vignette as an example of how the Expert crosses professional and personal boundaries as she seeks justification for her own position:

A White academic colleague and personal friend was applying for a prominent departmental position. We have been friends for a decade, and I felt she was aware of my cultural responsibility and commitment to make a positive transformation for my people. During her research seminar, she discusses her research pathway and speaks briefly about the Indigenous cultural concepts and her intent to use them in her work but does not acknowledge the culture and people the concepts belong to. I remain silent as I am there as a friend not a critic, however, I am aware of the divide between our positions and that the knowledge referred to belongs to my people. I wait for acknowledgement or recognition of the people that the knowledge stems from, but there is none. I leave knowing my White friend has traded on my culture and peoples' knowledge. In personal conversation at a later date she raises her use of the cultural concepts and I remind her that it is not her knowledge to use and the appropriate process is to allow someone from the culture from which the knowledge belongs to own and represent as they see wise and fit. She is defensive, disagrees and attempts to justify her position. She would like to discuss the issue further and debrief with me about work she is beginning to do with Indigenous communities as well as seeking introductions to my Indigenous network. I am disappointed that her understanding of my culture is only skin deep and at the resulting oppression and domination. The issue is unresolved, and I am now wary of the relationship. Another barrier is raised.

This is one case of the Expert trading on her association with an Indigenous woman academic to authorize her right to speak to and about Indigenous issues. The use of informal situations and conversations to receive insight and mentoring on Indigenous cultures and issues often creates a dynamic where knowledge is gathered without the acknowledgement of the person sharing the knowledge or formal permission to use it at a later date.

At the same time, the question of what is "personal" for Indigenous women academics often becomes an issue for our White women colleagues. "Don't take it so personally" is a common refrain, to which we reply that this work will always be personal because of our cultural responsibilities to our communities and future generations (Smith, 1999). In the end, we cannot help but wonder at the irony—we are reprimanded for claiming what is "personal" when our "personal" insights are co-opted for their advancement and benefit.

## Scholarship as Kinship: Sister-Scholars in the Sacred Grove

We contemplated ending this chapter with the previous section. However, we need to take up the fact that the "advancement and benefit" noted above does not occur in a vacuum but in a distinct cultural context—that of the academy. Academic culture places a high value on critique and competition, but often in a way that celebrates the achievements of individuals working in isolation, discounting connectedness and responsibility. This culture is so pervasive that it may be difficult to acknowledge that there may be another way of being in this place. Consider this vignette about different understandings of relationships:

> A White female colleague, who was also new to this foreign country, lamented the fact that she believed I have more access to Indigenous scholars and contexts here "simply because you are Indigenous." She even went so far as to suggest that she did not understand why things were "just easier" for me. It seemed that all she could see was that she was being denied "access," while it was being granted freely to me. She did not see my efforts to acknowledge my relationships to the peoples of this place when I am asked to speak, let alone my efforts to demonstrate solidarity by supervising Indigenous students, volunteering to attend and contribute to Indigenous community events and working to connect Indigenous scholars to those in other countries. Many of my White women colleagues do not seem to understand that relationships come with opportunities to connect and significant responsibilities—that is kinship.

Contrary to analyses claiming that Indigenous cultures require the collective to win out over, or even suppress, individual voices and needs, kinship and sisterhood are about the interdependence of individual and group needs. Being a sister-scholar means that we have some "tie that binds"—a shared experience or vision that connects our paths such that what affects one, affects both—whether good or bad.

In order to develop shared experiences and visions about what it means to be a scholar, we need different ways of engaging in critique. In many institutions of higher education, we are trained to be critical, which too often translates into criticism that does not encourage, uplift or challenge. Most of us can probably point to situations in meetings and conferences, or as part of the peer-review process, where we stopped being able to hear feedback because of the manner in which it was given. Sometimes the criticism comes in the form of harsh, angry words, while at others it may be veiled as more passive-aggressive statements. Yet, in most cases it is hard to hear because the person giving the feedback has stopped showing care for the one receiving it and is seeking to demonstrate his/her knowledge or to correct, cut-down and put his/her colleague in her place. The polemic has taken priority over what is productive and purposeful. Depending on the context, stage of life or career and particular moment, such criticism can roll off our backs or cripple us. As confidence is such a big part of being in the academy, these kinds of interactions can be devastating when confidence is lacking. And for what, we ask? Who does it benefit when we mistreat and disrespect each other through such carelessness? In the name of rigor some would say, but we would argue that we can maintain high standards and expectations for research without cutting each other down. Controversy and argument for their own sake may serve to protect the status of an individual scholar or institution, but they are not sustainable and rarely impact society in a meaningful way.

It helps to think about the kinship model here. Whenever we are trying to get the tone of a critique right or to determine if a critique we received was given in the right spirit, we find it helpful to think of Elders, youth and other cultural mentoring relationships we might experience. As Indigenous scholars we acknowledge particular protocols of respect when speaking with Elders in our communities. For instance, we would not ask direct questions but instead "wonder about" certain things, creating the opportunity for an Elder to respond without the obligation to do so if it is not appropriate. We do not publically question any counsel they give, but instead ponder it in private so as to honor their cultural status and not undermine their relationships with others. Similarly, in our research writing, we would never criticize the work of our Elder scholars in the ways we may have been trained to do so in the academy, but instead take up their work with a spirit of respect and thoughtful engagement. The questions we bring are not so much about the validity or error in their knowledge as they are about how and why they may have come to such conclusions—what is the genealogy of their ideas, how did they come to know these things, from what position do they speak, what are the goals and purposes they are working towards? In this way, we come to understand more about their knowledges and truths, rather than disregarding or judging them against our own.

The point here is not that truth is relative, but that if we can learn to appreciate the process of coming to know, we may be able to engage one another's insights and perspectives with respect—learning from the elements that resonate and considering those that do not instead of dismissing them as untrue or without value. We are too careless with each other's ideas and with one another in the academy.

Sisterhood means we support each other to achieve; we celebrate one another's successes as our own; we look for ways to honor one another through nominations for awards, mentions in meetings with senior scholars or funders and links to like-minded people or projects; we review each other's work with care, in the same manner we would hope our work to be treated; we respect each other's time and allow each other to set boundaries and to say "no" to opportunities; we challenge each other's ideas so that we each become stronger scholars, as "iron sharpens iron"; and we watch out for one another, while being willing to speak truth even when it may be hard to hear. Above all we recognize that meaningful, impactful and sustainable development requires all of us to be working from our various institutions, experiences, histories and communities—no one person can do this work in isolation. We present one final vignette drawn from one of the authors' work to supervise graduate students, demonstrating how we can take risks while building partnerships as part of a collegial academic community:

> Recently I was invited to be one of two supervisors to a non-Indigenous student undertaking a doctorate, which would potentially involve the study of Indigenous culture. The other supervisor was a White woman. For me, the invitation presented issues of using an Indigenous supervisor for a non-Indigenous student when the university is already short of people to supervise Indigenous students and even shorter of supervisors to work with Indigenous students interested in working with Indigenous issues. Another issue present was the study of Indigenous culture by someone from outside the culture. I met with the student and the other supervisor where we openly discussed my concerns. It was agreed that the student would not study an Indigenous culture as it was inappropriate, and she would find another way to speak to the political issues that interested her. I agreed to work with the student and supervisor with an understanding that we need to build relationships of trust and truth in the academy. If we are to seek sisterhood then we must seek opportunities to create spaces to share, learn and progress together.

In this way, we acknowledge our responsibilities to challenge each other and take opportunities to share across our differences to enrich one another.

Even in our short time as part of the academy, we have seen a myriad of examples of how Indigenous women academics and other women scholars of Color act as sister-scholars. At most of the professional conferences we attend led by Indigenous academics, we come together for working meetings in cross-cultural, inter-generational groups so that we can learn to engage one another across place and age and be able to publish from these gatherings. One group of African American women scholars collectively approached a leading journal with a group of articles on a topic of importance to them. They told the editors of the journal, "Either you publish us all or we send this seminal work to a competing journal." We have also observed a strong culture of mentorship, where there is an expectation that we look out for, share insights and guide one another along the pathway.

This is all to say that it is being done and that the sisterhood of scholars is strong because that is how we know to *be* in this place as Indigenous women academics. Our time may be designated for our kin because they care for us and fill us up in ways that friends and acquaintances do not or choose not to commit. And yet, as one of our mentors above reminded us, we need sister-scholars among the ranks of White women academics. In the same breath that he explained why he mentors White women in the academy, he described *how* he mentors them. He said, "When I decide to take on a White female mentee, I explain to her that I am going to teach her how to work her way out of a job—to mentor Indigenous students to eventually fill her role and lead the academy into a new phase." It would be easy to misread this approach as one of replacing White women with Indigenous people in the academy, when it is more about the interdependence between different generations—a culture of succession planning that does not prioritize the present generation over the past or future, but acknowledges the distinct roles each must take.

In the same way, kinship and sisterhood are not necessarily about becoming more like each other. In developing kinship with White women scholars, we expect that there will be domains where they will bring insights we may never have considered; and vice versa. We work from what we know, in relationship with one another, to bring about shared ends. In this way, we challenge the calls for standardization and uphold the promise of true diversity.

## "All My Relations": Skinship and Other Ways of Being an Academic

If you know whence you came, there is really no limit to where you can go.

(Baldwin, 1963, p. 8)

I shared with a senior colleague, who I believed at the time was the only male colleague I could trust, how broken my spirit was. He began by berating me for my silence and fear ...He asked me who I was ... I responded by saying, "I am Hawaiian." You know, that one statement made all the difference in the world. Being Hawaiian means that you "live aloha." ... Our elders teach that coming to a situation with aloha, of giving and loving and embracing the breath of life, opens the heart and soothes the mind.

(Benham, in Cooper, Ortiz, Benham, & Scherr, 2002, p. 77)

The previous two sections explored personal and professional relationships with academic colleagues. Yet, for us as Indigenous women academics, being a scholar involves relationships that extend beyond institutions of higher education. The stakes are very high and the responsibilities are very deep. There is a daily struggle to walk in a place that often feels toxic, cold and hostile. It takes a toll on our bodies as women and as Indigenous people— there are whole other conversations we must be having about how this journey and stress tax our reproductive systems and bodily organs. And yet, we must rise above this because there is important work to do. This is a paradox, but maybe it does not have to be.

Over time, we have observed the way one of our mentors walks this pathway. She is one of the most accomplished Indigenous scholars in the world, who also contributes in major ways in her own home community. When asked how she navigates treacherous academic institutions with such ease, she responds, with no hesitation, that these institutions are not foreign places, "These are my institutions—built on my peoples' land. I belong here," she says. And yet, she is not institutionally bound—she goes where her vision takes her despite the millions in grant money she may leave behind. For her, it does not appear to be about the contract dollars, accolades, publications or status—yet she has earned each of these over time. When we share our research work with her, she presses us to identify the impact this work has had for real people. She always brings us back to the heart of the matter, reminding us to remember who we are and where we come from, that we are connected, always. Consider another reminder from a sister-scholar:

> I very clearly see my home in the academy from a perspective much larger than the institution ... I define home as a place (within) where I feel comforted, safe, and valued. Home for me is a network ... of womantors, academic mothers, supportive colleagues, and mentors, too ... They nurture my soul and being because they know me ... it is through connectedness that I see the greatest potential in changing the academy and empowering individuals.
> (Ortiz, in Cooper, Ortiz, Benham, & Scherr, 2002, pp. 79–80)

Connectedness is how we survive and thrive because it is who we are, and yet it is not always valued in the academy.

As a result, sometimes it is hard to stay focused on the tenure track and on what institutions of higher education tell us we need to do to be successful on their terms. This plays out at a disciplinary and faculty level where we often feel compelled to work across disciplines and sectors because the work we do in community is not limited only to education, but connects to health, energy, economics and justice in critical ways. We also recognize that Indigenous faculty have to be wary of the dual appointment scenario that can burn us out and limit advancement. It also plays out in terms of our advocacy agendas. Being one of very few Indigenous academics, we are often called upon by our families, community leaders and fellow scholars to take leadership and advocate for Indigenous wellbeing. In many instances, this means countless hours of informal consulting and volunteering, as well as policy work. Some manage these responsibilities alongside their research, teaching, and service roles, while others are "fast-tracked" into major national and international roles off the tenure-track because leadership and advocacy are needed.

This is all to say that *being a scholar* may look very different for Indigenous women academics, which may be hard to explain to other academics. We get a sense, however, that this may be generational as we have had several conversations with our Indigenous and non-Indigenous peers about the rapid changes we observe in the academy each year. When we first decided to begin this journey, we did so for three main reasons related to a belief that: 1) the world needs the knowledge of Indigenous peoples; 2) scholars have a responsibility to serve as stewards of human action and inaction; and 3) humans need to be in reciprocal relationships with each other and the Earth.

There is a fundamental attack on life in all its forms taking place across the world. It is manifesting in the universalizing and standardization of development globally, in the irresponsible consumption of the world's natural resources, and in the elimination of biological diversity through genetic modification of plants and food sources. Indigenous worldviews de-center humans and recognize the interdependence, and skinship, of human, nature and spirit in ways that can help right the imbalance and preserve diversity and life. As scholars, it is our responsibility to help foreground this knowledge but only in sites where it will be treated with respect and used to guide responsible behavior and decision-making. This knowledge teaches us that all living beings deserve our respect, so it is here that we must begin to heal and develop our relationships with White women academics because we are already connected. Still, we ask that our White women colleagues who choose to be in relationship with us take the time to reflect on who they are as White women, as academics, and as humans in this work because there are two sides to being in relationship—one is connection and the other is responsibility. We look forward to walking this path together.

## Notes

1  Special thanks to Dr. Lisa (Leigh) Patel Stevens for encouraging us to read this powerful essay and issuing us with such a crucial challenge.

## References

Baldwin, J. (1963). "My dungeon shook: Letter to my nephew on the one hundredth anniversary of the Emancipation" (pp. 3–10). In J. Baldwin, *The Fire Next Time*. New York: Dial Press.

Cooper, J. E., Ortiz, A. M., Benham, M. K. P., & Woods Scherr, M. (2002). "Finding a home in the academy: Confronting racism and ageism" (pp. 71–87), in Cooper & Stevens (Eds.), *Tenure in the Sacred Grove: Issues and strategies for women and minority faculty*. Albany: State University of New York Press.

Deloria, V., Jr. (1969). *Custer Died for Your Sins: An Indian manifesto*. Norman, OK: University of Oklahoma Press.

Deloria, V. ,Jr. (2004). "Marginal and submarginal" (pp. 16–30). In D. A. Mihesuah & A. C. Wilson (Eds.). *Indigenizing the Academy: Transforming scholarship and empowering communities*. Lincoln: University of Nebraska Press.

Denis, C. (1997). *We Are Not You: First Nations and Canadian modernity*. Toronto, ON: Broadview Press.

Fredericks, B. (in press). "Universities are not the safe places we would like to think they are, But they are getting safer: Indigenous women academics in higher education". *Journal of Australian Indigenous Issues*.

Grande, S. M. A. (2000). "American Indian geographies of power: At the crossroads of Indígena and Mestizaje". *Harvard Educational Review 70*: 467–498.

Grande, S. (2003). "Whitestream feminism and the colonialist project: A review of contemporary feminist pedagogy and praxis". *Educational Theory 53*(3): 329–346.

Hill Collins, P. (1990). *Black Feminist Thought: Knowledge, consciousness, and the politics of empowerment*. London: Unwin Hyman.

Irwin, K. (1992). "Becoming an academic: contradictions and dilemmas of a Maori feminist" (pp. 52–67). In S. Middleton & A. Jones, *Women and Education in Aotearoa 2*. Wellington: Bridget Williams Books.

Jolly, M. (1993). "Colonizing women: The maternal body and empire" (pp. 103-127). In S. Gunew & A. Yeatman (Eds.), *Feminism and the politics of difference*. St. Leonards, NSW: Allen & Unwin.

Martinez, E. (1993). "Beyond Black/White: The racisms of our time." *Social Justice 51/52* (1/2): 22–34.

Minh-ha, T. (1989). *Woman, Native, Other*. Indianapolis, IN: Indiana University Press.

Moreton-Robinson, A. (2002). *Talkin' Up to the White Woman: Aboriginal women and feminism*. St Lucia, QLD, Australia: University of Queensland Press.

Reed, B. (2008). "Race to the bottom." *The Nation*. May 19.

Smith, L. T. (1999). *Decolonising Methodologies: Research and Indigenous peoples*. London: Zed Books.

Williams, K. C. (1994). "Mapping the margins: Intersectionality, identity politics, and violence against women of color" (pp. 93–118). In M. A. Fineman & R.Mykitiuk (Eds.), *The Public Nature of Private Violence*. New York: Routledge.

# 4

# THE WHITENESS OF TRUTH
# AND THE PRESUMPTION
# OF INNOCENCE

*Karen L. Dace*

I began this morning doing something I have done too many times to count as a woman of Color in the academy—assuring another woman of Color that although some White women and men on our campus questioned her character, integrity and ability to behave professionally—I understood that it was her detractors who were the problem and that I would advocate on her behalf. Of course this is not how I planned to spend my morning. The plan was to begin this chapter. Interestingly, my conversation with Karla supports the argument I want to make here, an argument I have been making in my head for years: truth is white.

Having experienced the "academy" on predominantly White campuses as a student, faculty member and administrator, I have learned many lessons as an African American woman about what I have long termed the "whiteness of truth." In this chapter I explicate my "theory" that truth is indeed a wholly-owned subsidiary of White people. The purpose of this book—the un-restraining of the strained relationships between women of Color and White women—offers an opportunity to examine the ways in which White people, White women in particular, own the truth in ways that negate the realities of women and people of Color in the academic setting.

An obvious product of the whiteness of truth is the presumption of innocence. In short, if White women own the truth in every setting they can and will be "found innocent" of improper or racist motives, judgments, intentions and actions. Necessarily, since women of Color do not own the truth, we have been "found guilty" of being wild, untrustworthy, angry, crazy, violent, disrespectful and rude in a world where truth, whiteness and innocence walk in concert. Hence, it was easy for a group of White people on our campus to question Karla's professionalism, ability to keep a confidence and be trusted while ignoring numerous examples of their own multiple failures to do the same.

Lest the reader understand the questioning of Karla's integrity to be something trivial, I want to explain the insidious nature of truth when it is owned by Whites and never, or rarely, in the possession of people of Color. The untruths spoken about Karla were being used to justify her elimination from a project that would contribute to her professional development, placing her in line for greater responsibilities and promotion. The only thing required to halt Karla's professional growth was the speaking of a single untruth in the form of truth through White lips, the gentle nod of agreement from other Whites around the table and eventual "ah ha" or "oh" from everyone else in attendance. Of course, Karla may attempt to deny the untruth that has been spoken as truth. But, as someone whose skin color makes it impossible for her to own truth, Karla is not a credible witness. What's more, the "testimony" of Karla's shortcomings will travel with each person present, spreading across campus like a virus becoming part of every explanation for not working with, hiring, promoting or drawing upon Karla's expertise because "well, I can't recall the entire story, but I've been told that we simply can't trust Karla to…"

Whether the untruths spoken about women of Color take the form of "simple" and out-right lies or exaggerations *about* the behavior of women and men of Color or come as inaccurate statements that are *reactions to* people of Color who behave as if they are equal to White women by questioning, challenging, instructing, reprimanding or introducing new ideas, they have the power and potential to do irreparable professional and personal damage.

## Colored Truth

Some observations about the character, motives, demeanor and intelligence of women of Color and White women demonstrate the whiteness of truth, innocence of White women and guilt of people of Color. In this section I discuss these observations and the ways they work by providing actual examples from the frontlines of predominantly white institutions.

**Observation I: Having black or brown skin makes it impossible to be objective where race is concerned and/or when the potential for a dispute occurs between another person of Color and a White person. However, those with white skin can always be trusted to remain objective in these situations.**

I first experienced this "reality" during an interview for a position that would give me control of a rather large budget and decision-making power about key expenditures. The position had the potential to place people of Color at odds with one another (some of whom were women) and with White women although no one could come up with an example when such a problem occurred. Still, many of the White women involved in the interview process were concerned that such a problem could happen should the wrong candidate be given the position. Hence the importance of the question in a room full of White women and me, the lone Black-woman candidate for the position: "How are you going to handle being Black when you have to decide between spending limited resources on minorities versus us (White women)?"

There are so many problems with this question that it is difficult to know where to begin. Without missing a beat, the White woman posing the question discounted my gender, something I would argue was easy to do since, for so many White people, whiteness is required in order to be considered fully a woman. But that is a subject for another volume. She could have just as easily stated, "You know you all stick together and that means you will have to fight everything within you to be fair to us poor little White women." Since my childhood I had been taught that black was beautiful. In the academy, and elsewhere in the American psyche, I have learned that black is overpowering, overwhelming and reduces one's ability to reason, be fair and objective. Of course it would be difficult for me, or any other woman of Color, to think rationally when I might have to decide between my White "sisters" and my "real" brothers and sisters of Color. Interestingly, I appeared to be the only person in the room bothered by the question. Everyone else seemed to lean forward, waiting for me to promise that I would try, hard as it might be, to not allow my blackness to overtake my ability to treat White women fairly. I made no such promise but rather reprimanded the questioner for posing such an inappropriate question. One wonders whether the discussion after my departure centered around my refusal to address such a racist question as evidence of my bias against White women.

**Observation II: When women of Color talk about race they always do so with a not-so hidden agenda. However, when White women do the same it is out of the goodness of their hearts.**
This is not a new observation but was first identified by Peggy McIntosh (1988) as part of a lengthy list of white privileges. I suggest that this particular privilege necessarily leads to the assumption of white truth, innocence and purity of motive when White people find themselves involved in discussions about race. Perhaps the best example occurred during a meeting about a separate issue when the discussion turned to the inappropriate and potentially racist behavior of a White male faculty member during one of his classes. He had admitted to using a racial slur during a lecture and students, both of Color and White, complained to university administration. Although the purpose of our meeting was not to discuss this incident, the topic arose toward the end of our discussion. One of the White women present explained "when you take into consideration *who* he is married to, you know he is not biased." All of the White faculty members in the room nodded in agreement.

In other words, when a White person marries someone who is not White, s/he gets an automatic pass on the "racism test." Apparently, sleeping black or brown exempts White people from being viewed as racially biased. The notion that a White faculty member who uses racial slurs but sleeps brown or black cannot be biased suggests something about the inherent goodness and innocence of whiteness. It is almost as if the White woman who jumped to our colleague's defense was saying something about his generosity in marrying someone who is not White. Being willing to talk about race or marry a "race woman" or "race man" implies that Whites have somehow lowered themselves, marrying beneath their station, when they do not have to do so or discussing something of little or no real consequence to them. They are noble, these White men and women who take up the banner of race during meetings or sleep with Brown and Black women and men. Because they are so generous, there is nothing really in it for them when they talk about race or marry a person of Color, these White people get to "own" truth and trust and be presumed innocent of all racist offenses and motives. Additionally, having bi-racial children or a partner of Color seems to exempt White women and men from having to explain, acknowledge or apologize for racist behavior. It is almost as if their decision to be in a relationship that includes people of Color gives them an automatic "get out of jail free" card when they behave in ways that would be unacceptable for anyone else.

However, possessing black or brown skin necessarily makes one suspect as evident in the conversation I was engaged in about the status of the African American Studies Program on our campus when a White colleague began by explaining the need for our meeting: "We are here to discuss African American Studies because it is important and well, Karen, we know why *you* are interested in this program." Again, as an African American woman, I must have a bias when it comes to African American Studies. The presence of the Whites around the table is genuine, sincere. While I am present, in their minds, *because of my race;* my White colleagues are there *in spite of* their race and *because it is the right thing to do.*

**Observation III: Women of Color are inherently angry and intimidating. These qualities are often revealed when they express dissent, challenge or question the behavior of White women. Anger and intimidation make it difficult for Whites to accurately recall exchanges with women of Color. The exaggeration and misreporting of events and outright lies about women of Color "feel" true to White women and will, over time, become true in the minds of most hearers.**

Should a woman of Color dare to disagree with a White woman, whether during a public meeting or in private, she is often described as angry and intimidating. When a woman of Color offers new information that challenges the long-held opinion of Whites or asks a question about the practices and behavior of a White person, the woman of Color has crossed into dangerous and forbidden territory. As the following example illustrates, the "facts" of the exchange will be repeated again and again often portraying women of Color as attackers and White women as innocent victims.

As one of two organizers, both of us African American women, I was the instructor in a year-long workshop on best practices for incorporating diverse materials into university courses. During our first session, we arranged for students of Color to address the faculty participants to discuss their positive and negative classroom experiences when race, class and gender issues arose. We intentionally decided not to instruct the faculty members how to react to the stories they would hear. What I mean here is that I have yet to witness a discussion of any kind during which people of Color have been asked to be vulnerable in discussing race where they have not been challenged by White audience members. Confident that the "interruption" would occur, we planned to use it as a "teachable moment" explaining that the discomfort experienced when listening to examples of racism in one's community, workplace or campus often provokes some to question the reality of those experiences or label them as atypical. We thought we would use the "interruption" of the students' stories to demonstrate how students of Color can be silenced in the classroom by instructors and classmates and the role a professor can decide to play to make certain that every voice is heard.

An African American male graduate student discussed the differential treatment he witnessed when he was forced to miss the first class meeting at the start of a semester. He mentioned to another classmate that he had to withdraw from the course because the professor explained that it would be impossible for him to catch up after missing the first three-hour session. His friend, a White graduate student, was surprised to hear this since she also missed the first class but was allowed to remain in the class. As the African American male continued, a White woman faculty member in the audience began to speak "that happens to White people too, that happened to my sister." The graduate student continued speaking but was interrupted once more when the same White woman faculty member repeated "that happens to White people too, that happened to my sister." She then proceeded to tell her sister's story of being differentially treated by a White male professor.

Knowing that we had our interruption example or "teachable moment," we allowed the panel to resume once the White woman professor completed her sister's story. During the question and answer period an Asian American woman asked all of us to reflect on what happened when the student of Color tried to communicate his experiences and was interrupted. She explained that the White woman professor's need to tell a story that contradicted that of a person of Color helped to diminish the significance of the African American male's experience and placed the focus of attention on the White woman when students of Color had been asked to be vulnerable in a room full of mostly White faculty. As she spoke, the African American male graduate student thanked the Asian American woman for making the point.

I probably do not have to write that we never saw the White woman professor in the workshop again. Shortly after the Asian American woman's comment, we broke for lunch and the White woman literally ran from the room, in tears. At that point, I did something for which I continue to kick myself to this day—I ran after her, calling her name. In a series of emails to me, the other workshop coordinator and her dean, a White male, she expressed her outrage:

> I was taken aback by the personal attack made by another participant toward me last Wednesday during the workshop, and I was dismayed that neither you nor [the other coordinator] indicated that such behavior was inappropriate. Realizing that the attack was (at the very least tacitly) condoned, I decided I could not be comfortable participating in such an environment.

In addition to copying the dean of her college on the exchange, the White woman professor engaged numerous colleagues in discussion about how she was attacked by the Asian American woman while two African American women did nothing to protect her. She refused to acknowledge that she had actively dismissed the experience of the African American student. Although several attempts were made to bring her back to the discussion, she refused to be engaged. Well, she refused to engage the three women of Color involved. But she had no problem discussing the situation with other White men and women in the workshop and colleagues in her academic department. Many of those discussions were relayed to the rest of the workshop attendees when we debriefed the event. My last communication with the White woman professor included an attempt to acknowledge the difficulties associated with talking about race, the discomfort many of us feel and the need to press through it:

> I have to say that doing the work of diversity, including infusing our curriculum with diversity, is often uncomfortable, tense and challenging for both faculty and students. Had you remained in the session, you would have received information and participated in the discussion about tension and discomfort experienced in these classes. Honestly, opting out of the discussion is always the easiest route, an option not usually afforded marginalized groups. The students present in that room discussed classroom and campus events that they would love the opportunity to avoid, to walk out on. However, that is a privilege they are not afforded. This work takes both courage and commitment from all parties or everybody loses. I encourage you to talk with me about this issue.

Of course, she did not talk with me about the issue. She opted to disparage the work of the workshop and the three women of Color she held responsible for an attack on her privilege. I am happy to report that we had a very powerful discussion with the remainder of the participants during our next meeting. Many of the White participants agreed that the White woman's motives had been misunderstood. When she interrupted the African American male graduate student it was to show the similarity in mistreatment of students who are either White or of Color, some explained. In the end, many participants understood that interrupting the student with an example that contradicted his experience could be interpreted as dismissive and shut down communication in the classroom. Still, some of the participants, after talking at length with the White woman professor, expressed the very fragile position in which she continued to find herself because of the "attack." Remember, the so-called attack involved a woman of Color suggesting that we all reflect on what happened when someone on the panel, a student of Color, was interrupted during his presentation. Very little consideration was given the vulnerable position the student occupied by talking about his experiences on a predominantly White campus in a room full of White faculty members. Nearly one year later, our office was asked to develop a mandatory sexual harassment and discrimination training for the entire campus. Once again, we heard from the White woman faculty member in an email forwarded by her dean. She wanted to know if she could be exempted from the training since our office had treated her so poorly in the past. Again, the "truth" that she shares with her colleagues (and anyone who will listen) is one that disparages three women of Color and, by association, everything we touch.

## Acting White

I am convinced that the problem many women of Color face on predominantly White campuses stems from our belief that we are indeed equal to White people. Acting on that belief, we sometimes pose questions, challenge ideas, correct inaccuracies, draw attention to inequities and even expect to be paid the same wage as our White counterparts. Although there may be policies in place, mission and vision statements and the occasional speech by high-ranking administrators about the importance of every voice, culture, experience and way of being, the reality for many people of Color on predominantly White campuses does not match the rhetoric.

An exchange I had nearly 20 years ago with, of all people, a White nail technician helped me understand that while many White women and men *talk* about being inclusive their hearts (or maybe their minds) are not completely sold on the notion of equality. In an attempt to explain just how open and inclusive she is to all people, races and religions, the White woman nail technician relayed story after story of the numerous women of Color she had served. But there was one African American woman who left a "bad taste" in her mouth. The nail technician continued to tell me how that African American woman wanted her nails to be perfect in every way. "She kept telling me how she wanted things, that she wanted me to shape her nails this way and that way … she was treating me like *I* was Black!" Little did that African American customer know that in expecting to get what she paid for she was "acting White."

The mistake that women of Color often make on predominantly White campuses, is expecting their voices to be desired. Too many of our White colleagues want diversity if it means that they can attract people of Color who will be just like them in every way except the color of their skin. They forget that a diverse professorate, staff and student body should bring a diversity of opinion, outlook, ideas and experiences. That means that when a person of Color says something that a White person has not thought of or would not say, problems arise. When White women are on the receiving end of a question about their behavior, they are often shocked, offended and often feel attacked. Every time a woman of Color questions a White woman, she is acting like her equal, she is acting White. Unfortunately, in systems of privilege and power there just are not enough spaces for everyone to be White.

## Colored Realities

One of the most damaging consequences of whiteness and the white ownership of truth and innocence is the power to silence women of Color, stopping us "dead in our tracks," removing us from the discussion and rendering us incredible, untrustworthy and suspect. In *Feminist Theory: From Margin to Center*, bell hooks (2000) notes the not-so-subtle messages women of Color receive from White women in the feminist movement when their comments fail to toe the party line:

> When I participated in feminist groups, I found that white women adopted a condescending attitude towards me and other non-white participants. The condescension they directed at black women was one of the means they employed to remind us that the women's movement was "theirs"—that we were able to participate because they allowed it, even encouraged it; after all, we were needed to legitimate the process. They did not see us as equals. They did not treat us as equals. And though they expected us to provide first-hand accounts of black experience, they felt it was their role to decide if these experiences were authentic … If we dared to criticize the movement or to assume responsibility for reshaping feminist ideas and introducing new ideas, our voices were tuned out, dismissed, silenced. We could be heard only if our statements echoed the sentiments of the dominant discourse (pp. 12–13).

As hooks (2000) notes, in many academic settings, women of Color are merely window dressing, present to signal the openness of White women and men but not required to speak. Countless university committees include people of Color for the sole purpose of legitimizing a search process that fails to yield candidates of Color. White committee chairs and members can always assure outsiders that the process was unbiased because of the presence of a committee member of Color. However, should that committee member of Color point to the lack of diversity in the candidate pool, she or he may be silenced or ignored. Every time a person of Color is labeled problematic when she asks questions or introduces new ideas, the message is clear—the university is "theirs" (hooks, 2000, p. 12). We are invited guests who must mind our manners by remaining silent or risk being seen as obstacles and "in the way" of the real work of the committee.

Until White women and men can see the multiple ways they are negatively impacted through their sole ownership of truth and innocence, little will change for women and men of Color on college campuses. Although much attention is paid the importance of a diverse student body, faculty and staff, the realities of that diversity—different ideas, understandings, ways of knowing and being—prevents us all from benefitting from that diversity. When our White women colleagues take offense at our questions, disagreements or suggestions they not only shut down communication, they set in motion a "story" about these exchanges that negatively paints women of Color as mean, abrasive, inappropriate, radical, intimidating, etc., while White women are depicted as innocent victims of a ruthless tirade. When White men and women own truth, they get to call the shots in the academy. Too often those shots, or messages about their exchanges with women of Color, turn into weapons with the power to limit or destroy opportunities for growth and development.

Belief in the inherent inferiority of people of Color aids in the creation of destructive stories about them and their behavior that are accepted by other Whites. White women committed to this work must be willing to do what Papusa Molina (1990) recommends—work at the personal level, unlearning attitudes and behaviors of oppression (p. 329). But White women cannot unlearn what they deny exists. Too many White women and men in the academy assume their advanced degrees, service on diversity committees and willingness to mentor people of Color are evidence that they lack bias or are capable of acts of oppression. I am asking for a monumental shift in the way White women think about themselves and people of Color in order to allow all of us to be seen as legitimate parts of the academy with the right to be ourselves as we interact and engage one another. Barbara Smith (1990) makes this point beautifully:

> I am sure that many women here are telling themselves they aren't racist because they are capable of being civil to Black women, having been

raised by the parents to be anything but. It's not about merely being polite … Racism and racist behavior are our white patriarchal legacy. What is your fault is making no serious effort to change old patterns of contempt—to look at how you still believe yourselves to be superior to Third World women and how you communicate these attitudes in blatant and subtle ways (p. 26).

This is a call for White women to make a "serious effort to change" the academy and themselves. Whenever what we believe to be true about ourselves is questioned discomfort, uncertainty and perhaps embarrassment wash over us. In my mind, the key to successfully dealing with these feelings is to avoid allowing them to turn in to anger and resentment. Rather, those feelings provide an opportunity for exploration. White women dedicated to becoming our allies will have to resist giving in to and participating in these well-established systems designed to silence and discredit women of Color by portraying their dissension as inappropriate and threatening. What would happen if White women and men, when confronted with a difficult question from a person of Color about a plan or idea, reflected on their answers to the following:

- What am I feeling right now? Why?
- What would happen if I refused to take the question or comment personally?
- Am I able to suspend the frustration that I am feeling right now to actually hear what my colleague is saying to or asking of me?
- Have I really thought the issues through?
- Why am I unwilling to answer or consider the question being posed?

I always wondered how different the outcome might have been had the White woman professor mentioned above "stayed in the room" and participated in the powerful discussion that followed her interruption of the African American student. Interestingly, five months before the workshop, the same White woman professor visited my office expressing a desire to work with and mentor students of Color in her academic unit. She noticed that many of the students of Color in her classes were struggling with the material and wanted some guidance in approaching them. She admitted being concerned that students of Color would not view her as genuinely interested in their success. In an email to me after our initial meeting, the White woman faculty member articulated an appreciation of the complexities of the faculty-student relationship and explained, "I haven't wanted to make things worse by being too pushy, especially given the power differential … This is an area where, even when people try to understand, misunderstandings can occur." Yet, in just five months she managed to forget the power differential that once concerned her, having no problem interrupting an African American male student serving on a panel as a guest of the workshop. Although she expressed the desire to be vulnerable and genuine, as well as an appreciation for the possibility of being misunderstood, five months later she was no longer willing to "try hard" or deal with her behavior. It was easier to become the victim of Asian American and African American women while wallowing in the innocence of her whiteness than to confront and acknowledge her own behavior.

The ease of whiteness, of owning truth, along with the privilege of being found innocent in the presence of angry women of Color, is the root of the problem. My earnest hope and advice to White women who are truly interested in building relationships across racial lines is that they be open to the frustration, discomfort and embarrassment that result when pushed to think differently or accept information that counters long-held beliefs. I suspect that the discomfort does not last forever and that on the other side of all those feelings is a better understanding of situations, structures, white privilege and the possibility of a relationship with a woman of Color. Since refusing to engage is an act of power and privilege most women of Color do not have in their toolkits, it is White women who must be willing to move through the discomfort toward women of Color who have already made themselves vulnerable, making the first move by asking for a salary equal that of others, pointing out a possible error in a plan or asking for more information.

Finally, I hope that our White women colleagues will relinquish their sole ownership of truth and innocence and begin to interrogate "angry women of Color stories," asking for specifics and, when appropriate, pointing out possible alternate explanations. If White women in the academy are interested in becoming allies with women of Color, they must be willing to speak up for us when they hear outrageous stories about our behavior. White women must also be willing to hear us when we speak and move beyond being offended by our presence, ideas and questions. They must also be willing to accept and acknowledge women of Color as their equal and necessary partners in the academy. A sure sign that we see others as our equals is our acceptance of their views, questions and challenges as credible and worthy of consideration.

White women must be willing to "stay in the room" when it is easy and when it is difficult to do so. What I mean here is that, it might be easier to challenge someone complaining about women of Color "fighting" to receive equal pay, especially if you played no role in the decision-making process that lead to the inequitable pay. It will be harder when a woman of Color asks a White woman, who has communicated her commitment to creating genuine relationships across racial lines, how as the chair of a search committee she has managed not to identify any viable candidates of Color.

One of the problems associated with the presumption of innocence is the idea that White women cannot afford to be found to be human, that is to make mistakes, to totally "drop the ball" from time to time.

I understand I am asking White women to walk away from a system of power and privilege that not only gives them the upper hand with women of Color but further cements their solidarity with powerful White men who may also be at odds with women of Color. Perhaps these facts have caused so many of the women of Color I interact with in the academy to be doubtful about the prospect of improving relationships with the White women on their campuses. The realist in me knows that many White women will not reject the system of privilege and all of its benefits. The optimist in me looks forward to creating sustained professional and personal relationships with the White women courageous enough to try.

## References

hooks, b. (2000). *Feminist theory: from margin to center*. London: Pluto Press.

Molina, P. (1990). Recognizing, accepting and celebrating our differences. In G. Anzaldúa (Ed.), *Making face, making soul* (pp. 326–331). San Francisco: Aunt Lute Books.

McIntosh, M.V. (1988). "White privilege and male privilege: A personal account of coming to see correspondences through work in women's studies," Wellesley College Center for Research on Women.

Smith, B. (1990). Racism and women's studies. In G. Anzaldúa (Ed.), *Making face, making soul* (pp. 25–28). San Francisco: Aunt Lute Books.

# 5

# ON BECOMING ALLIES

## Opportunities and Challenges in Creating Alliances Between White Women and Women of Color in the Academy

*Marquita T. Chamblee*

### The Beginning

Any writing that I do about the relationships between women of Color and White women in the academy must be done from within my particular context. I have been in an administrative or staff role my entire 28-year career in higher education and have never held a tenure-track appointment. This background highlights what I believe is another important layer in the complexity of relationships between women in the academy—that differences in rank and position within the institution also influence how we interact with one another. How for example might interactions between an African American administrator and her White female administrative assistant differ from that between a White female administrator and an assistant of Color? Or, what is the nature of the relationship between an African American mid-level administrator and a White female faculty member? If both hold doctorates and similar years of experience in the academy but one is non-tenured and the other is in the tenure system, can they relate to one another as peers? In seeking to develop relationships or forge alliances between women of Color and White women, rank and potential power imbalances must be considered, as the cost or risk to one of the pair might be significantly higher than the cost to the other.

One other contextual consideration I want to raise that also affects the development of cross-race relationships between White women and women of Color in the academy is the size of the institution for which they work. My work experiences have situated me on large, multi-campus, state "flagship" institutions (over 30,000 students), mid-level state institutions (under 10,000 students), and small private, highly specialized institutions (under 500 students). Size does matter in terms of availability and quality of relationships. At larger institutions, there is at least the potential for diversity and quantity of people with whom one can develop mentoring, ally, peer, or other relationships, both within and across race. At a smaller school you are somewhat confined to seeking out relationships drawn from a small subset of that group. Regardless of the institutional size, opportunities for isolation or connection, self-containment or collaboration exist for women of Color seeking to work their way up the ranks in academia.

Given these contexts I want to outline a few themes I've observed as White women and women of Color of various ranks and roles in institutions interact, and explore whether or not there was the opportunity to create alliances. I will offer examples of ways in which White women's silence—intentional or otherwise—helps to maintain the status quo of white male supremacy in the academy and erect barriers to developing relationships. Throughout I will explore scenarios in which cross-race relationships between women of Color and White women might have made a difference.

Some of the complexity in writing about the relationships between women of Color and White women is derived from the fact that so much of what happens between us is intangible and defies definition. It dwells in the realm of instinct, feeling, intuition, outside the bounds of rationality, intellectualism and logic in which so much of academia exists. My hope is to lift the veil a bit and allow us to glimpse the possibilities.

## The Right (Privilege) to Remain Silent

Throughout my career in academia, I have worked primarily for White male administrators, except for a three-year stint during which I worked for a White woman. In that time I have seen numerous examples of White female administrators continually deferring to White men in matters affecting people of Color and other under-represented groups. Part of what I have observed is this: White women are often in positions of authority from which they could be allies to women (or men) of Color. However, at times when they could use their privilege in causes affecting people of Color, they choose to remain silent or fail to act. They often do not advocate for people of Color either individually or collectively if their engaging in advocacy brings them into conflict with their White male counterparts or superiors. And in the worst case, they turn into antagonists, actually supporting a white male supremacist culture in opposition to a person of Color. The following example illustrates this point.

I was part of a senior administrative team that managed a large, multi-department unit at a research institution. My role was as an interim associate vice president, but because I was not tenured I couldn't actually *be* an associate vice president in title. That is another story. This team, comprised six associate vice presidents and the vice president, included three women—two of Color (including me)—and four men, all White.

During one of our regular meetings, Don, the vice president, told us he wanted our opinion on something. He was thinking about promoting a man from an annual contract to a permanent, high-level administrative position with tenure. One of the team, Linda, an African American woman, raised some concerns about the individual they were considering promoting. She asserted that the person in question didn't have the requisite credentials—he was untenured (and hadn't even been on the tenure track), lacked the academic portfolio necessary to be effective in the role, and thus should not be considered. Her assertion was consistent with other previous team decisions about such promotions. We often did not allow candidates to skirt around any of the various hoops required for promotion, tenure or administrative appointments.

Don replied, trying to justify making an exception in this case. His remarks were followed by comments from one of Linda's peers James, another of the associate vice presidents, who supported Don. I was growing uncomfortable with the exchange, but wasn't quite certain how to interrupt. In fact, I agreed with Linda. It was clear that Don had not really wanted our opinion; he wanted us to endorse his decision.

But Linda wasn't letting it go. Both James and Don became increasingly irritated with her for getting in their way. Finally Robin, a White woman, turned to Linda and said, "Linda, what Don is trying to say is that he can suspend the normal process in order to make the appointment." I looked at Robin a little stunned. I had expected that she would offer a neutral or supportive perspective that would defuse the situation. I wasn't expecting her to side with the boys. For her to interpret for Linda what Don was saying, as if she was incapable of understanding was incredibly disrespectful and insulting. Linda looked over at Robin and replied, "I know what we *can* do. My issue is whether or not we *should* do it."

At this point in the meeting, Don suggested we take a 15-minute break. I followed Linda back to her office and encouraged her to drop it.

"He's already made up his mind to put Bill in that position, Linda. You're just digging yourself in even deeper with Don than you already are." I had been concerned about Linda since she'd joined the administrative team. The two of us were the highest-ranking African American administrators in the unit, which made us high profile. Linda's assertive style hadn't played too well with the men on the team. They weren't used to being challenged and thus had begun excluding Linda from key decisions in which she should have been involved.

"What Don's proposing isn't right. You know they're just putting Bill in there because he's another one of their golden boys, not because he has the qualifications or has earned the job."

"*I* know that, Linda. But they're going to do what they're going to do. You have to decide if this is a hill you're willing to die on or if you want to live to fight another day."

On my way back to my own office I asked myself, "What are you doing? Are you asking Linda to sell out?" Had I decided to "go along to get along?"

Shaking my head at myself I made my way back to the meeting. To my dismay, Linda picked back up where she'd left off, re-raising her objections to the proposed appointment. When Don started in again with his justifications, I spoke up. To this day I don't remember exactly what I said. What I recall is that I suggested an alternative wherein the candidate could be vetted first without simply putting him into the position. What happened next is something I'll never forget. Don turned and made a statement to me in tone and energy that virtually cut my legs out from under me. Though I can't remember the words themselves, I experienced the tone as demeaning and intimidating. It almost felt like a physical blow. It was the first time in my life I can remember dissociating. My body was there and I talked and interacted throughout the remainder of the meeting; but my mind and spirit had left the room.

In the end, they of course, appointed Bill to a position for which my guess is they would have never considered placing a woman or a person of Color with the same or slightly better record. I learned that I could not depend on Robin to advocate for issues affecting people of Color, especially if such advocacy put her in conflict with White men.

It's important to understand the background of the story in order to grasp why I would look to Robin as a potential ally and then ultimately write her off. In her role as associate vice president, Robin had authorized a team of folks in her unit to create and implement a widespread diversity training program at agencies across the state as well as on campus. She went through the specialized two-day diversity workshop they created and participated in the train-the-trainers session that, in essence, prepared her to lead the seminar. She talked *a lot* about diversity, anti-racism, homophobia and related issues. In spite of all that training, I never was too comfortable with her. I never had the sense that she really understood the impact of the "isms" and white privilege at anything more than a superficial level.

During sidebar conversations with Robin, she often spoke of how important it was that Don do his personal work around issues of race, power and privilege. Yet, she failed to acknowledge that she might need to continue doing her own work in the area as well. In the meeting scenario described earlier, she had numerous opportunities to be an ally to the woman of Color who was making a valid argument against the white male system in place in the department. Surely it was evident to her that the old boy network was in operation—hadn't she seen it herself in the years she'd been on the administrative team? She not only remained silent, but added insult to injury by siding with the White men and correcting the woman of Color.

In addition to her failure to speak and act as an ally in administrative team settings, she also frequently failed to use her privilege—actually her authority—to promote a staff person in her department to a higher position. He had the years of experience and a master's degree, but she would not buck the trend and promote a person without a doctoral degree. She had defended Don when he wanted to suspend the rules to promote someone who didn't meet all the requirements, but would not promote her own Latino staff member to a position for which he was, in all other ways, well qualified. When she had the opportunity and the authority to do the right thing, she remained silent and refused to act.

What can we learn from Robin's case about when, why, and how to engage in effective ally relationship building? When I think about my experiences with White women in the academy, I begin to wonder how many White women serve at the pleasure of White male oppressors and don't speak for fear of losing places of influence? How many of them are silent because they, too, are operating from a position of disadvantage? Are they so rooted in their own survival that they are unable to advocate too passionately for anything or anyone else, especially a person of Color? Or do they keep silent on matters affecting people of Color because they are saving their political capital for concerns about which they are more passionate? As a woman of Color, part of the assessment I need to do in looking for allies among White female colleagues is to consider the question of cost—what it potentially costs them to ally with me or the causes I'm concerned with and what I can bring to the table that could help offset those costs.

For White women, it's important to recognize how their skin color grants them systemic privilege and explore how to use that privilege in support of those without it. Writing about how White people can become allies for people of Color, Kendall (2006), elaborates:

> Allies are able to articulate how various patterns of oppression have served to keep them in privileged positions or to withhold opportunities they might otherwise have. For many of us, this means exploring and owning our dual roles as oppressor and oppressed, as uncomfortable as that might be. I need to see how my whiteness opens doors to institutions or opportunities that most probably would not have opened so easily otherwise. We need to understand that, as White women, we are given access to power and resources because of racial similarities to and our relationships with White men. And we often receive those privileges at the expense of people of color, both male and female. While we certainly experience systemic discrimination as women, our skin color makes us less threatening to the group that holds institutional power. (p. 150)

It is also important for White women exploring what it means to be an ally to examine when, where and how they are silent in their interactions with white male power structures. Silence is a powerful tool for maintaining systems of oppression.

## Comrades in the Struggle

I believe it is possible to develop a valuable ally relationship with a White woman who has power in an institution. But in preparing to do so one has to evaluate a number of important factors. It is not enough that the person is situated in a leadership position from which she can advocate for particular issues or causes, although this is certainly helpful. Also, it is not enough that she has been through training and educational programming around issues of power and privilege. Possessing a personal commitment to understanding these issues and continuing to do the self work is a vital requirement for a would-be ally. How that ally fits in the overall power structure of the institution is critical to her ability to be an effective ally.

I worked closely with Joan, a White female administrator who was on the senior leadership team of the institution. Although we both reported to the chief executive officer (CEO), she was on his senior cabinet and I was not. That was problematic in that my role at the institution was as its chief diversity officer (CDO). My belief has always been that a CDO must sit on the senior leadership team where issues related to budget and finances, hiring and promotion, strategic planning, and other institution-wide concerns are addressed. Nevertheless, one would hope that having an ally on the inside would be almost as good. Unfortunately, that did not prove to be the case.

Although Joan, my ally, held a leadership position at the institution, the senior leadership team comprised primarily White men. The lone person of Color, a Latino, rarely broke ranks with the White men; rather, he stood solidly behind the CEO. In essence, he didn't make waves. Joan was often outmaneuvered and excluded from various hallway meetings (because her office was on a different floor than the other vice presidents). There was, of course, no intent to exclude her, or so they said, but exclude her they did. While Joan and I were able to do good work together in the areas for which she was responsible—her areas of responsibility at the institution were enormous—her introverted personality rendered Joan less effective in the face of white male supremacy. What we did manage to accomplish around issues of racial and social justice we did either by carefully aligning what we were doing with some of the CEO's pet ideas (he referred to them as "victories") or by covertly working around him.

There were perhaps times when Joan could have chosen to speak up and did not do so. There were more times when she did speak and was ignored.

There were certainly places in which she could and did take actions on areas directly under her authority that made a difference in the institution's antiracism work. And while I felt confident that she was personally committed to the work I was doing as chief diversity officer, I am not certain of the extent to which she was able to translate that personal commitment into institutional change when it meant going up against "the boys."

In this case, our alliance served only to make us comrades and co-miserators in the struggle. We would complain, then plot how to work around the CEO and sometimes we could garner support by working on one of the other vice presidents to gain their support. But most of the time we were forced to operate against the grain of the institution and both of us were ground down in the process. When Joan completed her term as vice president, she stepped down to return to the faculty rather than accept an appointment to a second term.

After Joan's term ended, she was replaced by another White woman. This new vice president had a direct, no-nonsense, straightforward temperament. She was less inhibited about going toe-to-toe with "the boys" on a variety of matters and many people looked forward to seeing how the new configuration would work. From my perspective, her personal knowledge of issues of racism and privilege was set in an intellectual, academic context rather than a deep personal understanding and commitment. While we worked together on a couple of important projects, I didn't have the sense that I had in her an ally with a deep enough awareness of the challenges to be an advocate in meetings with the men. Although she brought a much stronger voice to the table and was rarely, if ever, dismissed or outmaneuvered by the men, the cost of doing business that way took a significant toll on her health. She subsequently went on sabbatical and is due to retire from the institution.

We can learn from Joan's situation a bit more about silence. Unlike Robin, Joan had the will and the commitment to speak up and chose to do so. While Robin *chose* to be silent, Joan, because of a number of institutional factors was *silenced*, rendering her too less effective as an ally. Robin wouldn't, Joan couldn't. As a person of Color, I was able to work with Joan to advance the work of social justice on campus, but that was accomplished primarily through covert action. While covert action is still action, the impact on the campus was not as broadly evident. Because we worked in a fairly small institution, it was difficult to create a critical mass of people from various levels in the institution who could have supported Joan in her advocacy. Getting more powerful people on board would have helped reduce the costs to Joan and to me, but there simply wasn't a large enough pool from which to draw. Institutional size and structure were an important factor in our ability to be effective agents of change.

## White Female Antiracist Activist Allies

A few years ago I worked for a graduate institution where a number of the entering students had gone through various forms of white antiracism training. Originally, I hoped these students would complement my work, believing their training provided a level of knowledge and awareness lacking in many campus members. In some ways, this was true—they were knowledgeable about things like white privilege and systems of white supremacy and had thought a lot about whiteness in general. A group of these students gathered on a regular basis to talk about whiteness and its role in their lives and future vocation. They read, studied and participated in ongoing racial and social justice workshops and activities. Over time I grew concerned because they seemed to be mostly talking amongst themselves and evidence of their specialized training and knowledge was not radiating outward to impact more of the campus. Interestingly, I also didn't notice much interaction between these highly trained White students and students of Color. I didn't see from them a real understanding of what it means to be an ally to people of Color.

Lisa, a White, late-20-something graduate student who spent significant time during her undergraduate work participating in and learning from various trainings for White antiracists, began facilitating trainings and leading a small antiracist group on the campus. What I saw from her was a deep commitment to understanding and working with these issues, but what I believe was missing was grounding in practical experience in terms of being an ally to people of Color. I saw her befriend Tamara, a woman of Color, and over the next few years watched her advocate for her in the name of racial justice even at times when Tamara was in the wrong.

I've seen it happen before. As White people learn more about white privilege and the supremacy of whiteness, many want to connect with people of Color to learn from their experiences, develop relationships, perhaps to become allies. This is not necessarily bad but it is important to explore one's motivation.

Lisa befriended Tamara, a fellow student who spoke passionately and frequently about the racism she was experiencing on campus. While it is true that racism was a serious issue on the campus, Tamara, as often happens to people of Color, was victimized by it and it became such a focus for her experience at the institution that it affected her ability to function and succeed as a student. She alienated nearly every administrator and faculty member, including those people of Color who would normally have been most committed to her success. Through it all, Lisa remained a staunch friend and ally. When Tamara cried foul during various encounters on campus, Lisa stepped in, sometimes "going after" people without bothering to get details or others' perspectives. Her primary source of direct information about the racism occurring on campus and the basis for her advocacy came from one individual person of Color, Tamara.

In *Uprooting Racism: How White People Can Work for Racial Justice*, Kivel (2002) admonishes White people to exercise judgment when allying themselves with people of Color:

> We don't need to believe or accept as true everything people of color say. There is no one voice in any community, much less in the complex and diverse communities of color spanning our country. We do need to listen carefully to the voices of people of color so that we understand and give credence to their experience. We can then evaluate the content of what they are saying by what we know about how racism works and by our own critical thinking and progressive political analysis. (p. 94)

I cannot speak to whether Lisa did a critical, progressive political analysis of Tamara's words or behaviors. But, from where I stood, Lisa's seemingly unquestioning advocacy for Tamara caused me to question her ability to be an effective ally for people of Color. The focus of her advocacy appeared to be personal rather than institutional. Kendall (2006) makes a number of important distinctions between the types of relationships we form with other people: colleagues/peers, friends, allies. She also distinguishes between being an ally to a person versus being an ally to an issue:

> Focusing my alliance on a person leads me to relationship and friendship. I make certain decisions and act in specific ways because I am in relationship with her or him. Concentrating my alliance-building energy on issues pushes me to a very different place: I have to study, to learn, to refine what I know and what I need to know so that my actions and behaviors move us closer to the social and institutional change we, as allies, are striving for. Allying myself with an individual, then, occurs because of who that person is in relation to the issue with which I have allegiance. (p. 145)

Given that context, Lisa's connection with Tamara appears to be more of a friendship or alliance to an individual than the issue of racial and social justice on campus. This doesn't mean that Lisa should not have defended her friend; it does mean that she could not necessarily generalize the particular experiences of an individual to the actions that needed to be taken on behalf of the larger group of people of Color on campus. Being a better ally in the fight against racism on campus might have meant asking questions—both of herself and of Tamara—to clarify whether she needed to offer moral support to her friend or to carefully raise the larger issue with a wider group of people.

Like Robin and Joan, Lisa could have been an effective ally to women of Color on campus. She had the training and education in matters of race and white privilege, and chose to use her voice in advocacy against racism. She also had access to a group of other White antiracist activists who could have been a greater force for good in the push for racial justice. Unfortunately, she was operating from limited data (the issues and experiences of a single individual) and in choosing to ally herself with Tamara, Lisa was often dismissed right along with Tamara by the people in power at the institution.

## On Becoming Allies

Throughout this chapter, I explored three basic archetypes of White women as potential allies of women of Color. There are a number of other possibilities; some are described in many stories and case studies outlined by others throughout this book. What is clear from many of the issues and scenarios raised in this book is the complexity of relationships between White women and women of Color, in the academy as well as in the broader community. What is required for creating ally relationships and how one begins the process involves a number of important elements—different for women of Color and White women.

Many women of Color begin by drawing on our assessment skills. We may begin by identifying our would-be ally and the sources of her power on campus—where she is situated in the institution and how vital her role is to the work of advancing issues affecting people of Color or other "under-represented" or marginalized groups on campus. Who are the power brokers around her and what can we learn about her connections to and interactions with them? It includes evaluating our would-be ally from a variety of different vantage points, collecting as much information as possible that might give us clues as to her background, motivations, favorite issues, roles in her department and across campus, how much she has to lose or gain by allying herself to a particular issue.

Sometimes this requires months of watching her in action—where she sits at meetings, who she interacts with formally and informally, what personality traits she displays in different settings and circumstances, how she behaves toward or in the presence (or absence) of people of Color. We pay close attention to the intuitive "vibe" we get from our own personal interactions with her. We may not always have the luxury of time to do thorough research, but preliminary assessment is important. We follow that up with carefully wading into interactions with this person and the painstaking process of establishing and building the trust that is foundational to effective and authentic ally relationships.

White women should expect to be constantly evaluated and re-evaluated. Women of Color have experienced the Robins, Joans, Lisas and a whole lot of other White women who could have been allies but, in one way or another, fell short. Thinking through your motivation for becoming an ally, deepening your understanding of the dynamics of power and privilege in your institutional setting (and your role in contributing to those dynamics), and creating the trust needed to be a good ally requires a lot of hard work.[1] As is true for women of Color, you have to assess a number of factors in deciding to enter into a cross-race ally relationship, beginning with an honest evaluation of the costs and benefits, both to you and your potential ally. You must be committed to engaging in ongoing learning about race, power and privilege, willing to listen as non-defensively as possible to the painful truths expressed by people of Color oppressed by systems of white supremacy, humble enough to acknowledge your mistakes and learn from them, and willing to resist the urge to flee when things get messy and difficult.

I believe that it is possible to create meaningful, mutually beneficial, authentic relationships with White women in the academy. It requires courage, commitment and a sincere belief that it is the right thing to do in pursuit of creating a more just, equitable, inclusive and empowering community for us all.

## Notes

1 In *Understanding White Privilege*, Frances Kendall (2006) invites White people who would be allies to explore fully what it means to be an ally. In the final chapter of the book, "Becoming an Ally and Building Authentic Relationships Across Race," she gives a primer outlining for would-be White allies the various qualities and characteristics of becoming an ally as well as issues to consider when choosing to ally oneself with a person or issue.

## References

Kendall, F. (2006). *Understanding White Privilege: Creating pathways to authentic relationships across race*. New York: Routledge.

Kivel, P. (2002). *Uprooting Racism: How white people can work for racial justice*. Gabriola Island, BC: New Society Publishers.

# 6

# A LATINA *TESTIMONIO*

## Challenges as an Academic, Issues of Difference, and a Call for Solidarity with White Female Academics

*Theresa L. Torres*

This chapter contains a series of vignettes of the conversations and experiences of exclusion that come from my life as a Latina who is a faculty member at a largely white university. These experiences are part of an on-going discourse surrounding the issues of difference: race, ethnicity, class and privilege, which I analyze from a critical race theoretical framework.

In the 1970s critical race theory (CRT) was developed by legal scholars as a way to identify the role of race and racism in the subordination of people, particularly people of Color, and became a basis for promoting the end of racism within the legal system. Similarly, some scholars also employ CRT to advocate for change within educational institutions and other social structures.

CRT assists scholars who wish to critically work for positive systemic change, which is a central theme of this book. Chicano Studies scholar Daniel G. Solórzano (1998) notes five themes central to this theory. First, critical race theorists maintain that race and racism intersect and are pervasive within society. Although class is also an important factor within systems of oppression, class alone cannot account for all experiences of oppression. Second, Solórzano (1998) argues that employing CRT "challenges the traditional claims of educational systems and its institutions to objectivity, meritocracy, color and gender blindness, race and gender neutrality, and equal opportunity" (p. 122). Solórzano and other CRT scholars maintain that traditional claims are a façade for hegemony that perpetuates the subordination of people of Color and the continuation of white privilege. Third, critical race theorists are committed to social justice through systemic change to eradicate racism and the development of equitable educational structures. Fourth, CRT values and validates the experiences of people of

Color, e.g., storytelling, biographies, personal and familial histories and/or narratives. Using these counter-hegemonic forms of scholarship allows for the development of new research and insights grounded in the lives and experiences of all who are oppressed and whose voices have been excluded. Fifth, CRT is interdisciplinary and engages a variety of scholarship and methodologies in the study of important historical, cultural and social contexts within research (Solórzano, 1998). Employing a CRT framework is an invaluable means for understanding the differences among women of Color and White women within the academy.

In my career as a professor, my goal as an educator is clear. I am committed to work for social justice. In my classes, I address these issues critically and discuss the role of race, ethnicity, gender, sex and class. Many of the students are open to frank discussions about issues of "difference," and I often hear later from students who talk about how those discussions helped them broaden their view of society. My pedagogy is focused on engaging the students within the urban environment, so that they can apply what we have studied. Many of the White students tell me they were never allowed to go to certain parts of the city where they have lived. They realize that this parentally-imposed shield of protection obscures and redefines certain communities, along with their residents, while upholding the myth that we live in an equal society.

In some ways my work with the students is much easier than being a colleague in a largely white institution. While administrators, especially those who are people of Color or have worked in diverse settings, are more open to issues of difference and creating new forms of engagement within the broader urban community, my colleagues, the faculty, remain insulated from the issues of difference and knowingly or unknowingly create distance between themselves and the diverse realities that exist in the slow diversification of our student body and the wider diversity in the urban environment outside the doors of the university. I am often amazed that White faculty can teach about these issues from an academic perspective but do not seem to engage it in their own lives.

## Vignette One

At a dinner party with White colleagues, Bridget asked me about my current research project. I explained that I was interviewing a local Latina, Rose, as part of my research on Latina leaders and assessing their construction of leadership styles. Rose organized local community members who succeeded in removing a leader of the Minutemen from the city parks board. Bridget looked at me as if I had offended her and said, "I cannot believe how anyone could have viewed the 'Minutemen woman' as a threat. The woman is a sweet grandmother who would not hurt a fly." She was repeating arguments that were part of the dominant media's view of the Minutemen leader. This image belies the truth about Minutemen groups. In their research on these groups, the Southern Poverty Law Center identified them as a hate group, since their members regularly serve as armed patrols along the southern border looking for undocumented immigrants. Members of these groups have been suspected of killing immigrants. The fact that they cover the border with Mexico and not Canada also reveals the racial message underlying their commitment to "keeping the borders safe." They only want to keep one border safe from "Mexicans," which is a reference for all people of Latin American descent.

Those "sweet grandmother" images were challenged when she resigned from the parks board and sent a scathing letter to the media blasting those who opposed her. She made racist comments about immigrants and Mexicans, in general, as well as deriding some of the local Mexican American leaders.

As I started to explain to Bridget that she must have missed the "sweet grandmother's" public letter of resignation, the hostess interrupted me, turning to the person next to me and asked, "How do you like living in Kansas City?" I was stunned. I felt like my place at the table had been removed. I was being silenced for offending an assumed rule that race should not be discussed. I realized that she had assumed that as a light-skinned Latina my race was not part of who I am!

Later I thought about the experience and the way that my colleagues silenced me. I have reflected on the implications of silencing and the effects this has on the work that we do. Both of these women are feminist scholars and their lack of awareness of these issues creates silence and distance among us. It creates isolation and rejection of the person who is different for being so. The difficulties we have in being able to talk about these issues are often due to the fears surrounding the realities that divide our epistemologies. I often wonder why is it so difficult to address these with openness to hear one another. Why are we afraid of these conversations?

## Vignette Two

During a meeting with my feminist research group, several of the White female faculty were bemoaning the fact that while we have been trying for years to get the university to fund our projects, the university had just announced they were sponsoring a research project on the Latina/o community. After several minutes of discussion, one of the women realized that I was present, the only Latina faculty member in our group, so she turned to me. "We understand why the university has done this, since the Hispanic community has put pressure on the university to start the research program." I am the only faculty of Color, except for my Latin American colleague, who is active within our group and she was not present. I recognize their constraints and want to help them to see their own blinders and how they allow the dominant culture within the university to shut down any potential for getting their research agenda supported.

The feminist research program has had a number of setbacks. All of the members are aware of the saga of how we lost our funding and support. While I accepted they believed they were stymied by the university administration, I have never accepted the reasons they gave for not trying harder to rally support for funding. This was the first time I addressed them on this issue. "We do not have to accept this delay in funding our research. We could follow the route of the Latina/o group by getting community support to pressure the administration. We could point out their lack of consistency in not honoring the process set up that they require all programs to fulfill in order to get funding."

One of the leaders of the group said, "I cannot challenge the administration since I am not tenured. I would lose my job." I understand her concerns and was not speaking to her specifically, since at that time, I did not have tenure. As the only Latina faculty born in the U.S. on the faculty in our division of the university, I have had to mediate some difficult situations between the university and the Latina/o community, so as not to end relationships with the administration. I do understand her concern for being in the middle. I have been able to balance this position for the benefit of both the university and the community. This balancing act is not without risks.

Nevertheless, I believe that the very reason I am present on this campus is because I have a voice, one that I worked hard to acquire. I received my education and place at the table, not based on my on merit alone, nor for myself alone. If I refuse to speak up for those without a voice or a place at the table, I am not acknowledging or honoring all of those who fought for me to sit there. In other words, I have a responsibility to take the risk to speak. I have done so because I know the history of the Chicano and Women's movements, which includes historical examples of women of Color *and* White women. None of the women in that room, feminist scholars, seemed to be aware of the historical reality of protest and sacrifice in the social movements that supported the growth of feminist studies and the importance of the inclusion of women in the university. By ignoring the important role of protest and the sacrifices that others have made for us, we perpetuate the silencing not only of ourselves but those who came before us and future generations of women—White and of Color.

I turned to the other members of the committee and said, "Is there a way that we could raise the issue as a need so that the larger community might support us?" Immediately several of them said that they could not see any of their local groups ever "pushing" the administration to fund our research program. The faculty argued that their supporters are not that "kind" of women. A senior untenured member spoke from her vantage point of many years. She turned to me directly, "Roberta is telling the truth. Her job would be on the line if the administration found out that she had anything to do with engaging women in the community to 'push for funding.' "

Before I could explain that I understood Roberta's position and the limits of her job, a tenured faculty member said, "We [faculty] understand that Hispanics are a 'special case' since they are discriminated against in society, but no one sees our group [White women] as a 'special case.' Just look at the number of female faculty we have on campus." I was appalled! No longer able to contain my amazement, I exclaimed:

> Women do not experience discrimination? While we see a number of female faculty on campus, this does not mean that we are not discriminated against. Review the statistics of women's income compared to men. We make 77 cents to every dollar a man makes. A female faculty member makes even less, 62 cents to every dollar a male faculty member makes! If you don't believe me check out the American Association of University Women website on women's salaries and then go to the newspaper's website and search for our university's salaries. These are a matter of public record and you can compare what you make to your male colleagues. I have done so and realized the salary inequities existed at the time I was first hired. This inequity existed although I did not accept the first salary offer made to me, which is what many female professors do.

No one said anything after I spoke. I felt the tension in the room. In breaking my silence and speaking from my experience of dealing with systems that do not always listen to our requests or acknowledge our needs, I made the group of White feminist scholars uncomfortable. The irony is that they do not have to be so afraid. At a later meeting to discuss the Latina/o research grant, the provost, a White woman, said she expected the feminist research group to be "beating up on her" any day now since they had been trying to get funding for many years and should have been the first in line. I smiled when she spoke and thought about how the feminist group's fear of retaliation had stopped them from organizing and rallying the academic and local community for programmatic support. In their acquiescence, they created their own silencing. They have accepted the myth that their power is not their own; it only comes from the hegemonic systems that grant it. Therefore, they believe they only have the power if they play "nice" and do not ruffle any feathers. Yet, even the provost expected the white women faculty to use their collective bargaining power to challenge her lack of support.

Paolo Friere (1970) explains that oppressed people often remain so even after leaving the oppressed situation. They internalize oppression by accepting the myths of the oppressor. The White women above illustrate an acceptance of the myths that accompany sexism and oppression. They no longer question inequities for fear of losing what power they have, since they believe that they have power only if others, the administration in this case, grant it to them.

I discussed this case with an African American colleague of mine. We are in different departments but have found a kindred spirit in each other. We believe this is an example of what I call "a fear of asking." The previous example demonstrates the way white privilege blinds a number of White women to the need for struggle. Women of Color can teach White women in the academy how white privilege works to silence their voices. Working together we can help White women see their own blinders.

Women of Color know from firsthand experience that assuming you will be positively rewarded, especially on your first try, is a privilege that we do not have, namely white privilege. Experience has taught us that getting a negative response is to be expected and we can learn from each "no." Every negative response should be met with a series of questions. What were the reasons given for the "no?" How can I counter this? How many potential roadblocks exist? Also, one should never assume that the second request will receive an affirmative response. A guiding principle I work with is that it takes *at least* two negatives before one receives one positive response. This strategy is based on learning the reasons for every "no" understanding the hidden messages not communicated in that response. In the academy, every denial of a request provides information about and enhances our understanding of those in power and the positions they take.

One reason women, particularly women of Color, receive negative responses to our ideas and queries stems from a fear of retaliation or the "special case" mentality on the part of those in power. Institutional leaders may fear that other marginalized groups will retaliate when they see another oppressed group receiving what looks like special treatment. In reality, such treatment is not "special" at all. Rather, many of these requests are attempts to bring equity to institutions where the playing field is far from even for all its the members. Additionally, those in authority generally see sharing power with the oppressed as a direct attack on their power base. Working with a false (or at least, faulty) assumption found in a patriarchal society, they view the world through the lens of limitation. This exclusionary view of power, a binary of who is in power versus who is excluded, creates the illusion that in order to be in control, one group must remain dominant while others must remain oppressed. Sharing power is impossible from this perspective since it assumes that the dominant group is at risk of becoming oppressed. The dominant group fears that any sharing of power ultimately will result in their loss of it.

I have to say, I have rarely seen those in power willingly share it without some push from the outside. Even then it is done grudgingly with the hope that after a brief period of appeasement, all will return to the "natural order of things" with the dominant in control.

In *The Color of Privilege*, Aida Hurtado (1996) discusses the importance of role reversals of power among White feminists and feminists of Color. She notes that since power requires responsibility and privilege, it also means freedom and restriction. The reversal of power is a way for those in dominant and subordinate positions to learn from each other's positions so that White feminists learn what it is like to have less power and feminists of Color experience the "seductive aspects of power" (Hurtado, 1996). For example, people of Color in authority may choose to forget those people of Color who have not had the same opportunities and fail to take the responsibility to advocate on their behalf by creating additional opportunities to empower them.

## Vignette Three

Sarah's story illumines how white privilege limits our ability to work together as equal partners in the academy. As a new faculty member, with unique job expectations and requirements and whose salary comes from an external source, Sarah was placed in an academic unit per university regulations. When she started, Sarah, a White woman, was given a number of challenging requirements: a higher demand for research and publication, as well as speaking to and lobbying various publics, locally and nationally. Nevertheless, her academic unit ignores Sarah's unique status and the fact that her position is not a regular tenure/tenure-track professorship. I often run into Sarah and see how frantic she is to meet the varied and overwhelming requirements of her job. After the conversation with my feminist research group about the blinders they have regarding their own discrimination, I began to think about the ways that all women, White and of Color, are silenced in the workplace and how we tend to accept this as our reality. Sarah told me she accepted her situation since she wants to show her colleagues within her unit that she is a team player. At the same time, she explained that she wants to change the situation and that she regretted her decision to "play along."

What does this have to do with white privilege? The advantages of white privilege keep White women in their place for fear of losing their status as "good" players. They are not the "angry" women of Color, who dare to raise questions and ask why the status quo has to continue. What is holding back the feminist research faculty from requesting funds to hire a director? Is it the belief of their equal status with White men, since they argued they are not a "special case" or an oppressed group? Is their reluctance to ask the result of the fear that they might be seen as oppositional, confrontational, or worse yet, a "special case?"

When our White colleagues label African American women and Latinas as "angry women," who "push" the administration and are oppositional and confrontational, they are committing acts of racial microaggression. These acts are the daily verbal, behavioral, and environmental experiences that "communicate hostile, derogatory, or negative racial slights and insults toward people of Color" (Sue *et al.*, 2007, p. 271). No matter the intent, their daily presence in the lives of people of Color has long-term effects on the psychological and physical health of victims of these experiences.

Our predecessors, women whose voices, lives and work laid the foundation upon which we all stand, struggled to gain access to the jobs and status we all have today and were not afraid to be both challenging and confrontational. If they did experience fear, the cost of remaining silent outweighed that associated with accepting the silence being forced upon them. We stand on their shoulders, White women and women of Color. My first Latina mentor gave me that image and it remains with me today. When we began our relationship, Maria asked me to tell her about the women who fostered my inner strength. I told her stories of my grandmother, mother, aunts and teachers who supported me. I gain strength from the image of all of the women on whose shoulders I stand. They are my ancestors and role models who fought for the civil and intellectual rights of all women: Gloria Anzaldúa, Rosa Parks, Sojourner Truth, Audre Lorde, Delores Huerta, Elizabeth Cady Stanton, Susan B. Anthony ...

My interpretation of this lack of privilege as a position for freedom is similar to that of other Chicana feminists. Hurtado (1996) refers to other Chicana feminists, Maria Lugones and Gloria Anzaldúa, whose writings describe this absence of privilege as an in-between social space, as limen (pp. 84–86). Being freed of the "traditional order" of social position as the outsider, these Chicana feminists see their lack of social position as a place for liberation since this allows them the space to create new possibilities for overcoming oppression by creating new forms of social positions and liberation.

Previously, I worked for a university that did not allow intellectual freedom. At the time of my hire, I had to sign a document that stated I would not teach anything that was contrary to the Catholic Church's teachings. As a feminist, this meant that I could not speak about women priests, social injustices towards women, gays, etc. I stayed at that institution for a few years and realized that although I knew that I did not agree with what I taught, the silencing of my own voice, beliefs and lack of academic freedom began to change me in ways that domesticated my spirit and caused me to lose a sense of myself. No job is worth that experience. My time at that Catholic university, while difficult, was ultimately freeing for it taught me a valuable lesson about the price one pays for accepting the silencing of one's voice.

## Vignette Four

The final example comes from an experience with a White female colleague who has been a very good friend of mine, yet who has unintentionally silenced me on a number of occasions and has done so publicly. At a meeting to discuss Latina/o issues in the community and within the university, my White female colleague corrected me. She also took over the meeting with another White woman to speak about immigrant issues and the university's position. The rest of the Latina/o community leaders (I was one of two Latina/o faculty present) were shocked by the manner in which the two White women spoke to the administrators, particularly to one of the administrators, an African American man who had been absent from his position due to his recent illness and stay in hospital. In a room full of Latina/o community activists, political, business and education leaders and experts, white privilege empowered these White women, while in the minority, to represent one group of Color and reprimand the other.

After the meeting, a couple of the administrators, both women of Color, took me aside and told me that they were angry at the two White women for their treatment of the university officials, and that their actions were demeaning to all of the Latina/o leaders present. "As liberal progressives, these White women should have known better. They were very condescending to us and to you in particular." Before they spoke to me, I felt as though I needed to replay all that had happened, since it belied my trust in my friend. I was shocked by my friend's actions and her boundary violations. I had a feeling of being verbally assaulted, although I was not the person who was on the receiving end. I was strongly encouraged by the women of Color to challenge the two White women since they may have harmed the good will of the administration in dealing with our issues, one of which was to get a Latina/o research project started and continue our annual fundraising for Latina/o scholarships to the university and on-going support for a host of outreach programs to the Latina/o community. Later the Latina/o community leaders and I spoke about how embarrassed and angry we were by the actions of the White women at the meeting. Their actions were also potentially harmful to the overall goals of the group.

When I called my White colleague and explained that she and her friend may have caused serious harm, she interrupted me before I could finish. I stopped her. "As your friend and one who has never before challenged you in any of your actions or even your thinking, I ask you to listen and hear me out." I told her about the potential harm and how I believed she had a good message but took the wrong forum and method. I understood that she was probably upset with me and asked her to withhold her response until she was no longer angry. A week later she told me she understood my points. While she did not fully agree, she recognized that her communication style, and that of the other White woman, during the meeting should have been different. Further, my friend explained that she did not understand my position. She said, "I don't think of you as a Latina." I know that she meant well, but her denial of my reality and my own chosen identity cut to the core of the essence of why we were not able to communicate. Her statement was a racial microaggression that is a covert racist means of denial of the issues and constructs of racism in society. My friend's actions of "correcting" the Latina/o leaders and university administration about immigration issues were ways of silencing us and challenging our integrity. By her actions she revealed her latent racial dominance and control. Believing herself to be a progressive liberal who was acting on behalf of Latina/o immigrants, she sought dominance and control while unaware of her own racist actions. The invisibility of covert racism is insidious for its ability to create self-doubt and psychic harm. This has a more harmful effect for people of Color than overt racism due to the hidden nature of the acts and the belief of perpetrators who claim they are not racists (Sue *et al.*, 2007).

I believe that we, especially faculty—women of Color and White women—need to address these issues of difference directly and stop being afraid to face the difficult conversations. I know that initially when I stepped out of my world of denial about the inequities of race, class, gender and sexuality I was afraid and, at times, felt immobile. Later, I realized it was the fear of the unknown and guilt that played on my ignorance and acceptance of the hegemonic discourse surrounding these issues. But I soon learned that immobilization and guilt were worse than any "supposed" fear that I had to face. As I walked into my feelings of discomfort, my fears of guilt were lifted and the immobilization was gone. I did not have to be held hostage by those challenges. The difficult conversations do not have to hold us hostage. Rather, they can be a means for liberating us from our fears and the assumptions that prevent us from understanding one another.

My *testimonio* is offered as a means for dialogue and insight as to the ways that communication can create new avenues for understanding and can assist in removing the inequities and oppression that exists among us. These examples are given to explain the challenges and my reasons for staying the course, to promote justice and equity within academia so that together we can pay it forward to the next generation of scholars and to students.

## References

Freire, Paulo (1970). *Pedagogy of the Oppressed*. New York: Continuum.
Hurtado, Aida (1996). *The Color of Privilege: Three blasphemies on race and feminism*. Ann Arbor: University of Michigan.

Solórzano, D.G. (1998). Critical race theory, racial and gender microaggressions, and experiences of Chicana and Chicano scholars. *Qualitative Studies of Education*, 11(1), 121–136.

Sue, D. W., Capodilupo, C., Torino, G., Bucceri, J., Holder, A., Nadal, K., & Esquilin, M. (2007). Racial microaggressions in everyday life: Implications for clinical practice. *American Psychologist*, 62, 271–286.

# 7

# WHAT DO I DO WITH ALL OF YOUR TEARS?

*Karen L. Dace*

> ... many women, not only women of color and not only academics, do not want to be "just women," not only because something important is left out, but also because it means being in a category with "her," the useless white woman whose first reaction when the going gets rough is to cry.
>
> (Catharine A. MacKinnon, 1997, p. 21)

Although Catharine A. MacKinnon's (1997) discussion above is part of an argument for a more expansive understanding of what it means to be a woman and the very narrow ways the academy and legal scholars define "woman," it also points to a behavior found in white womanhood that is particularly problematic for women of Color in the academy—crying on the part of White women in professional settings. I am referring particularly to the tears that erupt in conversations involving race. During difficult dialogues, challenging moments that call into question her commitment to equity or shed some light on what others might perceive as her bias, every White woman has one weapon that can shut a meeting down in mere seconds, thus ending an uncomfortable moment (for her) while ushering in anger and resentment from women of Color in the room. Many of us know that the moment a White woman begins to cry during a meeting, no matter the significance of the issue prior to the waterworks, the meeting is over. Often, the issue under discussion is never re-introduced for fear of more tears and discomfort.

As I struggled with this chapter, I kept thinking of the countless tears I have been privileged to witness in the privacy of my office, over coffee at a local restaurant, or late at night on my home phone. These are not the tears of papers, journals, conference panels or book chapters because they do not emanate from White women. Like many of you reading this chapter, I have been in more meetings than I care to count during which a White woman has burst into tears rather than respond to a challenging question or simply began crying while attempting to talk about race. However, those tears do not begin to approach in number those I have experienced while listening to women of Color—American Indian, Asian American, Chicana and African American—as they relayed stories of their treatment, often at the hands of their White women colleagues.

As I began re-thinking this chapter, I thought an appropriate alternative title might be "I Wish *Our* Tears Mattered." I simply do not believe the same behavior—crying during a professional meeting on the part of a woman of Color—would meet with the same rush to comfort, suspension of the discussion underway or insistence that the "offending" party apologize immediately. White supremacy makes the tears of White women important while rendering those of women of Color inconsequential, invisible and, in the minds of many, impossible. This is helped by the very public nature of White women's tears versus the privacy required for those of women of Color. While creating "safe zones" for White women to cry, supremacy on predominantly White campuses drives the tears of women of Color underground.

For 12 years, due to an administrative appointment which has sometimes empowered me to successfully advocate for marginalized students, staff and faculty on two predominantly White campuses, I have had the sad privilege of seeing and hearing women of Color cry as they recall an exchange with colleagues, express frustration, anger and hopelessness or discuss how they are grappling with unfair treatment in the academy, often, but not exclusively, at the hands of White women. While I could recount numerous occasions during which a White woman has "used" tears to shift attention away from the subject at hand and toward her own need for affirmation, I will do very little of that here. Rather, I have chosen to focus on three women of Color who have given so much of themselves to an academy that repays them with the kind of emotional pain that elicits tears.

## The Tracks of Our Tears

I will never forget the sight of Jean, sitting in my office, shaking as she placed the anonymously-penned letter in my hands. Our campus was famous for what I referred to as "drive-by" emails, notes and letters often intended to do harm but sometimes to be helpful. The author identified her/himself as a whistle blower who witnessed a series of troubling events but understood that she or he could easily become a target. The letter, placed in Jean's office mailbox, confirmed what she long suspected. There was a plan underway to undermine and discredit Jean in hopes of having sufficient evidence to have her fired. Although membership in the professorate cannot fully protect women of Color, it provides more shelter than the non-tenure track jobs most women hold on college campuses. Jean, an African American woman in her late 50s, known for the high quality of her work, held an administrative title with several years of experience in her profession. Perhaps it was the confidence with which she walked the halls, the professionalism she exhibited in meetings, the meticulous manner in which she wrote reports or her attendance at university events when not required by her job to do so that caught the attention of her superior, a younger White woman with limited experience and expertise. Whatever the reason for her resentment, the letter outlined a plan that would ensure Jean's dismissal by making certain she did not receive necessary information to complete assignments and eliminating direct contact with university personnel that relied upon her expertise. The author went further to explain that Jean's boss planned to take evidence of her poor performance to her superiors and human resources professionals to begin the dismissal process.

As we discussed the letter and our next steps, Jean lost the battle to hold back the tears. They were not so much tears of hurt, I think, as they were angry and frustrated tears. She had become a target because she performed the duties assigned to her well, refusing to make apologies for her abilities. Jean's demeanor never betrayed the fear many of her co-workers exhibited when interacting with her supervisor. She spoke with a quiet clarity, poise and determination absent from many of the younger men and women in her department. As she sat there, recent events made perfect but wicked sense. The anonymous letter helped Jean make sense of a recent directive that, until further notice, her boss would interact with each external department representative rather than Jean and pass on the necessary information. It was not, after all, a mistake that her boss failed or forgot to pass pertinent information on to Jean, resulting in a less than successful project. Jean was not losing her mind, just her job, potentially. The author of the letter wanted Jean to know about the plan, explained that she or he was searching for another job and, should she or he become successful, would pass on the evidence of this elaborate plan to Jean.

Jean's tears had the most disturbing and profound impact on me. I think it was her age, as I explained to my superior, that made Jean's tears most painful. As we sat in his office, I shared the anonymous letter and explained my personal frustration. Clearly, Jean is "not old enough to be my mother." But she was older than me. And, like me, Jean is an African American woman. In her tears I think I saw evidence that no matter how long or hard people of Color work, we remain targets of white supremacy until we leave or are pushed off of predominantly white campuses. Jean's experience showed me that the battles I fight both as an African American woman and an administrator and as part of my job expectations will never end. If someone of Jean's stature and age could be penalized for being talented, professional and confident in an African American woman's body, there can be no safe place for people of Color in the academy. In my administrative role I had rarely been asked for help by someone older than me. Of the handful of "older" university employees seeking my assistance, Jean was the only one who had cried. There is something painfully sad about someone you consider to be your elder—a class of people who, in most cultures, merit respect— so hurt by racism that they cry in your presence. While I am not certain, I suspect there was a certain embarrassment on Jean's part and maybe some on my part as well. Weren't our roles reversed? Shouldn't I, the younger of the two, be going to her for assistance and support? As I explained to my boss, although some people have cried in my office, "I don't ever want to see *that*"—an elder brought to tears at the hands of white supremacy—"again."

Ana and I met at a local coffee spot to discuss her decision to leave the university. So hurt by her experience, she had absolutely no desire to step foot on campus, the site of such pain. Like Jean, Ana held an administrative staff position not afforded the protection of the professorate. Prior to joining our university, Ana, a Latina, enjoyed a successful career at another institution where she earned a reputation for professionalism, team work and success. Heavily recruited to switch universities, Ana made the difficult decision to make the move and for a couple of years enjoyed tremendous success. Celebrated both on and off campus, she received high performance evaluations and quickly became involved in the local Latina/o community. However, everything changed when a White student suggested that Ana was not treating her fairly. Further, the student's parents contacted Ana's boss demanding her dismissal. Although Ana offered evidence that contradicted the student, her immediate supervisor, a White woman, explained "these are credible people" and suggested that Ana "just admit that you did these things; it will be easier on you if you do." Several of Ana's co-workers spoke up in her defense and she pleaded with her boss to contact other students who could support her side of the story. Her boss refused to speak to any of the potential witnesses and continued to suggest that Ana's credibility could not compare with that of the student and her parents.

What exactly was it about this student and her parents that made them "credible people" and consequently rendered Ana incredible? How could Ana have, after working for several years with outstanding ratings and student evaluations, become an overnight ogre capable of singling out one student for mistreatment? As I have argued elsewhere in this book, I suspect the problem stems from the whiteness of truth, the presumption of innocence on the part of Whites and the necessary assumption that people of Color are guilty of any and all claims made about them by Whites, even when that White person is a student with seeming less power and status.

As a result of the student's accusations, Ana's boss changed her working arrangements, limited her interaction with students and created new policies and restrictions for Ana's work. Later, Ana learned that none of her colleagues were made to adhere to these new policies although she was informed the new rules were for all staff at her level in the department. Ana cried, off and on, throughout the telling of her story, apologizing along the way. "I don't do this; I'm not a crier," she wept. But these experiences, which seemed to come out of nowhere, caused Ana to do something very foreign to her nature. She loved her job, she thoroughly enjoyed working with students and had done so for nearly 20 years without incident. Ana was confused. How could all of her years of work, high performance evaluations and record of success in developing students be dismissed by one complaint from a disgruntled student?

Through tears, Ana explained that her demeanor changed. She found herself dreading coming to work, crying at home at the thought of working with the students or interacting with her boss. Gradually, Ana's work was affected and she admits that she became bad at her job for the first and only time during her career. Now, the once stellar evaluations were sub-par and she felt she had let herself and the other students down. In her mind, the only viable choice was to resign from a job she once loved but had, in the period of a few months, grown to dread. So horrible was this experience that Ana decided to leave the field altogether, vowing never again to work in the college setting.

Sharing other women's stories and moments of deep sadness is not something I take lightly. Prior to publishing this piece, I sought approval from both Jean and Ana. I also thought it only "right" that I share my own "private" tears as a way of moving from the position of observing and reporting about others to one that places me on the inside to be observed.

After five years of trying, a White woman administrator finally convinced the White men we reported to that she, not I, should be responsible for several areas and departments that reported directly to me. Among these programs was one of the most successful initiatives on our campus earning local and national attention for the positive impact we were having on students and the university. Yet, one afternoon, one of our White male superiors explained that he had "some bad news" to share with me. The two White men in charge and the White woman administrator decided to move one-half of my responsibility areas to the White woman who so desperately wanted them in her portfolio of responsibility. There would be no discussion. The decision had been made, without my input, and there would be no reversal. When I offered to meet with them to discuss the decision, I was told there would be no meeting. I was the only person who saw such a need and had been overruled. My mind went back to a conversation I had with the White woman administrator three or four years earlier during which she made it clear that "it made better sense" that *one* of my areas of responsibility be transferred to her control. In fact, she had already identified the person in her administration who could assume responsibility of that department immediately. Foolishly, I assumed that when I said "thanks, but no thanks" the discussion ended. It had, of course, continued until she succeeded in taking the original department she wanted and some newer programs created during my tenure. She continued a discussion about me without me and, apparently, no one in these meetings found that odd, inappropriate, unprofessional, unethical or just plain wrong.

Like Jean and Ana, I am not one who cries or is overly emotional so I was surprised at the appearance of my tears and caught off guard whenever they materialized. Also, similar to both Ana and Jean, I was confused about the behavior that brought about my tears and began questioning myself. What had I done to merit this treatment? Were there signs that I was inadequate at my job? If all of the very public and private compliments my boss paid were genuine, what happened to make this other administrator finally successful in her campaign to take over major portions of my job? As I mulled these questions over in my head while cleaning my home, I cried. In discussing this decision with my friend and mentor, I cried. When my academic department chair and good friend, a White woman, visited my office to express concern about me amid all of the changes, suddenly I was in tears. During a meeting with a man of Color in one of the offices that was to be moved from my control, I cried as he expressed his concern and confusion about the situation. Sitting in the car one Monday morning trying to gather the strength and will to walk through the doors of the administrative building, I fought back tears while informing an old friend and former graduate school officemate, also a White woman, "I just don't want to go to work anymore."

These three stories are representative of many I could relay about the pain imposed on women of Color on predominantly white campuses by White women and men. However, unlike the very public tears of White women, these are private tears and almost never revealed in the presence of the person who has caused them. And, if women of Color had their way, they would never be displayed around those we love and trust. I will not attempt to speak for Ana and Jean, but I felt the need to be strong for those who looked to me for leadership. As I revealed above, I unexpectedly cried in front of a subordinate of Color during a very trying period in my professional career. Although the tears came and went quickly, I found myself "ordering" him not to tell anyone that I had cried. It was important for me to appear confident even when I was being treated unfairly and others might have thought those tears warranted. I suspect many women of Color do not want to "let the people down" who look to them for leadership, guidance and strength. From my perspective, there were a number of people who reported to me who were scared, angry and confused about the changes. I think they looked to me for some sign that everything would be alright, that they would be alright. The appearance of tears on my part could not create the confidence they needed and I regretted showing my sadness in that way.

## Allies or Opponents

There are at least three lessons to be learned from the study of "raced" tears. Those lessons are explored below and followed by recommendations for women in the academic setting desirous of creating alliances across race.

### *Lesson 1: Never Let Them See You Cry (If You Are a Woman of Color)*

While both women of Color and White women may cry in the academy, the circumstances of those tears are not the same. White women, most likely, cry privately but it is their public tears which come when questioned, pressed or challenged around issues of race that are problematic for women of Color. The absence of public tears from women of Color may be the result of a need, whether real or self-imposed, to present a positive and controlled demeanor no matter the challenge. A strong motivator driving our tears underground may be our need to protect ourselves from the White people who cause them. That is, by showing our hurt and pain in the presence of the people causing our tears, we may give them the upper hand in the struggle. In every exchange, interaction and meeting I had with the White woman administrator who wanted to take over my responsibilities, I never showed anything but the utmost professionalism, confidence and determination. I may have cried in safe, private spaces, but publicly I always walked with my head high when in the presence of the White woman who conspired against me. Anything less might have communicated that she had been victorious in more than taking away some of my areas of responsibility. While she might have been temporarily successful in removing units from my control, I never once concluded or intentionally communicated that she had a right to do so, that I had waved the white flag in defeat, or had given her any justification for her behavior. I believed just one tear in her presence would have signaled my total defeat to the White woman administrator and I was most determined to never give her that satisfaction. And, while my tears were brought about by the removal of a major portion of my job, the private tears I cried had little to do with the White woman administrator. I suspect Jean's and Ana's tears were not a response to the White women who conspired against them. Rather, our tears were a natural response to the realization that even in this millennium, people of Color can be subject to the whims of white supremacy; that White women and men can participate in horrible acts against people of Color in professional settings without retribution; that "life" as many an African American mother has explained to her children "is not fair." Although we may intellectually know that life is not fair, that racism still exists and that given the choice many White people will support other Whites even when their actions are unfair, Jean, Ana and I were all caught off guard by the actions of these White women. As we were moving forward in our careers, doing our jobs and representing the university professionally there were White women working against us and the shock of that reality brought us to tears. It's not that prior to the events that made us cry we ever thought these White women liked us, were our friends and allies or even wished us well. It just never occurred to us that they would devise such wicked plans and no one in authority would stop them or come to our aid.

### Lesson 2: Depending Upon Race, Tears Are Either a First Response or a Last Resort

Unlike the White woman MacKinnon (1997) describes at the start of this chapter, tears are not the "first reaction when the going gets rough" for women of Color. In an email exchange about this chapter, Liz Leckie, a White woman and contributor to this book wrote:

> When I have cried in public, I usually get some version of what I think I need/want ... sympathy ... let off the hook ... apologies ... I bet if you were to ask many white women they would tell you that as white girls they learn to cry to avoid punishment or correction for doing something wrong. It seems to be working the same for us as white women in conversations about race ... we say something that needs to be challenged or corrected and instantly the tears start coming and even though the correction may come, it is often softer than the wrongdoing really warrants.

Following this line of thinking, resorting to tears is one of the tactics available to White women involved in uncomfortable and challenging discussions about race that, while momentarily embarrassing, makes others sympathetic and softens whatever correction may come. For women of Color, however, crying is not the first reaction but a last resort. Since we dare not cry in front of the person responsible for our tears and may feel the need to be strong for others who count on us, women of Color may not think of crying as an option or behavior appropriate for any professional situation. This is why Ana constantly apologized even as she shared her experiences of mistreatment at the hand of her superior. It is the reason I made my subordinate promise not to tell anyone else that I cried. While little White girls understand from their upbringing that crying helps one escape from punishment, at some point women of Color learn a different lesson. Even in the privacy of my office, I could see Jean fighting to keep the tears from falling. In truth, she never gave in to them completely. All three of us composed ourselves quickly and got back to the issue(s) at hand rather than stopping the discussion and waiting for comfort and apologies.

For us, tears were an interruption of something important that needed to be figured out, understood, remedied. For many White women, tears become the interruption prayed for, a respite from some uncomfortable situation. While the tears of White women may be intentionally or unintentionally strategic and used early in "battle," they merely get in the way of important work for many women of Color and cannot really be viewed as weapons for warfare. The very last thing I wanted to do each time I did so was to cry.

### Lesson 3: "Raced" Tears Elicit Comfort or Contempt

One of the more interesting differences between the tears of women of Color and White women in the academy is the corporate response to them. Liz Leckie explained above that as a White woman she has been comforted and received apologies after crying publicly. The private nature of our tears precludes such apologies for women of Color although it is doubtful that the very people responsible for our injury would be moved to act accordingly anyway. Any woman of Color who has ever asked a question or made a comment that reduced a White woman to tears can attest to the cold stares and glares she receives from most of the other White women and men in the room. In addition to being labeled as "that angry Black woman who made Amy cry," many women of Color may be ostracized on campus, excluded from future meetings, uninvited to gatherings and ignored the next time she raises her hand to speak in a meeting. All of this is done to send the message that her behavior is unacceptable and she must be disciplined. I was heartbroken during a recent diversity conference as I listened to one woman of Color after another describe how she had been made to apologize to White women when her question or comment made them cry. Most disturbing were the instances when their men of Color superiors forced them to apologize for, in the course of doing their jobs with diligence, "making" a White co-worker cry. How much more painful must the punishment be for women of Color when the person giving it is also a person of Color coming to the aid of a White woman in need. My heart aches for women of Color in this situation.

Because, for the most part, our tears are absent, White women have not been required to apologize to women of Color. Just as I am not suggesting that women of Color should apologize in the situations outlined above, I am not calling for a flood of apologies from White women. But it does occur to me that many other White women and men are aware of the bad behavior of White women and choose to remain silent. Even the person willing to inform Jean of the plot to ruin her career could not do so openly. Ana's boss had a superior who silently allowed her mistreatment to drive her to resign her position. I am also not suggesting that racism is the source of this poor treatment. That is, race may not be the motivator that caused the

White women described above to behave the way they did with Jean, Ana or me. However, I do believe race played a vital role in the fact that such bad behavior went unchecked. In short, I do not want to suggest that the White woman administrator who worked for years to take over major portions of my job did so because I am an African American woman. Nor am I suggesting that race was not a motivating factor. But I do believe the fact that I am African American made her behavior more palatable for other senior administrators. In this way, race may not have been the motivating factor but it was a conduit, if you will, for others to look the other way or stomach her actions. Racial hierarchies and castes, along with stereotypical views about women of Color as super-strong, angry, suspect, untrustworthy and different, create the space where other Whites with the authority to intervene choose to remain silent. Although all of the White women in the scenarios described above were known for their "strong" personalities, centuries of racist and stereotypical depictions of Latinas and African American women make the playing field uneven with women of Color perceived as a much stronger group that can fend for themselves. This creates an interesting juxtaposition in which women of Color are often disciplined in the academy by being made to apologize for asking questions and White women go unpunished for creating circumstances that wreak havoc in the lives of women of Color.

According to Liz Leckie, the interpretation of the rare tears of women of Color on the part of White women differs from their own: "The painful fact is that in white circles, [the tears of women of Color are] talked about as a version of 'playing the race card.'" For many people of Color, the phrase "playing the race card" is recognized as a means by which our White colleagues dismiss, belittle and ignore significant experiences we believe to be quite significant. In the pages above I have identified public crying as a near taboo for many women of Color engaged in campus battles with White women and men. In more than 20 years in the professorate or as a college administrator, I cannot recall ever being in the presence of a woman of Color who cried *during* an unpleasant exchange *with* her White colleagues. One might expect the infrequency of such tears as an indication that their rare appearance merits some attention, compassion and empathy. This may not be the case. Perhaps the reason White women see crying on the part of women of Color as manipulative is because they recognize it as a tactic they have employed successfully. Hence, their tears are interpreted as genuine and innocent while those of women of Color are a last-ditch effort to use their race to get their way. Although White women may characterize the tears of a woman of Color as an example of "playing the race card," it appears that the tears of White women trump those of women of Color every time.

When White women require comfort for their own tears but hold disdain for those of women of Color, they are, in effect, asserting their superiority of cause, import and femininity. Sole ownership of womanhood affords

White women the power to have their tears valued while devaluing those of women of Color. It makes it possible for White women to expect support as they give in to their emotions and ensure that women of Color do not do the same. White women effectively use their tears to avoid punishment while having power to discipline women of Color for displaying the same vulnerability. Race, however, renders the vulnerabilities different, unequal. For, while White women may indeed escape punishment by crying in public settings, women of Color are subject to both wrath and defeat when they cry in the presence of Whites whose behavior has brought about their pain.

## From Here to an Alliance?

At first glance, this appears to be an "anti-ally" essay. As a realist, I know that some women of Color and White women may never form alliances. This essay is intended for those who desire to create those rare cross-race alliances. The three White women discussed above are not the intended focus here; the White women (and men) who work alongside them are the intended audience. Specifically, it is the White people with power who sit or stand by silently while claiming a will to work across race and support people of Color I that hope to reach. Below, in no particular order, are suggestions for both women of Color and White women on "what to do with all of the tears" in the academy as they struggle to become allies.

- **Acknowledge One Another's Humanity**. Women of Color must acknowledge that tears may be a natural response to being caught off guard when questioned about race, one's commitment to equity, etc. It is quite possible that White women who cry when pressed find themselves genuinely hurt by the implication that they are not truly committed to eradicating racism. When we acknowledge one another's humanity, we create a space for people to express themselves in a manner that suits them best. We give them time to compose themselves and we get right back to business once the tears have been shed. In this way, we do not deny someone's reaction to a difficult question nor do we permit that reaction to signal the end of a difficult discussion—a break, maybe, but not the end.

  White women who acknowledge the humanity of women of Color accept that women of Color are not super-human, emotionless or incapable of feeling the pain of white supremacy. If tears can come at the posing of a difficult question about race for a White woman, why wouldn't they erupt out of frustration, humiliation and confusion resulting from mistreatment from a woman of Color? This is not an appeal for sympathy toward or pity of women of Color but for civility on our campuses. White women should not expect women of Color to cry in their presence when they have perpetrated hurtful acts against them. But White women should not assume that the absence of tears is an indication that women of Color have a higher tolerance for pain, insult, injury, plots against them, and the like. White women who use their own tears to play the ultimate race card should not be insulted or infuriated when a woman of Color gives in to her own tears.

• **Remove the Stigma Associated With Emotion.** I hope we can create space for everyone to express emotion. Bring the tears when necessary but fight the inclination to allow their presence to signal the end of a difficult conversation. Work through them, understanding the subject of race can be hard and uncomfortable for everyone in the room. Allow time for composure to return and get back to the issue as soon as possible. After all, if a subject is one that brings someone to tears, it is likely a matter of import that should not be brushed aside because some find the topic or someone's tears uncomfortable. Similarly, we must not create climates where everyone is expected to know all things about every subject. If a White woman is not prepared to address a hard-hitting question, she should be able to ask for more time to explore the issue rather than be required to be all knowing or to come up with an answer "on the spot." Creating such a climate requires the effort of all women as we cannot expect or count on the men on our campuses to do this work. If such a climate is to come about, it will be the result of women working together to create that change.

• **White Women Must "Woman Up."** Progressive Whites in authority must assume responsibility for correcting the bad behavior of other Whites in their organizations. Interestingly, some Whites with limited power seem more willing to support women of Color in these times than those with the greatest power and ability. While some White women and men spoke up for Jean, Ana and me during our struggles, very few White women in authority challenged the behavior of their "sisters" publicly. It is imperative that women with power understand that silence is not always golden. In fact, doing nothing while other women are under attack is detrimental to all women in the academy. Our silence while others are being mistreated communicates our approval.

Often, women of Color involved in campus battles with Whites hear quietly from other Whites who recognize the unfairness of our treatment. Jean's anonymous letter is one example of this kind of support. It is much like the story in the New Testament of the Bible where Nicodemus, a leader with tremendous authority, respect and power is thoroughly impressed by Jesus but cannot risk being seen in his presence so he goes to him secretly, at night. Women of Color have more than enough "secret" allies in the academy. In fact, many of us find one secret ally to be one too many. It is time for the courageous White women to step forward and speak up about the unjust treatment they witness. Doing so may bring about a different kind of crying from White women—born out of empathetic knowledge of and frustration about the institutional and personal systems that make universities a battlefield for many women of Color. It may also lead to a new source of tears for women of Color—stemming from an appreciation of the risks taken by the White women who emerge as public allies and advocates.

## Reference

MacKinnon, C. A., (1997). From practice to theory, or what is a white woman anyway? In R. Delgado & J. Stefancic (Eds.), *Critical White Studies: Looking behind the mirror* (pp. 300–303). Philadelphia: Temple University Press.

# Part III

# WHITE WOMEN TALK

# 8

# TOO MUCH HISTORY
# BETWEEN US

*Peggy McIntosh*

When African American and White women work in higher education in the United States, we are working in institutions which were built on the exclusion of all of us. But we were excluded to different degrees, and those differences in degree persist no matter how much we all may appear to be "in," now. Women of Color and White women want to get and keep jobs and gain institutional power and respect, but the contest is not equal. Our different histories of exclusion affect our day-by-day relations to the institutions we are in, and to each other. Our different histories affect pay, promotion, press, praise, prizes, publications and the power of tenure and job stability. Whiteness gives me an undeserved edge in the competitions of the academy as in the society as a whole. Being persons of Color usually gives my colleagues an undeserved disadvantage. Allying can feel personally workable but the deep impediments to it are systemic, psychological and historical. I cannot assume that if I have a friendship with a woman of Color I am truly allying with her. Our systemic histories work through us still, and the white social structures around us relentlessly pressure us toward different locations in life and outcomes within the academy.

Because of the differences in our access to systemic power, I think that at a deep level no woman of Color can trust me—and I cannot trust her—without a lot of careful and intentional work. There is too much history between us. It comes up to the present and is lodged in our heads and hearts whether or not we want it to be. But I am grateful for the coaching that Black and White women have given me on how to use power to share power—to be an ally.

For example, once I got a large three-year grant from the Andrew W. Mellon Foundation for feminist professional development work with college teachers. Pat Bell-Scott, an African American colleague of mine at the Wellesley College Center for Research on Women, came to my office and said, "Peggy, you owe it to us to give at least two of the five big grants each year to women of Color." I said I would. And I did. But I had not thought of this. This is part of the "history between us" in my chapter title—white oblivion to the presence, deservedness and worth of women of Color. As a White woman in the academy, I had a much better chance of getting such a grant at that time, but sharing its power had not occurred to me. I could not be trusted to think of sharing the wealth.

During the seminars that this Mellon grant made possible, a White woman, Margaret Andersen of the University of Delaware, tutored me on the worth of one of the well-known scholars of Color to whom I had given one of the major grants. Margaret said, "Peggy, you are letting Gloria Hull sit in the seminar but you are not recognizing her. She should be a resource for everyone else in the room." Her tone of voice implied she was asking, "What is wrong with you?" Letting women of Color into this previously white space addressed one problem, but assuming they have nothing to bring is another huge problem. I had felt that giving this well-known African American scholar access to the seminar was enough. I had not yet learned that access is just the beginning. Gloria Hull (who is now Akasha Hull) had the potential to change the seminar and make it more useful for everyone there. Indeed she did, as an insightful, vivid and deeply informed participant. My facilitator assumptions had to change, to expect and recognize this. Moreover, Akasha later published a brilliant, multiethnic, path-breaking paper entitled "Reading literature by U.S. third world women" based on her work during the 1983–4 grant year.

Once I was at an academic retreat for women from several colleges to talk and write together about multicultural work. The chores were divided up so that we had teams for shopping, cooking, cleaning up, taking out trash, etc. One afternoon I had no chores coming up so I told my colleagues that I was going upstairs to take a nap and asked them to wake me up when dinner was served. Later that evening two African American colleagues took me aside and said, "Peggy we like you. But that word 'served!'" And I saw how the history of servitude and their race went together in my grandmother's Confederate family and in my immediate past. No wonder they were offended by this class- and race-based word. They dared to tutor me on my insensitivity or my assumptions. Victor Lewis of the film *The Color of Fear* says that non-dominant people have to suffer paying the tuition for members of dominant groups to learn to see themselves and their systems. This was a case in point.

Another major coaching I received from a woman of Color came in 1984, when my office neighbor at the University of Denver said casually one day, "I wouldn't want to be White if you paid me five million dollars." This astounded me at the time. It got me thinking for the first time about whiteness as something other than normal—and also desirable. Among other gifts, it gave me this insight on how to be an ally: do not assume the person of Color you are allying with wants to be in your life circumstances or your culture. Nevertheless, she may want you to use your resources in the system to change things. This same colleague told me when we were on a search committee together, "Don't pick a weak Black woman just because she is Black. It just sets us all back." As we talked she often asked, "Why do you say that?" These were her ways of teaching me to know myself better and my power better. She was coaching me on the "politics of location" (Rich, 1986).

Once, at a gathering of National SEED Project seminar leaders in northern California hosted by fellow co-director Brenda Flyswithhawks, those on the planning committee asked that she and I conduct a 90-minute open conversation with each other so participants could see what was on our minds. We were happy to do this. In the course of the conversation Brenda said something about how she was learning to trust White people. I suddenly found myself telling her, "Brenda, don't trust me." She said, "Even you, Peggy?" She knew my white privilege work, so she thought I was onto myself as a White person. I said, "No, don't trust me, Brenda. I will betray you." She asked, "What do you mean?" An example jumped into my mind. I said, "Ever since we arrived here yesterday [at Santa Rosa Junior College] I have been oohing and aahing over the fact that your college is located on the site of W. Atlee Burpee's farms—the experimental gardens where he developed all those fantastic fruits and vegetables. But I completely forgot about the fact that this is Indian land. Your ancestors were here centuries before he got here, but I had wiped that knowledge out of my brain." We continued the conversation, and afterward a SEED seminar leader who is also a police captain in a nearby town expressed how upset he was with my response. He said that Brenda had offered me a gift which I had rejected. I can understand his feeling, that I had disrespected the generosity of a woman of Color, and at the same time I feel it was the right thing for me to do—to act on my sudden insight that I was not trustworthy. It has nothing to do with whether or not I am a good person. It has everything to do with the racism deep in me, handed down through the generations, that wipes out the knowledge of the near-genocide that the ancestors of SEED Project Co-director Brenda Flyswithhawks escaped only by hiding out in the caves of North Carolina. It was white privilege for me to forget this, and to forget it even in her company.

If I want to be an ally—or a friend—with women of Color, of any ethnicity, I need to give up the idea of being trustworthy and try instead to stay in honest relation. I need to give up the wish for comfort or relaxation around people of Color. Instead, I need an attentiveness that brings sincerity and that may allow us to work together. I cannot imagine that a woman of Color is comfortable with me and I don't expect her to be. But when I am tutored by a person of Color I am grateful that he or she took the risk.

So what can I do with my combination of ignorance and power as a member of the "in" group in the academy? At times, I can be an ally-translator for people of Color. As a White person with a Ph.D., I know the insider language of White male academic institutions. I have learned to survive and even thrive within the academic conventions of speech and behavior, teaching and testing, categorizing and conceptualizing, which pervade the academic world and that come from my White ancestors' legacies. I often chafe under them, even while being successful at them. I remind myself again and again that the foundational exclusions of the whole academic system have become internalized as part of my psychic system. When I speak the academy's language, I tend to perpetuate its policies of exclusion, consciously or unconsciously. After years of being tutored to see my whiteness and the unearned advantages it gives me, I know that academic conventions I was trained in are set against my actual values and my current ways of seeing and experiencing the world; they do not honor or use the worth or wisdom of White women, men and women of Color, and other people in most of the world. The knowledge system does not contain systemic self-awareness. But I can help nonwhites to cope and learn some of the skills needed to survive and possibly thrive in the white academy.

When I entered Radcliffe College in 1952, I did not feel I needed male allies because I did not feel the gender distance at first. Those were the days when I identified with Hamlet, not with Ophelia. I felt fortunate that I was "in," in the world we celebrated in songs at football games: 10,000 men of Harvard! I did not notice that I studied an all-male, all-white curriculum, and was taught by about 64 White male professors and one female discussion (section) leader in the art department. I did not realize that my sector of society—the women's half—was not really in the knowledge system at all. I felt honored to be at Harvard. But after blurting out an ignorant comment in a freshman class I vowed to keep silent—"never make a fool of myself in college again"—and from then on I was silent in class. Years later, I wrote an article about this entitled "Little Miss Muffett Asks a Political Question and Frightens Herself Away." From then on I wanted to crawl around at the feet of the professors and not be noticed—like a child under the dinner table listening to the grownups' conversation. I was both "in" and "out," but more "in" than a woman or man of Color could have hoped to be.

For I had been around White males all my life who, though they were not "professorial," had been to college. I had learned and absorbed their frames of reference by listening to them. I knew their language. My father and both of his brothers had been at Harvard, the same college I was now attending in the former "Annex," now called Radcliffe that Harvard had created for women. So I felt that if I would only keep my mouth shut from now on, and just do the work, I would be fine. And in terms of grades, I was. There was one light-skinned African American woman in my class. I never wondered how it was for her. I did not ask why she was the "only" Black woman. I saw her simply as an individual. She liked singing in the Choral Society which I think was a big respite for each of us. Perhaps she would have welcomed an ally, but I was busy trying to assimilate myself.

As I see it today, an African American female colleague in an academic setting where we might work together is most likely in an institution whose leadership avoids mention of the reality and the effects of chattel slavery, modern-day slavery, and of nonwhite populations around the world. Unless she is in one of the intentionally multicultural areas of the institution, she will be surrounded by silence about the negative effects of colonization around the world, in past centuries and in our own time. Her family's history in this country may date back to the time when it was a crime to teach a slave to read. That legacy, together with related economic injustice, may have kept her family out of higher education until recently. As she studies or teaches in a curriculum still deriving from my White ancestors, the work may be interesting and even engaging to her, but as a person with a heritage of her own she is even more out of the curricular picture than I was at Harvard's renamed Annex. Teachers and other students may doubt whether she can do the work on the traditional fields of knowledge.

Whereas when I went home from college for vacation, it was to a house full of books in a white neighborhood full of White students who were also writing term papers and studying for exams in white colleges. My parents understood what the requirements of college were, including how much and what kind of work one had to do to pass courses. Some of my ancestors' houses had had shelves of books for 300 years. Being "well read" was a mark of upper class status, and college was necessary to have that.

Despite my good intentions, when a woman of Color enters a group I am employed in, if I am aware of such possible differences as those in our family backgrounds, I will be tentative about saying anything that could make me sound insensitive or racist. This will produce in me a certain amount of fear, mistrust of the situation and of myself, confusion, evasion, wariness and caution. It will create what I see as interpersonal tension between me and my colleague of Color. I can't just blithely say anything that comes into my mind in her presence. How will I be heard? What am I doing in what I am saying, and what am I missing?

For many years these fears of messing up and the discomfort I have felt around people of Color made me retreat back into a seemingly safer white silence. I now think that the good side of this tentativeness is that at least I am not taking much for granted. If we are not friends, I know enough to know this. It is unlike being with my sister whom I take for granted. I can make lots of assumptions when I am with her. This is restful. With African American colleagues I do not take much for granted. This makes working together slower and more deliberate than with other colleagues. I can never

Table 8.1 Thirteen deadly habits of oppression in the workplace and nine "instead" habits

| Always being: | Instead behaviors |
|---|---|
| The Knower | Listening |
| The Manager | Learning |
| The Authority | Observing |
| The Authorizer | Relating |
| The Judge | Relaxing |
| The Jury | Reflecting |
| The Gatekeeper | Consulting |
| The Challenger | Connecting |
| The Competition | Settling down |
| The Speaker | |
| The Synthesizer | |
| The Generalizer | |
| The Clown | |

assume we are "on the same page." I am feeling my way and my colleagues of Color are too, and I do not know how they read me. I am not sure how I read them. This tentativeness is an improvement over the habits of certainty I used to use routinely to demonstrate that I was competent to be in charge in an academic setting. My tentativeness now with colleagues of Color may be seen as oppressive, may be seen as a kind of withholding, even secrecy, but I think it is better than being oppressively certain.

I have written a list of "13 deadly habits of workplace oppression" that I noticed in myself and in other people of dominant groups, and an alternative list of nine "instead" habits which come from a more relational sensibility and set of skills (Table 8.1). The 13 deadly habits come from *always* being the one in charge, or trying to be the one in charge. These habits are very assertive and they can be very offensive to anyone who isn't identified with authority or has not been given authority and feels the pain of this. Ironically and sadly, as a White person I was taught that these 13 habits were traits of excellence in public life. They showed which person knows the most, can manage people and ideas, is the authority on a subject and is a gatekeeper who knows how to keep the undesirables out and maintain the enclave. Those practicing the 13 deadly habits of workplace oppression were maintaining a gated community of the most powerful. I myself had no respect for the people who practiced the "instead" behaviors. Though I was assigned them as a woman, I did not think that they amounted to leadership or carried any particular virtue.

The deadly habits are embedded in public sector life in our culture so a person needs to be able to draw from them to be engaged in that sphere. But for working on race relations, they do not work. I feel the deadly habits are fatal for creating interracial relationships. Whereas all of us have characteristics that put us on both sides of this contrast, people who have "succeeded" in public life often build their entire personae around the deadly habits. For some, there is little incentive not to. What makes the habits deadly is that their actors think they should *always* play these roles. In *any* meeting they assume these roles. They have the impulse to take over. Even the role of the clown, though it may not look like power grabbing, is a form of it. The clown breaks up any conversation that is heading for territory dangerous to his or her ego, and makes jokes which derail the conversation.

Upper class White women of my generation and region in the U.S. were socialized to specialize disproportionately in the "instead" behaviors, regardless of how we felt about those roles. To be forced to play them meant that others could ride roughshod over us. A White woman who crossed from the "instead" behaviors which circumscribed her would usually be seen as an unnatural woman. This was bad enough. But a person of Color who crossed over would be read as dangerous. My colleagues of Color, for survival in the white academy, have often been forced to specialize, whether or not they wanted to, in the "instead" behaviors, in order to arouse less fear in White colleagues. They don't have white permission to develop and express their more assertive talents in white-dominated settings. I have had more license than my African American female colleagues to use the deadly habits because White colleagues will be likelier to give me the benefit of the doubt, while seeing African American assertiveness as threatening.

To be an ally to a woman of Color I need to be on both sides of chart. As a White and owning-class woman I need to stay on the relational side and listen and learn. I also need to use the dominant and controlling traits if I am going to challenge policy and practices, and try to redistribute power, money, credit and respect more evenly. Both sets of skills are useful if I am to use my power to weaken unjust power systems and use my privilege to weaken systems of privilege. I need to be able to fight when necessary, and to listen when necessary. When it comes to forming relationships with women of Color I have to use the "instead" skills, but to be an ally to women of Color in the world I also need the deadly habits.

So what I have I done, surrounded and filled with oppressive legacies but committed to social justice? My main contribution to institutional change, other than the white privilege work I have done, is the establishment of the National SEED Project on Inclusive Curriculum (Seeking Educational Equity and Diversity). This progressive professional development project for K-12 teachers is now in its 26th year. Building on the "instead" behaviors, it has created new structures for cross-racial interaction between people with unequal access to power, and as a result, has had transforming effects in changing individuals and institutions. The aim of SEED is to prepare educators to lead their own year-long, monthly SEED seminars to explore with their colleagues how to make their curriculum, teaching methods and school climates more gender-fair, multicultural, and inclusive of students from every background.

The staff members of the SEED Project intentionally create and use forms for interacting that enable "deeply personal group work." These forms undermine inherited imbalances of power and counteract academic and other pecking orders. When we address difficult and fraught subjects of race, class, sexuality, and gender violence, our relational strategies keep us allied and reduce fear. We avoid the deadly meeting habits that grow out of hierarchy and get in the way of people working together.

We emphasize time sharing, regardless of anyone's credentials or designated role in a group. We call for a balance of listening and speaking. We value experience over opinion, honesty over "polish," concreteness over abstraction. Our strategies require short comments rather than long intervals of speech. We do not allow interruption, argumentation, challenge, nor even echoing, piggy-backing, or seconding others' thoughts. They have allowed us to work on a shared task—the preparation and "holding" of teachers to be collegial leaders of adult development and social change in their own schools. As a result of our strategies of inclusion, the SEED Project is a magnet for teachers of Color, who say it is unlike anything else they have experienced in school. They trust SEED's processes, which reduce fear and allow White people and people of Color to work together on fraught subjects of privilege and oppression.

The SEED Project has strong theoretical and scholarly frameworks. It uses as its main mode of interaction a process I have named Serial Testimony. A facilitator states a theme or opens with a simple question. Each participant speaks in turn around a circle, uninterrupted, without response from other group members. Participants speak only from their own experience and without reference to what anyone else in the group has said. The facilitator times the speakers and stops them when their time is up. Serial Testimony does not aim to solve problems or create dialogue among participants. In fact, it is specifically designed to *not* create dialogue except in the unspoken thoughts in the heads of listeners. The purpose is not to network or piggy-back off others' comments, nor to take sides. Rather, Serial Testimony is for the contribution of each person's experience so that all will speak and all will be heard on a matter of shared interest or importance.

Serial Testimony can be used in any kind of meeting or classroom, and I believe strongly that meetings that do not follow this kind of intentional dismantling of the pyramids of power are doomed to repeat the old racial and gender patterns. I credit Serial Testimony with the fact that I have been able to develop friendly colleagueships and some deep personal friendships with women and men of Color in the SEED Project. Staff members love to be in the company of each other, with a shared sense that we are trying to transform teaching in a significant number of U.S. classrooms, so that teachers and students will not continue to be trapped in inequitable ways. We are freed ourselves by our processes. We ally with each other. I still do not trust myself, but I trust SEED processes, and because of them I feel I can hold others and be held myself in a process of mutual learning.

To some, Serial Testimony may seem an overly-structured mode of facilitation. But I call it "the autocratic administration of time in the service of democratic distribution of time." It requires participants to speak for themselves about their experiences rather than their opinions. It prevents single individual's views from becoming the focus of discussion. It brings each person into the conversation if they wish. The facilitator needs intellectual discipline and belief that when we hear from every single person in a group, the whole is greater than the sum of its parts.

Here are a few prompts from SEED's structured approach to fraught subjects, such as race, class, sexuality, and gender, using Serial Testimony. For the opening go-round, the facilitator might ask, "Who were you taught to look up to?" For the second go-round, the facilitator asks, "Who were you taught to look down on?" Subsequent prompts deepen the exploration.

Or, "What is a vivid moment you will always remember from your own schooling? Where are you? Who else is there? What is happening? How do you feel about it?"

Or, "What are some of the voices in your head from early childhood telling you how to be a boy or a girl?"

After people have repeatedly spoken in turn around a circle, without interruption, and without being asked to explain themselves, there is usually more trust in the group and less competition to be "on top of things" or be "right" or "smart." We de-emphasize debriefing and analysis of the kind that would allow participants to generalize, take sides, or single out some contributions for special mention. I find I can more confidently trust my capacity for ally-ship with people of Color *and* White people when we are in this mode, for it keeps us from being limited by the complex histories between us. In the SEED Project we teach K-12 teachers and parents to use these modes in classes and in institutional meetings so that what Emily Style (SEED Co-Director) calls "the textbooks of our lives" inform the conversation and the decision-making.

In the National SEED Project, the core staff who lead small groups daily in our week-long summer training workshop is composed of nine teachers of Color and five White teachers at the time of this writing. This ratio is very intentional and I am proud that staff members choose to be in the Project year after year. I believe that without our strategies for sharing time rigorously and circumventing argumentation, we 14 human beings could not be allies in any sense; we would take our places in the same old power hierarchies that have prevailed for centuries. The serious colleagueship and ally-ship that we have developed as a group of SEED leaders comes as a result of our commitment to the equalizing politics of Serial Testimony. Through it, we balance attention to "the scholarship in the selves and the scholarship on the shelves," as Emily Style explains. We use Serial Testimony in all of our summer staff meetings and for two and a half days in our planning meeting in the middle of the winter. It is the best thing I know for building, over time, respect, affection, and yes, even trust, between people of Color and White people.

Working closely with people of Color in this way has transformed my life. The structures for interaction in the National SEED Project have lessened the grip of the negative histories between us and among us, and have shown me the joy and meaning that comes from allying with each other. It sometimes surprises me that one of my chief contributions to large-scale systemic change in education is a project that rests on such an apparently simple and intimate process: letting the stories and experiences that we carry within bond us, give us systemic insight and embolden us to work as allies for social justice, in schools and in the world.

# References

Rich, A. (1986). *Blood, Bread and Poetry: Selected prose, 1979–1985*. New York: Norton.

# 9

# FRIENDS IN DEED, FRIENDSHIP *INDEED?*

*Liz Leckie*

What does it mean to be female allies and friends in the academy? How do female relationships form across race? How are they maintained? What happens when these relationships fall apart? What is the significance of female interracial friendship in the academy? Are these interracial relationships, *indeed,* friendships?

These are the questions that first came to me when I considered the possibility of friendship between White women and women of Color in the academy. As a university administrator, I immediately began to reflect on my relationships with women at work. As a White woman, my initial thoughts were about my female colleagues of Color; and I was swept up in affirmative beliefs that these relationships are *indeed* friendships. My confidence, however, shook as memories surfaced of the various relevant conversations I have had with White women at the academic institution where I work. I am reminded again that, like many White people, I live in a white fog that distorts my view of reality and creates a belief that life beyond the haze is unpredictable. Instead of making efforts to see this smog for what it is—human created and perpetuated—we unreflectively breathe in the damaging air of white entitlement and supremacy.

The title of this chapter—*Friends in Deed, Friendship Indeed?*—illustrates the collective and multiple ways in which White women talk to me, another White woman, about female interracial relationships. Here, I retell these exchanges to represent how my relationships—collegial or friendly—with women of Color are often constructed and misconstrued in the academy. I write these stories as invitations to my colleagues and myself to reflect on our white talk about female relationships across race.

I have made a deliberate decision to focus exclusively on comments made by White women as an act of disclosing how our unreflective statements can—perhaps unintentionally—reinforce white supremacy. In doing so, I heed the wisdom of bell hooks (1994) in her book, *Teaching to Transgress:*

*Education as the Practice of Freedom,* when she expresses her curiosities about why White women's writings about race often focus on Black women and women of Color while avoiding how White women's lives, works, and experiences are also about race. Although the stories that I tell bring into the light how White women's conversations are manifestations of how we recreate a world of white entitlement and interracial exclusion, I do so with the intention of lifting the haze and creating clearer opportunities for further conversation. Again, I turn to bell hook's (1995) advice in *Killing Rage: Ending Racism,* where she encourages women across races to find ways to work communally to change society. Specifically, she advises women to get to know one another better and learn how to acknowledge and respect each other's differences and similarities. However, we cannot do this if White women continue to hide in a veiled racial reality of their own creation and self-preservation.

Considering both of bell hook's declarations that women need to find ways to know each other better across race and White women's inclination to disregard the importance of race in our own lives, I offer the following stories to illuminate some of the subtle and seemingly innocent ways in which White women's talk is both raced and also inhibiting of interracial efforts to create collective change. I conclude this chapter with my ideas of what acts White women may need to change in order for women in the academy to begin to build the type of relationships that may have the potential of becoming alliances.

## Labeling Friends, Questioning Friendship

Many of my relationships with women of Color have been built and have grown in the academy. They began, and in many ways continue, as a result of the deeds or acts in which we have collaborated. We work and support each other "in deed." Many of my relationships with women of Color have not transcended our institutional deeds. Our talk is focused on the work at hand and we often know very little about our lives outside of the academy. As the following conversations illustrate, I question whether or not to identify these relationships as friendships because we have constrained our relationships, perhaps for good but unspoken reasons, within our professional obligations. Still, the work of white entitlement is to assert labels and create certainty where questions still exists.

### We're Looking for "Fun" Women …

After a campus-wide planning meeting for our upcoming student orientation events, I was asked by a group of White women to join them in training for and running a relay race to be held in a neighboring city sometime in the coming year. I laughed as I responded, "Thanks for the invitation, but I'm not a runner." One of the women responded and explained that it did not matter if I ran or not; they would still like me to join them. The purpose of running the race was to "get away from campus" and "have some fun." Another woman interjected that even if I didn't run they needed people who could drive the van while the others ran and rested, and they would love to have me join. Still, I did not respond with any real interest.

One of the women asked me if I knew of anyone else who might be interested in joining the team because they needed a few more participants for this effort to be realistic. I mentioned a colleague of ours, a self-identified Chicana, whose voice is active on our campus in conversations about social justice and who, unlike me, enjoys running. The immediate response from one of the women was that she did not know this colleague. Another woman in the group said she knew her and asked "but are you *friends*?" I answered— in far too much detail for the question—that I knew her from serving on a number of campus committees and that we saw each other and occasionally talked while working out in the campus recreation center.

One of the women clarified again that the main reason for running the relay was to have fun, and "we do not need anyone who is too serious about it joining." Another woman agreed. I asked them why they thought inviting our colleague would be a problem. I explained that our conversations were always quite enjoyable, and I found her to be "a fun person." Another woman interrupted me and said "Oh, that is not what we meant. We just want to make sure everyone who participates has a similar goal: *to have fun.*" I again reiterated that I felt our colleague, if asked and interested, would come with that goal, and the fact that she enjoys running would also be important since the race is about *running*—something that she enjoyed. I further suggested that she could likely make a greater contribution to the group than simply *driving the van.*

Later, when I shared this conversation to our Chicana colleague, she explained that she was not surprised, she was "aware of these women" and although they all knew her from various meetings they have attended together, they often did not talk to her except when it involved diversity efforts on our campus. I told her that, despite the pressure I felt to commit, I was not interested in participating and asked her to let me know if she wanted to run or if these women asked her to join.

She was not asked if she wanted to run, and I found out later that this group of women decided not to run the relay because they could not find enough people to participate.

Like in this story, some of our relationships in the academy become stuck within the institutional deeds we perform and rarely become alliances. These relationships become like contractual affiliations that only exist within particular institutional contexts. When I suggested that these White women invite a woman of Color to participate, they questioned and labeled my connection with our colleague. Perhaps this response is appropriate since interracial allies are uncommon, even though, as bell hooks asserts, many White women are in denial of this condition.

When my White female colleagues asked me if I knew anyone with similar interests, it is likely they made an assumption that I would suggest another woman like us, a White woman. This assumption is based on an unspoken white solidarity. In conversations like the one I illustrated here, race is not named; however, it is important to create and maintain white bonds through exclusionary alliances. These selective alliances create and maintain—unacknowledged—racial distance.

As I pressed my White female colleagues to explain why they would not consider inviting our Chicana colleague to join them, why they would not consider her fun, we were all dragged momentarily out of our white haze and forced to see more clearly the smog of white supremacy we all so willingly breathe. When this happens in conversations about interracial relationships, denial of the white haze enveloping our world is certain. As bell hooks (1995) teaches us, this talk creates and maintains racial distancing and hinders alliance building. It compromises the necessary work to know each other and learn about racial and personal differences *and similarities*. Talk, like this, does the everyday work of drawing boundaries around relationships and labeling *acceptable* race relations.

Frequently, I listen to White women label my relationships with women of Color as "friendships." These seemingly innocent constructions of our relationships often result in sizing up the women of Color for their willingness to work and create alliances with a White woman and me for my motives as a White woman. It is a fact that we come together in acts of solidarity to improve our institution for those who have been historically and continue to be under-represented and underserved. Perhaps, these relationships have the possibility of becoming friendships, but we have not explicitly named them so.

## Maybe Next Year …

I was asked to serve on a committee to help plan an annual leadership conference for eighth-grade young women. One of the goals that the committee had determined before I joined was to increase the diversity of the young women attendees. When the chair of the committee told me about this goal she made many suppositions about how she understood this to be a lofty goal and that she knew that as a committee they would have to start small. In time, she hoped, we would realize greater participant diversity.

As I looked around the room of all White women and through the list of participants, I noticed that they had not included women on our campus whose institutional responsibilities explicitly involved outreach and recruitment of under-represented and underserved populations—specifically young women of Color. For example, they had not invited the diversity officers in the School of Medicine or College of Nursing who organized K-16 pipeline programs for under-represented female students and women in the health sciences. They had not included representatives from the institution's Center for Ethnic Student Affairs who worked directly with students of Color to conduct annual outreach efforts in local public schools. I suggested that they might want to contact these women, include them in the planning and listen to their suggestions. I underscored that these women were experts on our campus in these efforts.

Initially, the members of the planning committee responded that they did not know who these women were. As I explained further why I felt these women's contributions would strengthen their conference—in particular to assist them in reaching their newly articulated goal of increasing the participant diversity—the women on the planning committee explained to me that "women from the community" were already attending the event. As they listed the female doctors and nurses who were participating, I recognized that the women that they had invited were White female medical professionals.

I pushed further and explained that while I understood including professionals from the community was very important, the women of Color I recommended worked on and had important connections to different communities. Further, they could help them with their articulated concerns that increasing diversity was a "lofty goal" requiring "small steps." The members of the planning committee graciously thanked me for my insights while simultaneously explaining that the event was only a few hours and it was too late in the process to change the program. They ended by suggesting that perhaps next year they could consider including "these women" earlier in the conference planning.

A couple of days later, I received an email from the committee chair informing me that they forgot to mention they had already invited women of Color to participate. The email explained that one woman of Color from the College of Engineering was scheduled to speak during the conference. The woman, however, was not a professional engineer. Similar to the women of Color I had suggested in our conversation, this woman was a staff member responsible for creating academic pipeline programs to recruit White female students and students of Color to the fields of engineering. The email concluded with this statement, "We have taken to heart your suggestions about including others from campus in our planning for this conference, and we will make every effort to include *your friends* [emphasis mine] in next year's event."

The following year when this same event planning committee convened, I was again contacted to participate. However, the committee did not contact any of the women of Color whose professional expertise was, and is, so imperative for striving toward inclusiveness in events such as this conference.

This story illustrates one of the ways that our work in the academy across race is broken. The actions of the White women planners did not reflect their stated goal of increasing the inclusion of young women of Color. It is too often the case that when white colleagues create programs in higher education where diversity is not the primary focus, inclusion of people of Color is an afterthought or that we seek the one woman of Color that we know to create the opportunity of inclusion for all people of Color. Making goals to increase diversity is an important part of our communal campus efforts. However, when we do not do the necessary work to re-envision programming that has been historically and continues to be exclusive, our talk and walk are misaligned. Again, as bell hooks (1995) articulated, it is in conversations like this one that race is important; however, there is an outright refusal to discuss race relations or give meaningful attention to the subject.

The ways that potential interracial relationships among women play out in academic settings are often predictable. Aimee Carrillo Rowe (2008) explains in *Power Lines: On the Subject of Feminist Alliances,* White women claim participation in diversity efforts to promote their own institutional status while simultaneously keeping women of Color at a distance. As this story illustrates, this maintenance of spatial distance can happen regardless of the institutional responsibilities or power that women of Color hold. The naming of our relationship as "friends" instead of professional colleagues, however well intended, marginalized these women of Color and minimized their professional work on our campus.

Labeling these relationships "friendships" simultaneously reinforced white bonding and solidarity between me and the other White women on the planning committee. When they informed me in the unsolicited email that they had already included a woman of Color in their planning efforts, this information was important to our relationship building because it informed me that they were actually already "thinking like me." The information—that had slipped their minds in the planning meeting—simply needed to be cleaned up and to put my raised concerns to rest. The women were seemingly negotiating with me about what needed to happen to make their conference more inclusive and simultaneously creating white bonds of approval. In addition to maintaining white solidarity, it is evident how white supremacist ideals shrouded our beliefs about women of Color. In our veiled white realities, women of Color in the academy became simply interchangeable and are disregarded for their individual talents and accomplishments.

These previous conversations also illustrate the unacknowledged priority of white bonding in our daily acts. In these stories, the White women were willing to abandon their goals and, whether intentionally or unknowingly, maintain the spatial distance across race. Aimee Carrillo Rowe (2008) writes about the zero-sum logic that drives alliance formation. For White women, alliance building, which is relationship building, is often considered strategic and intentional. Professional gains are calculated so that opportunities are extended to an exclusive few—whether these are on or off campus. Therefore, the focus of white solidarity is about creating and maintaining individual status, not necessarily institutional change. However, these examples also demonstrate how when confronted White women explicitly deny or renegotiate their acts. In doing so, we maintain and reproduce a racial status quo that is inclusive of some at the exclusion of others.

Unlike in the previous two stories, the few times when I have announced (explicitly or through my actions) my alliances and friendships with women of Color, they are often seen by White women as relationships that come at the expense of potentially damaging relationships with White female colleagues, as well as my own professional advancement. In these conversations, White women's shock is relayed in messages of surprise—or even offense—at these alliances. The tone that they use to talk to me about my relationships—even in front of women of Color—is interrogative. The statements that they make are coded with tones of disbelief, like "Really, you're friends?" and "How is it that you know her?" Occasionally, they underline their skepticism with sarcastic statements and pandering head nods. It is as if these White women are saying—indirectly—"Indeed! I can scarcely believe what I am hearing!"

### *You Look A Lot Better ...*

The day the former Associate Vice President for Diversity left our campus to pursue new career opportunities was one of the saddest in my professional life. To this day, she is still among the most important people I have met in my life. This woman has been instrumental in my professional and personal growth. I worked with and learned from her as we participated together on a number of campus committees. But, more importantly, she served as a member of my doctoral committee; and, even though she left our institution before I was finished, she made a commitment to be with me until the end. Like many who spoke and acknowledged her efforts at her good-bye tribute, I too was incredibly grateful to her and for her influence. Even though she sat in the room with us, I missed her already. I remember listening to the stories of her accomplishments on our campus and the lives that she touched, and I could not hold back the tears. I tried. But in a room full of people crying, I surrendered.

A few days later, I was tabling at a recruitment event for the university. I invited one of our campus undergraduate student leaders to join me to talk to incoming students about the opportunities at the university. During the event, one of our campus highest-level White female administrators walked by our table and paused. The last time I had seen her was at the good-bye celebration, but she had not said anything to me there. As she paused at our table, she said, "Liz, you look a lot better than the last time I saw you," as she drew a tear down the front of her face with her finger. I froze. I fell silent. I think after what seemed like too long, I uncomfortably nodded to acknowledge that I knew she was speaking to me.

After she left, the student who was with me asked what that was about. I explained that I was pretty emotional at the recent good-bye celebration for the Associate Vice President for Diversity. She responded, still concerned, and again asked "So, what was that about?" and she drew a similar tear down her face.

I explained in the only way I knew at the time. I did not tell the student that I thought I was being disciplined, that my exhibition of loyalty to a strong Black female leader and my willingness to freely show emotion had possibly threatened this powerful White female administrator. Honestly, I was engulfed by this act of professional discipline, and I'm not sure I could have articulated those thoughts so clearly at the time. I simply said, "I guess she wanted me to know that she saw me crying."

A few weeks later, however, the disciplining became more explicit when the same White woman administrator asked me during a campus meeting if I was planning on leaving the institution. I was surprised. I answered that I had no intention of leaving; that I needed to complete my degree. She responded, "Oh, I guess I figured that you would want to leave to go and work near *your friend*." Again, I had no response. I felt the weight of her power on our campus in this suggestion, and I simply responded by shaking my head "no." Regardless of her intent, I felt small and in that moment needed a friend.

This story again emphasizes the zero-sum logic (Carrillo Rowe, 2008) that guides White women's bonding and reinforces white solidarity. In particular, these conversations concerning the interracial relationships cultivated within the institution demonstrate how visible loyalty to people of Color threatens insecure white bonds. A response to this threat is the explicit disciplining of and imposing of white boundaries in ways that scrutinize specific behaviors, pokes fun at another's pain and diminishes the importance of interracial alliance-building efforts by renaming them "friendships." When loyalty exists across race, the assumption is that loyalty is diminished within race. This logic ultimately creates barriers in efforts to join together in communal efforts.

The act of labeling interracial relationships as "friendships" carries with it the historical and present beliefs of white supremacy and racial inferiority. This country has a history of renaming and labeling people of Color in ways that reinforce their inferiority. In this situation, the renaming of my relationship with the Associate Vice President for Diversity as "friend" instead of "advisor" or "mentor" or "professor," no matter how well meaning, removed this woman of Color from her position of respect and power in our institution and repositioned her as my equal, *my friend*. Whether or not we have a friendship is insignificant. White woman's entitlement to label and use labels to discipline behavior, however, is quite significant. This story teaches us about another barrier to female interracial alliances in the academy and how White women's talk creates and maintains obstacles to interracial relationships by explicitly belittling the importance of the women of Color and the work that they do in the academy.

The preceding conversations illustrate how White women used language to create and maintain white solidarity by holding tight to White female relationships exclusively, negotiating for white approval, and disciplining behaviors that are seen as violations of the boundaries of white solidarity. These efforts to enforce white racial alliances occur when White women are working on institutional efforts, off-campus relationship building and regardless of the institutional power that women of Color hold.

All of these stories also illustrate how White women create racial distance, through language, which maintains ambiguously fraught relationships with women of Color. Ambiguity concerning the desire for female interracial relationships in the academy occurs when certain women are included and others excluded, when relationships are relied upon in particular contexts for particular gains but do not extend outside of those contexts or when we use our institutional power to belittle and dismiss the actions of others. In *Killing Rage: Ending Racism,* bell hooks (1995) invites all women to question the ways that female xenophobia interferes with our efforts to end racism and sexism in order to work for communal change. As White women perhaps one of the most needed realizations is how our daily conversations about female interracial relationships in the academy announce, possibly unintentionally, the bonds of white solidarity and, often unacknowledged, declarations of racial distancing.

## Considering Deeds of Friendship: Observations and Recommendations

During my time in the academy, I have learned that my female friendships across races are less common yet more dense than the surface office relationships in which I, and many of my White female colleagues, frequently engage. My female friends of Color and I have created these relationships— sometimes friendships—through deliberate and sustained actions. We have built trust in our relationships by being honest with each other, by making mistakes and forgiving our failings, by supporting one another's efforts, and in some cases looking out for each other in the political landscape of our institutions. These relationships are born through purposeful action and in recurring deeds of friendship. Our relationships are *indeed* important to us.

Still, I cannot escape the white dense haze in which I was raised and continue to live. In writing these conversations, I am reminded of how thick this smog is. In reliving these conversations I see missed opportunities. Despite the learning that I have done to see the smog, I still fail to see how I am engulfed. For example, in retelling these stories there are spaces where I was invited to participate and failed to open up these spaces so that my colleagues of Color could also attend; moments where I fell silent and could have used my voice to speak up more clearly about the importance of interracial relationships in our academic lives; and times when I did not follow through and invite women of Color to participate in events on and off campus—instead, I left it to others to do so, and they did not.

From these conversations, we, as White women, learn that at the core of improving interracial relations in the academy, we may need to listen to our talk. We need to question the language choices that we comfortably use to label relationships; and in so doing, create alliances as well as distance. I underscore this recommendation by turning to writing of Carol C. Mukhopadhyay (2008) who asserts, "… language is one of the most systematic, subtle and significant vehicles for transmitting of racial ideology." As Mukhopadhyay writes and has been underscored by the conversations herein, the labels used in interracial relationships are not as innocent as we may want to pretend. The act of naming creates racial solidarity and distance, and investigating this talk may be an important vehicle to changing divisive racial ideology.

Listening to our everyday talk may make possible unveiling the motivations we have for entering into female interracial relationships in the academy. When we find that our motivations do not question the historical legacy of interracial relationships among White women and women of Color—especially, working relationships in the academy—we are invited to take pause. When, as these conversations illustrate, our motivations sustain individual gain at the cost of institutional change, we are again invited to recalibrate what we have claimed to be our desires and question whether or not it has been a genuine relationship/friendship that we have sought.

As these conversations teach us, we, as White women, also need to shift our attitudes to tolerate ambiguity rather than offer answers. An attitude that tolerates ambiguity means being open to what is uncertain, to question our xenophobia and to think outside of what we have learned about relationships among White women and women of Color. This includes being vulnerable to the unknown challenges and changes in self that a shift in attitude may bring.

Listening to our talk, questioning our motives and shifting our attitudes take dedication. This dedication is especially evident in the academy where we have learned to judge, evaluate and question one another's claims; to seek out validity and truth for professional gain; and in many instances, to fight for our personal agenda regardless of the cost to others. External validations and competitive attitudes that engulf our academic deeds and create the smog of white solidarity must be brought into the clearing in order for women to succeed in working across race. We must certainly challenge them if we are to *indeed* become allies.

## References

Carrillo Rowe, A. (2008). *Power Lines: On the subject of feminist alliances.* Durham, NC: Duke University Press.

hooks, b. (1994). *Teaching to Transgress: Education as the practice of freedom.* New York: Routledge.

hooks, b. (1995). *Killing Rage: Ending racism.* New York: Henry Holt and Company.

Mukhopadhyay, C. C. (2008). Getting rid of the word "Caucasian." In M. Pollock (Ed.), *Everyday Antiracism: Getting real about race in school* (pp. 12–16). New York: New Press.

# 10

# MOMENTS OF SUSPENSION AND OTHER INSTANCES OF WHITENESS IN THE ACADEMY

*Angelina E. Castagno*

A storm of legislation, legal challenges, national media attention, and community activism looms over Arizona in 2011. Within this context, there is no such thing as "business as usual" in the academy. The curricular approval process is just one space where race, racism, and whiteness are painfully apparent. This chapter explores one White woman's story of introducing a new course on critical whiteness studies within a public university in Arizona in the middle of this storm.

My purposes in this chapter are multiple. By describing in detail an event within a predominantly White university that advances a commitment to diversity in its mission statement, I hope to highlight the complexities of working for greater justice and equity around issues of race. I also hope to highlight how whiteness operates in both explicit and implicit ways, but always protects dominant interests. In addition, I hope to illustrate how working within predominantly White groups composed of self-identified liberal and diversity-supporting people can be extremely difficult. This difficulty is particularly evident when contrasted to working within groups composed primarily of people of Color and White allies who have an explicit commitment to anti-racist work. And finally, I attempt to vividly describe my own responses and reactions to all of this—which I have come to think about as "moments of suspension." These moments of suspension highlight some of the barriers, stresses, privileges and assumptions that frame my experience.

## A New Course, But a Familiar Pattern

When I first came to the university in 2006 as an assistant professor in the Department of Educational Leadership, I had aspirations of eventually teaching a class on critical whiteness studies. As I found my footing within this new university, I began to get more involved with groups that seemed important. I joined the Commission on Ethnic Diversity; I founded and helped facilitate a group within the College of Education concerned about issues of social justice; and I was invited to join the Ethnic Studies Steering Committee. Through conversations with all of these entities and significant support from Ethnic Studies, I developed a course called "Whiteness in U.S. Schools and Society." Faculty in my own area of Educational Foundations and faculty in Ethnic Studies agreed that the course should be cross-listed, and that I should test the waters by offering it as an "experimental" class in spring 2008.

Offering an experimental course formally requires faculty approval from the department, but in the past, when faculty have brought requests before the Educational Leadership Department for temporary approval, very little discussion ensued and it was viewed as an opportunity for a faculty member to try something new before seeking full course approval. However, when I brought the whiteness course to the department, this pattern was broken. Many of the senior faculty members immediately raised concerns about the course. First, they suggested the course title and material of "whiteness" was "too political" and would likely open up the department to outside criticism. Second, some felt issues of race should be embedded in all classes, rendering a separate course that looked specifically at race unnecessary. Third, limited department resources needed to be focused on offering core courses rather than "extra" classes that "students don't really need." As the conversation progressed, these same objections were raised by many people but were always coupled with comments about how the department is "committed to diversity," the faculty members "agree that our students need to have an awareness of issues of prejudice and discrimination," but that "we already cover that in other classes." In the end, the course was approved with the minimum number of votes needed to pass, but the approval was for the course only to be offered one time and then I had to come back to the department for further approval.

During this department meeting and vote, I was jolted into that already familiar feeling of suspension. Was I naïve to have thought that a course on whiteness would be embraced by my department colleagues? Did other faculty members really believe that we were adequately addressing race and racism in other classes? Why were the few colleagues of Color in my department not speaking up more forcefully in support of the course? But then again, why should I expect them to, when most of my White colleagues weren't doing so either? When it was time to vote, every faculty member of Color voted for the course along with a couple White faculty members. Every faculty member who voted against the course or "abstained" from the vote was White. And then something interesting happened—two of the faculty members who voted against the course stated that they "wanted the record to reflect" their reasons for voting that way, and in both cases the faculty members believed we simply didn't have the resources to offer a new course. The sensation of being suspended only intensified at that moment as I tried to make sense of what I had just heard, particularly considering that I had never heard someone request that our meeting minutes reflect reasoning behind votes, nor had I ever heard the resource rationale used against a new course proposal.

The course was a success. It had substantial enrollment, received very high evaluations and both the students and I believed it was a course that ought to be offered regularly. After discussions with Ethnic Studies and Foundations faculty, I spent part of the summer of 2010 completing the necessary paperwork to move the course through the formal curriculum approval process. Between the time I offered the course experimentally and the subsequent struggle to get it approved as a "real course," a number of significant events occurred in Arizona. Due to massive state budget shortfalls, the state legislature slashed funding to all public schools and universities in the state. We saw hiring searches cancelled, travel money evaporate, programs disappear, class sizes increase and repeated efforts to "streamline" and make "more efficient" the work of the university. Also in mid-May 2010, on the heels of Senate Bill 1070, the Arizona Governor signed House Bill 2281 into law. Often referred to as "the anti-ethnic studies bill," the legislation threatens to withhold funding from noncompliant schools. The bill specifically targets elementary and secondary schools and does not make mention of higher education. More recently, the current Arizona Attorney General and State Superintendent have indicated that they will "go after" university ethnic studies programs and colleges of education that prepare K-12 teachers with ethnic-studies-related teaching approaches.

## Forging Ahead, With Expected Stalls

When I sent the course approval paperwork to our department chair and the Ethnic Studies chair one month before it needed to be submitted to the appropriate college-level committees, I immediately received an e-mail from the chair of Educational Leadership stating:

> There has been some concern and informal discussion amongst faculty regarding the title of the course, specifically the word Whiteness. This is something that we should have a departmental discussion about prior to sending it on to the next level ... I do not want this course approval to be something which is divisive within our department ... With the heightened sensitivity at the Governor and legislative levels, I would not like to have our department and college be placed under the microscope because of one word in a course title ... How important is the word Whiteness to the course and could something else replace it?

My e-mail response stated, "my perspective is that the word 'whiteness' is absolutely central to the course, it does not target any particular group of people, it is not unique to our department (there are whiteness classes, books, etc., across the nation), and that calling it something different would be antithetical to the course itself." I copied my colleagues in Educational Foundations on my reply in order to keep them informed. Within hours, a senior colleague, Dr. Thomas, replied with the following note, which he further copied to three other senior, White, male colleagues within our department:

> What a State! We have a governor who is assured of election because she signs an immigration bill that the Federal government says is racist, we have a sheriff in Maricopa County who threatens arrest to any government official that does not agree with his heavy-handed approach to handling immigrants, we have a State Superintendent that puts a bill through the legislature that threatens to withhold state funds to any district that teaches a course that would ever question the actions of our government in treating other races, we have a legislator who represents our East Valley area who will propose a bill next year to deny children born in this country citizenship because of the Color of their skin. I suspect that a course that proposes to teach about Whiteness would get noticed by our legislature. All it would take would be one student to accuse our college of preaching hatred for the white race and I would hate to see the appropriations for [our university] for the next year. I think you should change the title.

Also within the hour, one of the other senior colleagues in my department, Dr. George, replied, "I agree with [Dr. Thomas'] assessment re: change in the title (given the current political mind set of state officials)." I tried to clarify the critique by asking, "is the ONLY issue with the course title? In other words, is there agreement that this course is needed and should move forward (but just with a new name, according to some)?" I received no response.

Another moment of suspension came when Dr. Thomas sent the e-mail detailing the current context of Arizona and then concluding that the course title needed to be changed. Here was someone articulating the context in a very similar way that I would have done myself and yet coming to the opposite conclusion. While suspended here, I felt a detached amusement stemming from at least two places. On the surface, my amusement was of the sort that suggests "I know better than him and he is just a typical White guy trapped in the system." This source of amusement allows me to position myself above my colleague so as to not be sucked into his way of thinking. But below the surface, my amusement stems from the fact that this colleague occupies a higher-status position than me in multiple ways. I cannot help but feel small next to him, a male full-professor who is almost twice my age. The persistent sexism, deskilling, and disempowerment that structures the university context leads me to develop coping strategies to get through seemingly small occurrences that weigh heavily because of the bigger picture. The concept of microaggressions is helpful in understanding this (Solorzano, 1998; Solorzano, Ceja, & Yosso, 2000). Although I do not experience microaggressions based on race, I do experience them related to my gender, age, and occupational status, and my tendency to respond to situations like the one above with amusement is probably one way I have learned to cope with the university context given my own positioning within it.

I also knew that I shouldn't be surprised by Dr. Thomas' e-mail. After all, White liberals have become adept at articulating a problem and justifying a less-than-progressive response. While complaining that conservatives miss the boat on what the problems actually are, liberals come to very similar conclusions about what ought to be done. How was I to respond to this e-mail? Or, as a good colleague and fellow White person similarly pissed off about the context we all found ourselves in, was I not supposed to respond? As I tried to gain some footing, I was further destabilized by the silence of my other colleagues who self-identify as progressive and anti-racist. Where were the other voices? And what were those silences screaming?

At the same time, there was an e-mail conversation happening among my colleagues in Ethnic Studies. This group is primarily composed of faculty and staff of Color, with a small number of White faculty (like myself). The responses via e-mail from this group were all consistent with my own perspective. They included:

> I think sticking to your guns about keeping whiteness in the title is important.
>
> (White male)

> [D]on't give up the ship.
>
> (African American male)

> [W]e have to stand up for the educational mission and not compromise it. If the substance of the course is okay, it is hypocritical to try to camouflage the title just because it may catch the attention of any ill-willed legislator.
>
> (Asian American male)

> It is my opinion that when people want to control you they will bring up issues that are designed to illicit fear. So talking about potential funding loss in these tough economic times is designed to control people. We need to stand strong and NOT BE CONTROLLED!
>
> (African American female).

The Ethnic Studies group was clear in their desire to move the course forward, but they were at a standstill while the Educational Leadership faculty decided how to proceed.

The Foundations subgroup within Educational Leadership decided to meet to discuss a strategy since the course was scheduled to be on our Educational Leadership department agenda early in the fall 2011 semester. In an effort to find common ground so that we could move something forward as a program, the Foundations faculty agreed to a course called "Racism in U.S. schools and society: Examining whiteness and constructions of race." We discussed that this had a broader appeal that would allow whatever faculty member was teaching it to decide how exactly to frame the conversation and what readings to include, but that the course would still maintain some examination of whiteness.

This course, reached through compromise among the Foundations faculty, is what was sent to our full department for review and discussion. A couple days before the department meeting, Dr. Thomas, who originally voiced concern about the title, sent me an e-mail saying "Thank you for responding on the title of the course, I think that it softens the impact by appearing more an intellectual exercise. The content is still the same, the bibliography for it is extensive." Others indicated to me that they supported the course—some with the old title and some with the new title. I didn't expect a unanimous vote, but I did expect a majority to vote for the course.

When the course came up for discussion, Dr. George restated his concerns and said he "could not support the course with whiteness anywhere in the title." He discussed the current context in Arizona and nationally and emphasized that he thought a course on race and racism "was essential" but that "we shouldn't open ourselves up as a target." I shared that another state university has two courses with whiteness in the title and that our institution's legal counsel explicitly said that we need not be concerned with university funding tied to one course. Dr. George disputed what legal counsel told me since he "personally knew" many of our state's legislators. He reiterated that we "want to win the war, not the small battles, and this is a battle that we need not open ourselves up to."

Then one of my Foundations colleagues, Dr. Glibb, voiced his opposition to the course because he felt whiteness was a "narrow approach to studying race" that only represented a critical race theory perspective and because he thought it was "too sophisticated" for the students at our institution. He then made a motion that we vote on a course titled "Race and racism in U.S. schools and society" that had "essentially the same syllabus" but did "not include whiteness in the title or course description and objectives." I voiced my opposition to this, saying that I thought it was dishonest and not a fair representation of the course that had been designed. I asked that we vote on the initial course, but since a motion had already been made, we had to resolve that motion first. Dr. Glibb's motion passed with five in favor, three opposed (including myself), and four abstentions for people who were not present. I again called for a motion to vote on the original course, but my motion could not be considered given the outcome of the first motion. In wrapping up the conversation, Dr. Glibb commented that he wanted to see a course that "included greater faculty input and that was designed expressly with the needs of the EDL department and College of Education in mind." He implied that the course I initiated did not come about with full faculty input and that it was more aligned with Ethnic Studies' needs rather than our own.

## Multiple Moments of Suspension

I was represented as constructing a course without the input of my colleagues, which only included one perspective on race and as being overly concerned with the Ethnic Studies Program needs rather than my own department. It is interesting how all three of these critiques were framed in an academically-appropriate way and, hence, taken for granted as legitimate forms of critique within the university context. Was it true that I had done most of the work on designing this course? Yes. Was it true that it wasn't done collaboratively? I'm not sure. I sought my colleagues' input many times over the previous two years, but they very rarely responded, so I moved forward. What I did hear was support, so I assumed folks were on board. It seemed far too coincidental that now, when the course was supposed to be at the end of the process, I was hearing so much input and concern over the way the process had unfolded. Perhaps I was just being paranoid or hyper-sensitive since, from my perspective, we are living whiteness and whiteness is exactly what was going on through all of this.

At times in these types of encounters, I find myself choosing silence. This is another space of suspension because silence often results in the protection and perpetuation of whiteness (Castagno, 2008). What is most disconcerting is that when I am in a situation where I cannot say what I want to say and what I know needs to be said, and yet I'm not willing to say something related in a gentler way, I end up saying nothing. This occurred when Dr. George said "I want to win the war, not worry about small battles." There are at least two problems with this. First, perhaps the small battles are how to engage the war and, ultimately, win it. By not waging small battles and experiencing victory, you risk not getting anything done, becoming overwhelmed by the largeness of the war, and in the end, the opposition wins. Furthermore, not worrying about the small battles is probably a privilege only some of us have. I wanted to say this to my colleague, but instead I chose silence.

I also chose silence when my senior colleagues adopted what I perceived to be hypocrisies in their own ideologies. Dr. George and Dr. Glibb have both been ardent supporters of "academic freedom" in past meetings, but I heard nothing of this issue in the meeting about this course. Both have also voiced strong opinions about "full faculty input and participation," and yet Dr. Glibb put forward a motion on a course that he developed on his own as a reactionary move against my course (despite the fact that "my course" had actually been modified as a way to find some common ground between my own and Dr. Glibb's perspective). Every faculty member in my department has at some point commented on "doing what's best for our students," and yet in this instance the initial and primary concerns revolved around playing it safe with politicians and bickering over various theoretical approaches. As I think about what we might call "double standards" or "hypocritical stances," I'm again stuck. This is yet another beautiful enactment of whiteness. As an ideology, whiteness' boundaries shift in order to accommodate seeming contradictions. Whiteness accomplishes this so skillfully it is frightening.

## Shining a Light on Whiteness

In addition to the ways whiteness is embodied and engaged through the people, language, relationships and feelings I've described above, whiteness is also operating in less tangible ways throughout this incident. First, Harris (1993) explains that historically, rights were achieved through individual property ownership, and whiteness became conflated with property so that Whites came to own our whiteness. Viewing whiteness as property helps explain how and why it is that White people came to expect and protect the rights and privileges associated with whiteness and, therefore, with individualism. Meaning is determined, rationalized and legitimated by powerful Whites who maintain legal and moral imperatives centered on individualism. In this particular incident, whiteness' exclusive right to determine meaning is evident in the determination of a race-based class being "too political." The unspoken assumption is that colorblind and supposedly race-neutral approaches are apolitical and, therefore, inherently better. But decisions to ignore or obscure race are just as political as decisions to center race. Whiteness' exclusive right to determine meaning is also evident in later concerns about the very concept of whiteness in a course title or as a course focus. Maintaining the obscurity of whiteness also maintains the power of whiteness. Thus, whiteness shapes what is determined as the norm and defines what is acceptable. Since whiteness structures what is truth and since colorblindness is valued as an ideology of whiteness, issues of race and racism get silenced.

Second, this incident highlights the assumption of a zero-sum game in which the dominant group expects and relies on entitlements as normal (Harris, 1993). Because certain entitlements and privileges are assumed to be normal and natural, they are very difficult to let go. As Lipsitz (1998) points out, we have a "possessive investment" in whiteness because we devote time and energy to whiteness, maintain our privilege by guarding it from others, and use our whiteness to accumulate more advantages and privileges. In this particular incident, faculty are invested in the business-as-usual approach to curricular offerings and program development. In their view, the program serves students well and there is little reason to change it. Changing the program by offering different coursework with a more critical and race-based perspective may devalue the investment they have in the current program since their traditional courses may no longer be those most highly valued.

Finally, objections to the course are couched in a well-intentioned, liberal framework of being "committed to diversity"—which allows the predominantly white department to believe they are taking the moral highroad. Instead, the discourse becomes meaningless since it is expected and normalized, and the policies and practices that are implemented serve as structural barriers to greater racial justice. Whiteness serves as a "pervasive ideology justifying dominance of one group over others" (Maher & Tetreault, 1998, p. 139). So in this case, maintaining that one is committed to diversity is all that is needed to justify and rationalize a policy/practice that does nothing to disrupt the current pattern of White people dominating this particular academic field. This discourse of being committed to diversity is one of the ways whiteness is engaged because it allows White people to feel good about the world and our role within it.

## Other Moments of Suspension

Moments of suspension are not limited to this particular curricular approval issue. A recurring moment of suspension occurs when colleagues of Color articulate what I perceive to be less racially-progressive ideas than I hold. Examples that are not uncommon in my academic field include opinions about how families and communities of Color "don't care about their kids' education," "anyone can get ahead in this country if they just work hard," and "teachers ought to treat every student as an individual." When I find myself confronted by these and similar ideas by colleagues of Color I have a harder time responding than when I'm confronted with the very same ideas by White colleagues. Intellectually I know there are many reasons for this and it's not a simple issue, but emotionally and socially I often feel stuck in that familiar place of suspension.

On the one hand, it is a White liberal perspective to "give people of Color a pass." I know that racist messages and images are so entrenched in U.S. society that we are all impacted by them. As Tatum (1997) explains, it's like the smog in the air we breathe and people of Color are no less affected by that smog than White people (though we are all affected in different ways). I also know that racial dominance has historically, and currently, resulted in the silencing of particular perspectives, voices, and knowledges. As a person committed to working against dominance and towards greater equity, I am very aware of the need to ensure space for typically marginalized perspectives, voices and knowledges. Further, I know that when people do not feel supported and welcomed, they may cope by trying to fit in with the norm. All of these reasons lead to my enactment of whiteness by not saying anything. On the other hand, I know I am enacting whiteness and taking a White liberal stance by not saying anything and, therefore, that I am engaging and reproducing the very dominance I abhor. I also know that my silence places greater value on one person's voice or perspective in one of these instances than on the larger system of whiteness. I know the right thing to do is to hear the person but also to respond in a way that brings their error to the front of our awareness. I continue to work on following this knowledge through in practice.

Another moment of suspension recently occurred in a conversation with two White female colleagues about the promotion and tenure process and how to "tell my story." We were talking about whether and how to frame issues that might be politically charged. As an example, I explained that one of my career goals upon entering the university was to learn more and be honest about racism within the academy. I wasn't sure that was something I should include in my tenure portfolio. The most senior woman in our group advised me to "frame it as wanting to support diversity, be inclusive, advance multiculturalism or something along those lines," and the other woman agreed with this approach as a "more positive" way to frame the issue. But herein lies the problem: as White women, we are supposed to be positive, nurturing and not rock the boat. If part of my story as a young faculty member has been about being frank about racism, I cannot also maintain a commitment to always being positive, maintaining group stability and nurturing my colleagues and the institution. I had a moment of suspension because the choice was so clearly laid out for me, the "obvious" path was marked. Yet, I felt unable or perhaps unwilling to take it.

## Being Grounded, but Always by Choice

Part of coping with some of the issues I've identified throughout this chapter is deciding the time and place when one will engage an issue and when it is "not worth it." This, however, is another aspect of whiteness. Just like Dr. George, I have more leeway in choosing not to engage a particular battle than most people of Color. Indeed, if and when I choose to not go to battle, most of those around me probably don't even take notice since the normal course of events is not disrupted. In other words, I am expected to not engage.

As a friend reminded me, however, everybody is a White liberal in certain contexts. It is a White liberal stance to play the game within university contexts and frame issues with words like "diversity" and "multiculturalism" rather than "race" and "whiteness." I have certainly adopted this stance many times and, for me, it is most often in the context of my extended family and friend circles. I am less likely to adopt this stance with my work colleagues, but I know that others may make these decisions in very different ways than I do. Does making these kinds of decisions and choosing when and where to take a White liberal stance mean that one is compromising who they are? Does it make one's commitment to racial justice less real?

As a White woman working within a predominantly White university context, I struggle with these moments of suspension, when to stay suspended and when to abort. Being suspended is unstable. I am neither sure of myself nor sure of others. I am neither grounded nor light. Being suspended is agitating. I want some closure but it is out of my hands. Or maybe it is in my hands but I'm unable or unwilling to seize it. I am frustrated with others and with myself. Being suspended is confusing. Just when I think I understand something or someone, I realize I don't. I try to make sense of what I'm seeing or hearing, but the dots just won't connect. Being suspended is disempowering. I don't have the footing to move in any particular direction and I'm not sure how to (re)gain that footing. But being suspended is also easy. I don't have to move. I can wait in limbo—wait for something, even if I'm not sure what, so I don't need to spend too much time or energy thinking about it. Being suspended is a way for me to maintain dominance. If nothing moves or changes, business as usual continues. Perhaps, then, part of me wants to remain suspended. Maybe it is the easiest difficult spot to be in as a White woman.

I'm often struck by how clear cut my friends and colleagues of Color believe a situation to be—particularly when it is about what White people need to do or not do. With this curricular approval issue, for example, it is men and women of Color who simply say I must persist. It is White men and women who complicate it—even those who say persist, parse that advice with other "things to consider." I do this myself. Recognizing that I do this creates another opportunity for suspension. By complicating a matter, and then recognizing that I'm complicating a matter, I put myself in that place of suspension. I can continue to tell myself that it really is complicated and that I need to work through it. Or I can cut the strings holding me in limbo, fall back to the ground with a heavy thump, and do what obviously needs to be done. It is that simple.

## References and Further Reading

Castagno, A. (2008). "I don't want to hear that!" Legitimating whiteness through silence in schools. *Anthropology and Education Quarterly*, 39(3), 314–333.
Gillborn, D. (2007). *Racism and Education: Coincidence or conspiracy?* New York: Routledge.

Harris, C. (1993). Whiteness as property. *Harvard Law Review*, 106(8), 1707–1791.

Leonardo, Z. (2009). *Race, Whiteness, and Education*. New York: Routledge.

Lipsitz, G. (1998). *The Possessive Investment in Whiteness: How white people profit form identity politics*. Philadelphia: Temple University Press.

Maher, F., & Tetreault, M. (1998). "They got the paradigm and painted it white": Whiteness and pedagogies of positionality. In J. Kincheloe, S. Sheinberg, N. Rodriguez & R. Chennault (Eds.), *White Reign: Deploying whiteness in America* (pp. 137–158). New York: St. Martin's Griffin.

Solorzano, D. (1998). Critical race theory, race and gender microaggressions, and the experience of Chicana and Chicano scholars. *Qualitative Studies in Education*, 11(1), 121–136.

Solorzano, D., Ceja, M., & Yosso, T. (2000). Critical race theory, racial microaggressions, and campus racial climate: The experiences of African American college students. *Journal of Negro Education*, 69(1/2), 60–73.

Tatum, B. (1997). *Why Are All the Black Kids Sitting Together in the Cafeteria? And other conversations about race*. New York: Harper Collins.

# 11

# USING TENURE AS A WHITE WOMAN

## Speaking Truth to Power

*Marybeth Gasman*

When most people look at my curriculum vitae they make the assumption that I am an African American woman. Of course my name makes people wonder, but names are not always an accurate signifier for race. The truth is that I am White. However, I've never quite been able to relate to other White women in the ways that society says I should. I have White female friends but not a lot of them and none of my closest friends are White women, with the exception of my daughter and my mom. I used to question this fact but as I have grown older, I have realized that friends are where you find them— much like love.

In this chapter, I discuss my role as a White woman who studies race in the academy. I examine my ability to use my status, including my tenured status, to make change that can have a positive impact on faculty and students of Color, especially African Americans. I also explore the limitations of my role and the reactions to my role by both Whites and people of Color.

## Growing up Rural and White

I grew up in a family of 10 children in a very rural area of the Upper Peninsula of Michigan. We were horribly poor. I often tell people, "We were so poor that when my mom made chipped beef on toast, there wasn't any beef." My mom did the best she could on about $7,000 a year. People often ask how 10 children and their parents could survive on so little money—the answer: we grew and made everything. As a child, I learned how to can fruits, make jams and jellies, wax vegetables for winter, cut sides of meat, gut fish and deer and bake pies. Ironically, as an adult I do not eat meat and my husband is the cook in the house (enough is enough). As children, we entertained ourselves. We did not have a television or any fancy games; we made up games. We climbed apple trees and shook them for fun, flooded the backyard to make an ice rink during winter, played "kick the can" and rode the tractor for sport. I remember making homes for my blond, bikini-clad Barbies out of old record albums and tape. My little sister and I entertained each other for hours with these make-shift Barbie homes.

We had no idea that we were poor. Of course our parents knew, but we kids thought everyone lived this way. It was not until eighth grade when our house burned to the ground and we had to live in temporary housing in a nearby small city that we realized we were poor. I noticed what others had and the access that money gave people. It was then that I discovered that I was on free lunch and that my school uniforms had been worn by my brothers and sisters before I wore them. I wondered why my blouses were not white and why my tights had holes in the knees. I did not say much about my thoughts and feelings to anyone because I knew it would hurt my mom and dad.

My mom was lovely although she cried a lot. She tried her best to hide her tears but her struggle was hard. My father was an adequate husband. Yet, he was resentful and jealous of the accomplishments of others. He was bitter and this emotion resulted in very little love shown toward my mother. Instead, he verbally abused her, labeling her stupid because of her lack of education. She did what she needed to raise her children and get through the madness that had her trapped in a life she had never envisioned. Perhaps what I admire most about my mom and why I am talking about her in an essay about using one's whiteness to speak truth to power is that she spoke up and pushed back. In a provincial town, where most people conformed and took part in hatred and bigotry, my mom did not.

Sadly, my father did. When I wrote that he was bitter earlier, I was referring to his hatred of others, be they Blacks, Latinos or Asians. Native Americans were spared for some reason (more than likely, my mother says because my father was actually part American Indian). I grew up hearing my father say nigger, spic, jap and chink. But I also grew up with a mother who told me that these words were wrong and hurtful. She washed our mouths out with soap if we ever repeated these words. I saw my older brothers endure the *Zest* or *Dove* bar many times. In my heart I knew those words were wrong and did not say them. My mom told us that hatred of someone based on race, color or wealth was wrong. Of note, there were *no* African Americans, Latinos or Asians living in our town or within 150 miles from us at any point during my childhood (and even today—the town has not changed much). But that didn't stop my father or many of the other residents of our town from hating these racial and ethnic groups. Oh, they were fun to laugh at on *Sanford and Son* and *Chico and the Man,* but you wouldn't want "those people" as friends. Minorities were easy targets.

My father did anything he could to convince us that African Americans were bad and that we should always hold them suspect. "Martin Luther

King was a rabble rouser and didn't really believe in peaceful protest." "Malcolm X was anti-American." "Blacks are dirty and lazy; they just want a hand out." Ironically, my father was always trying to get government cheese and he stole from his employer time and time again. Many of my school teachers reinforced these stereotypical, racist ideas. I learned nothing about African American history and culture with the exception of slavery (and that was romanticized, whisked over and, of course, there was no blame to be had). I heard teachers say derogatory things about Blacks. My Catholic grade school had a slave auction and was not apologetic about it. As a small child, I didn't see a problem with the slave auction. I didn't even know what slavery was, let alone the horrors of Jim Crow. Our local coffee shop was called "Little Black Sambo's" and had a young African boy being chased by a tiger on the sign and on the menus. I thought Sambo was cute. The local bakery had big fat cookie jars decorated like a Black woman. I dug my hand in for a cookie, never thinking twice about the image on the jar. I went to "Sambo's" and the bakery with my father; my mother never took me to these places.

As my mom saw my father's influence on her children, she worked to counter it—ever so patiently. She told us not to listen to him. She confided in us—telling us how my dad blamed minorities for his lack of success, for his problems. She told us that she had grown up in Flint, Michigan, living next door to a Black family and that they were "just like you and me." When she married my father she had no idea that he held such racist views. Many of these views did not surface for years and by that time she had too many kids to make it on her own. She felt trapped. And as a result, she endured his hostile and shameful verbiage. Through our mother, some of us learned that prejudice is wrong and that we should speak up for others and confront injustice. Unfortunately, not all of my siblings learned this lesson—some of them harbor horrible thoughts and school their children in racist ideas. I no longer speak to these siblings—a choice I had to make when I had my own child.

Because of my mother and despite growing up in a racist and exclusionary environment, I chose to pursue a research agenda and scholarly life dedicated to issues of race. It makes sense to my mother. My father couldn't understand until very late in his life why his daughter would care so much about equity. In the spirit of true irony, my father had a stroke and we placed him in a nursing home near my sister in Tennessee. Unlike the Upper Peninsula of Michigan, there are African Americans in Tennessee and my father's roommate in the nursing home (he had a roommate because he could not afford a private room) was an African American man. Although disgusted and belligerent about the idea at first, my father grew to love the man and the man's family. They became close friends and when I would visit him, the two of them would be sitting in rocking chairs laughing and sharing stories.

A few months before my father died, he told me that he had been wrong about Blacks. He cried in my arms about the life of anger and hatred he had lived for over 80 years; he was proud of me for standing up against his racist beliefs. Sadly, he never acknowledged the work of my mother—a poor, abused, White woman who could have grown bitter—to push back against his influence over her children; he continued to resent her.

Given the example of my mother (and my father for that matter), my interest in race and equity might make sense. Despite not knowing anyone of another race or ethnicity (outside of Native Americans) until graduate school, I felt compelled to make a difference in the world. I idealistically believed (and still believe) that we should "be the change we want to see." I make no apologies for having this perspective. Yes, it might color my viewpoint—it might make a difference in what I choose to research. But it does not mean that I will cover up findings to appease my ideology. It does not mean that I'll avoid asking questions that run counter to my hopes. I believe that it is entirely possible to pursue a research agenda steeped in a commitment to justice.

## Pushing Back and Making Change

I am a firm believer in doing research about which you are passionate and with which you can make a difference. Issues of race, class and gender have been salient in my life. Growing up in poverty with a trapped mother and a racist father gives me a unique insight into these issues—not the only insight, but an interesting one. For example, I could have become the type of person who carries the "pulled myself up by my bootstraps" narrative, questioning the work ethic of minorities. I know many White women who carry this narrative. I do not hold this perspective because I have come to understand that racial prejudice is much harder to overcome in the United States; whereas Whites can mask class differences.

Although the majority of my research is focused on Historically Black Colleges and Universities (HBCUs) and African American philanthropy, for this essay, I want to focus on the research that I have done related to students of Color. This research interest grew out of my experience at the University of Pennsylvania, an elite, Ivy League institution with a less than desirable percentage of African American students (interestingly, people from the Caribbean and Africa are counted in this group). When I first arrived at Penn, I encountered a barrage of students who sought solace from their past experiences within my department. Faculty members, who have long since retired, drove them crazy. One young woman, who now teaches at another Ivy League institution, was told she was "dead in the water" upon admission—that she would never make it at Penn. Of course, when she graduated with distinction, she was a "phoenix rising from the ashes." Other

African American students were discouraged from studying topics related to race. Classes revolved around White, Eurocentric ideas and rarely did anyone notice. Above all of that, admissions decisions were made with no commitment to bringing in a diverse class and as a result, I found myself looking out upon a sea of whiteness in the classroom.

I care deeply about the future make up of the professoriate because I believe firmly in equity. I also believe that a diverse professoriate is the responsibility of all faculty and not just faculty of Color. As such, I have focused much of my scholarly efforts on issues that will help bolster the future professoriate. Interestingly, my actions here are connected to my historical work on Black colleges. My dissertation was on an African American leader of a Black college named Charles Spurgeon Johnson. One of his goals was to change the face of the academy and to prepare future scholars and leaders. I decided to follow his lead. Of course, making a decision to change the status quo is not without its critics. Those who want to protect the status quo guard it with their lives. Taking on these individuals can mean coming to terms with your sense of integrity. Although I am fortunate to have, for the most part, good colleagues at Penn, there have been times during which I had to assert my perspective on equity in order to stop the extreme perpetuation of privilege.

One of my first efforts to make change at Penn relates to admissions decisions. I was uncomfortable teaching an all-White class and as such, I banded together with one of my White, male colleagues to make much-needed change. I knew that we would have more power working together. We conspired on ways to increase not only diversity in the applicant pool, but how to push back against our senior colleagues who wanted to maintain the status quo. When the time came for the meeting in which admissions decisions were made, we pushed back at our colleague who had separated the candidates into acceptable and non-acceptable. Of course, the majority of the non-acceptable students were students of Color. Together, we forced our colleagues to review each candidate in a holistic way, emphasizing the need for a diverse class and our commitment to access for more than merely White students from the Northeast. Our efforts started out slowly, with some success, but eventually (today), we had the most diverse programs in our school. Our cohorts are truly representative of the nation as a whole. Moreover, our faculty, which has changed and is much more diverse in terms of race and gender, is now committed to enrolling a diverse class. We no longer have to push with such intensity.

Based on my knowledge of higher education and especially the experiences of African American students both within Black colleges and historically White institutions, I know that learning in an environment that embraces one's ideals and culture is beneficial. In addition, as someone who also wants to be part of an environment that cares about issues of race and tries to move forward in its ability to understand and manage these issues, I wanted to create an open conversation around race. With the help of the Dean of Students in my school, we started a Race in the Academy series that showcased research on race and also highlighted films and plays pertaining to race. Although the attendance was slow in the beginning, it picked up and students began to look forward to the events. They saw the gatherings as a safe space in which they could share their thoughts and frustrations. Of note, White students participated in these events as often as African Americans and saw them as a supplement to their classroom instruction. When the Race in the Academy series started there was some backlash from a few faculty and staff members who "didn't think race was a problem" or "wanted to see more talks on Whiteness because that is a race as well." We tried our best to embrace these faculty members and offer programs that met their needs too. Unlike some scholars, I believe that people who are resistant to change and the infusion of conversations around race should be included in discussions. The only way for learning to take place is through exposure. That said, with some faculty, we just could not change their minds.

Over time perhaps we have changed minds. Shortly after the launching of the Race in the Academy series, with the support of our dean at the time, we began a series of informal discussions about race among the faculty. We met once a month over breakfast and talked about issues of race in our research, teaching and interactions with students and each other. Interestingly, different people showed up for the discussion every month. Sometimes those people who we knew were committed attended; we knew they were committed from student comments, from their research and from their actions in the school. Other times those people who never spoke up in a meeting or never attended any race-related events showed up. They did not talk, but they listened to the conversation. I think that just listening to others talk about the manifestations of race was helpful to those who live in fear of taking a risk. These monthly conversations about race and the Race in the Academy series bring the conversation to the surface and it bubbles up and from time to time there is a breakthrough.

Recently, I feel that we had a breakthrough in terms of an individual's understanding of her own perpetuation of oppression. During a faculty meeting, we had a discussion about issues of race in the classroom and one White, female professor who is notorious for ignoring these issues, silencing others, and making deeply insensitive comments to students, spoke up. She said, in a trembling voice, something so important: "How do I know if I am one of the people making our African American students feel uncomfortable? I think I might be but how will I know unless someone tells me?" Interestingly, this professor is one of the most powerful faculty members in our school and commands immense respect externally and within the university—yet, she does not know how to manage her thoughts about race and does not know how to facilitate conversations around this issue in the classroom. She did, however, take the first step and admit her inability. Bringing issues of race (as well as class, gender, and sexuality—which is something we do) out into the open is vital and creates an environment in which people (eventually) feel comfortable asking for help, admitting fault and expressing a desire to change. For those of us doing research related to race, it is crucial that we create these opportunities in our local environments. It's not *just* enough to do research—the research should engender change.

Perhaps the area in which a professor and researcher can have the most impact is in his or her teaching. Of course, this is a choice. One can merely present information and let students take from it what they want and move forward. Or one can present information and ask probing questions to make students think—critically think. Or one can teach with a particular ideological approach and ignore other perspectives. I want to make it clear that although I believe in discussing issues of race in the classroom, I do not believe in jamming an ideology down students' throats. I use the second approach I described above.

For example, in my History of American Higher Education course, I provide students with readings that speak to issues of race, class, gender, sexuality, ethnicity and religion. Within these readings, I present many sides of each issue and a variety of perspectives. So, if I am teaching about the civil rights and student protests of the 1960s, I present readings from the right, left and center. I want students to analyze these readings and understand the various perspectives. I want them to study the language—there is a difference between calling students "activists" and "radicals," for instance. Why are the different words used and how does the use of one word rather than the other color the reader's perspective?

In addition to presenting different perspectives, I try to push students to understand their role in the world and more specifically, in American history. So often, students think that they are powerless. Not true! I provide my students with many examples of how students have changed many aspects of academe as well as the larger society. One need look no further than the Black college students who sat at a lunch counter in Greensboro, North Carolina and endured ridicule and abuse in order to desegregate eating facilities (and so much more) (Branch, 1989). Students have had a great impact on the make up of the faculty at many colleges and universities, pushing for greater diversity. They have also shaped the curricula, asking for offerings that represent their perspectives and serve their needs. Sometimes students doubt the ability of one person to make change. In response, I talk about those well-known individuals who have led movements for change: Nelson Mandela, Martin Luther King, Jr., Caesar Chavez, among others. But I also talk about those leaders, many people of Color but also Whites, who have made change on a daily basis within their local communities, schools and universities. The readings I provide to students focus on these people and their efforts. I also talk about the ways that I have pushed back to make positive change as a White woman. Of course, regardless of one's politics, all of my students now have a contemporary example of how one person can make a difference and make great change—Barack Obama—a person who started out making change in local communities and is now the leader of the United States. And, of note, students at colleges and universities across the country are partially responsible for Obama's success—students who many assumed were passive and lacked any inclination to step up and take responsibility for their country.

Although I only tell the students once that I want them to live their lives for something bigger than themselves, I secretly hope that my message will get through to them. I hope that they will choose to fight for justice in many areas—some do, some don't. I try to role model this behavior.

From time to time, students do not like my approach to teaching history. They are angered that I don't teach the traditional "White men and wars" curriculum. When I was younger, those students who disagreed with my approach got on my nerves—got under my skin. However, now I just let people know on the first day of class that my approach to teaching history is an inclusive approach. I let them know that I want each student to see him- or herself represented in the readings. And I bluntly let students know that they might want to drop the class if they are not comfortable with this approach. Rarely do people drop. Rumor has it that my class pushes people to think differently—that students leave feeling refreshed and energized about making change. They may not agree with everything I say, but they understand that "to be educated is to be conscientiously uncomfortable" (Peterkin, 2008, n.p.).

## The Power of Tenure

Thus far, all of the examples I have given in this essay took place before I had tenure. I have always been a fighter and a feisty one and as such, when I started at Penn, I told the dean at the time that although I respected tenure, I did not want it so badly that I would sacrifice my integrity over issues of equality and equity. She agreed and supported me. I felt empowered by her support and as a result, I was probably much more outspoken than most of my junior colleagues at the time, regardless of race. That said, I do realize that there is a certain safety in whiteness and my femaleness and I typically recommend that all faculty members choose their battles when standing up against faculty colleagues. I did not fight back against every little thing but chose which incidents and topics I wanted to speak out on—these typically involved race, gender, class, and sexuality, and every so often, religion. My motto as an untenured professor was always this: "If you are productive, it is hard for someone to take your voice away." Productivity was a protective shield for me as it is harder to get rid of someone who publishes a lot and brings in substantial grant funding.

Upon receiving tenure, I did feel slightly more empowered and I have to admit that tenured professors who remain tight lipped frustrate me. I did not work extremely hard to get tenure only to be silent about that which I feel strongly. On one particular occasion, I was happy to have the security of tenure. Our school had just finished selecting the year's round of Ph.D. students and the administration distributed a list of the students, noting their race, gender and other particulars. I noticed that the percentage of students of Color was down significantly from the year before and after studying the list, I realized what had happened. Without oversight from a higher level, each of the divisions in the school had relied on the other divisions to bring in the students of Color—the result: very few students of Color. I wrote an email to our dean and he agreed, stating that he had noticed the same thing when he saw the list of students. When we had our school-wide faculty meeting that month, the dean raised the lack of diversity in the Ph.D. cohort for discussion and I decided it was an opportune moment to speak up. After listening to faculty members make statements such as "I want to recruit students that I feel comfortable mentoring" and "I want to advise students who do research that is similar to mine," I spoke up. I asked how we could in good conscience keep what Penn had to offer for Whites only, and for that matter only affluent Whites. I explained that if we only mentored people who were "like us" the academy would remain exactly the same (realizing that some people would like the academy to stay the same). I said that I was ashamed that our Ph.D. cohort lacked diversity and that based on the few years prior, I thought we had reached an understanding as a faculty that there was great value in having a diverse Ph.D. cohort and in essence, preparing a diverse professoriate. When I made these comments, I saw a few eyes rolling but, interestingly, afterwards I received quite a few supportive emails from faculty members. I wish they had spoken up during the actual meeting; however, some people will never do this even if their research is related to race or social justice.

Another incident that took place after I received tenure pertained to the recruitment of faculty of Color. While serving on several search committees for faculty positions, I began to notice that there was not a systemic approach to recruiting faculty of Color; it was haphazard at best. Curious, as usual, I secured funding from the dean's office to conduct a study on our institution's policies and practices for recruiting faculty of Color. I met with all of the faculty members who had served as chairs of search committees as well as members of the administration and faculty of Color who had come through the recruitment process in the past five years. If I had been untenured, I might have been uncomfortable conducting the interviews as some of my colleagues were hostile in their views on race-based recruiting (most colleagues were supportive even if they didn't quite understand how to recruit a diverse faculty). I learned an incredible amount about what we do and don't do at Penn to ensure a diverse faculty. In addition to writing several peer-reviewed articles, an op-ed and a scholarly essay with the data from the study, I also talked with my dean. I told him about my findings and my concerns that we had no system in place—save an unwritten rule: "no more than two white men on a search committee." To my surprise, he was incredibly supportive and in the subsequent year, he continued to ask my perspective on faculty recruitment. Of note, he purchased books on faculty recruitment for search committee chairs, wrote letters to them stressing the importance of recruiting a diverse faculty, and made sure that they received training to help them reach candidates of Color. Through the efforts of our faculty of Color and supportive White allies, we have been able to make slow, yet substantive change within our school.

## Concluding Thoughts

My race, class and gender have shaped the way that I approach scholarship, teaching and service within the academy. Rather than merely pushing paper and pencil, I aim to push students, my colleagues, and the policies of the academy that exclude, oppress and discriminate. I aim to push for change and progress regardless of the "sage" advice from older colleagues that researchers should be just that—researchers, keeping their noses out of activism. I urge future scholars to consider pushing back against the status quo. When you use empirical research to back up your opinions and perspectives, you can rest assured and feel confident that your actions are justified. Those who have tenure, regardless of race, need to work together to make the academy a better place for all faculty and students.

## References and Further Reading

Anderson, J. (1988). *The Education of Blacks in the South, 1860–1935*. Chapel Hill: NC, University of North Carolina Press.

Branch, T. (1989). *Parting the Waters: America in the King years, 1954–1963*. New York: Simon & Schuster.

Gasman, M. (2007). Truth, generalizations, and stigmas: An analysis of the media's coverage of Morris Brown College and Black colleges overall, *Review of Black Political Economy*, 34(2), 111–135.

Gasman, M. (2009). Much ado about Morris Brown College. *Diverse Issues in Higher Education Blog*.

Gasman, M. & Sedgwick, K. (2005). *Uplifting a People: African American philanthropy and education*. New York: Peter Lang.

hooks, b. (1994) *Teaching to Transgress*. New York, Routledge.

Lincoln, Y. S. (2000) The practices and politics of interpretation, in: N. K. Denzin & Y. S. Lincoln (Eds) *The Handbook of Qualitative Research* (California, Sage Publications).

Meizhu, L., Leondar-Wright, B., and Robles, B. (2006). *Color of Wealth: The story behind the U.S. racial wealth divide.* New York: The New School.

Peterkin, D. (2008). Entry made on Teagle Foundation Blog.

Tierney, W. G. & Salle, M. (2008). Do organizational structures and strategies increase faculty diversity: A cultural analysis. *American Academic*, 4(1).

Part IV

# WOMEN OF COLOR AND WHITE WOMEN IN CONVERSATION

12

# ARE WE THERE YET?

## Trust, Faith, and the Power of a Common Goal

*Kristi Ryujin and Martha Sonntag Bradley*

In this chapter we, Kristi (an Asian American woman) and Martha (a White woman), discuss a conflict involving race, gender and power that had the potential to ruin any possibility of creating a cross-race alliance and institutional change. Rather than taking "the easy way out," we decided to fight to become allies. This is our story.

### The Beginning: Kristi's View

I don't recall what the day was like when Abigail entered my office. It seemed a rather average day at the university. Abigail was coming to meet with me about what many faculty and staff at the university wanted—to get their hands on my scholars, students of Color. This was not always the case as many at the U thought of our student scholars as less than capable—the university was doing something noble for these kids—giving them a hand out. While folks were generally supportive, they doubted these students would graduate or make any difference in the overall institution. The program was meeting what they saw as their "commitment to diversity." What they didn't count on was the tenacity of these diverse students and the handful of committed faculty and staff who worked to support them.

Abigail looked like so many of the students, staff and faculty at the U: a young, White woman dressed in preppy clothes and very bleached blond hair. I think she was used to being received very positively as a representative of the university's elite Honors Program. As a member of the university's staff for 20 years, I had come to know Honors as an organization committed to supporting its White, upper class and male students. My interest was piqued when Abigail contacted me to discuss recruiting my students into Honors. In the past, I assisted the few students who showed interest in Honors. I recall a young Latina who was interested in taking Honors Writing. She had an excellent high school GPA, but her ACT score did not meet the program's admission standards. I sent Dr. Bradley, Director of Honors, an email requesting admission for this particular student detailing her skills and her response was "we will give her a chance." I remember thinking to myself, "no, she'll give *you* a chance."

This history explains my surprise to have Honors courting me and my students. When Abigail entered the office I asked her about herself—how long had she been working for the university, her educational background and how long she had been recruiting diverse students. Trust is a big thing with me. My students are like my children, I want to know who they are playing with, are they good people and do they respect and like them. I think Abigail thought this would be an easy sell—"we're offering your students this very special opportunity ..." and that I should be grateful. The look on her face of stunned disbelief when I asked, "How many faculty of Color teach in Honors, and how many students of Color are there?" was amusing. This might have been the first time anyone had questioned an offer from Honors. I went on to ask what they were willing to do to alter their classrooms to be more welcoming to diverse students. Abigail seemed unprepared for this line of questioning and defensive about the impressions I had about the Honors program. To her credit, she stayed in the conversation and we discussed creating a training opportunity for Honors faculty. She left the meeting committed to discussing this idea with her boss, Dr. Bradley.

I entered this relationship hoping to ensure a better environment for diverse students and improve the Honors Program. Abigail organized a meeting with Dr. Bradley, and I invited a few key student leaders and two faculty members of Color, Professors Fuentes and Lowery. It was a typical meeting about diversity with White faculty talking about the good things they had done for us. I recall with uncomfortable clarity the story that ensued. Honors had recently recruited Upward Bound students, largely students of Color. Dr. Bradley talked about all the work that the program had put into this effort. She ended this "uplifting" story by giving the White Honors students credit for the success of the Upward Bound cohort. My students exchanged glances of disappointment and irritation about Dr. Bradley's comments. I felt like their eyes were shouting, "You're going to stop this right? You're going to challenge this racist bitch!" There was an uncomfortable silence as I looked at my students and my faculty colleagues. My response was direct, but polite as I began to explain how her story and others like it demonstrate the need for a training program so that Honors would be prepared for the talented diverse students we would be bringing. In addition, Honors would need to challenge the culture of its organization so that the faculty, staff and leadership could begin to alter the oppressive practices that create barriers to access and success for students of Color. The students were not shocked by Dr. Bradley's comments—taking credit for the achievement of people of Color by Whites is not a new phenomenon in colleges or other institutions. However, to be asked to attend such a meeting to begin the recruitment of diverse students where the director makes this fundamental mistake after professing a commitment to diversity does not bode well. Often "good White liberals" spend significant time talking about the plight of "colored folk," but fail to act, "some may want change, but almost all white liberals want to achieve it without cost or pain" (Bennett, 1964). After I offered what I perceived as a very gentle critique of Dr. Bradley's comments explaining how her statement was offensive, her face flushed with what I believed to be anger but now understand was embarrassment and she retreated from the conversation by excusing herself for another meeting. No resolution came from that meeting and we were farther apart than when we began.

What I continue to struggle with when working with White women, ironically, is paternalism. It's the "do-gooder syndrome," that they are somehow saving us from ourselves—that without them, we would be boats without oars, lost at sea. The issue of propriety is perplexing. When White women are racist and offensive and we challenge them, we are being rude, disrespectful, unprofessional. The expectation that women of Color will maintain a commitment to what hooks (1994) describes as "bourgeois decorum," adds to the challenges of working with White women. My "incivility" (Mayo, 2001) or unwillingness to operate within established/ accepted forms of communication where racist comments are brushed over, ignored or labeled as something else, pushed my status to the extreme margin labeling me "other-other." White women's willingness to stay silent within white supremacy and then mandate our complicity both covertly and overtly exacerbates the problem. White women's enculturation into whiteness ensures their privileged status while relegating them to the position of subordinate. It is this "trade" for privileged white status that betrays their feminist interests and separates them from women of Color.

Later, I heard Abigail and Dr. Bradley called me a "bitch" and "unprofessional," respectively. When White women claim they have been attacked, whether it is metaphorically or literally, someone will pay. Historically people of Color have been lynched for this "betrayal," "not knowing one's place," but for me the damage was less physical. Instead, my professional reputation was impacted when word reached senior academic affairs officials. It is here that White women are most dangerous as their claims are always heard by White men, powerful White men with authority to alter both the professional and personal lives of people of Color. White women's trade-off of gender subordination for race supremacy is reified and white supremacy protected.

Typically, this would be the end of the story. I contacted my boss, Dr. Barrie, angry and upset. No matter how many times I am criticized for doing this work, I am never immune to the dis-ease it creates. Dr. Barrie gave me permission to end the relationship. I had been down this road before working with individuals who claimed to value diversity but, upon realizing this work requires effort and commitment, walk away. Luckily for both Dr. Bradley and me, Dr. Lowery intervened. Drs. Lowery and Bradley met the following day. Dr. Lowery described Dr. Bradley as defensive, offended and hurt by my comments. He listened and suggested that she and I meet and work it out. He asked her to think about what she had said in that meeting and the true meaning of her words. "Race talk" is often coded in the academy to preserve the illusion of collegiality. She didn't refer to the students as students of Color, she referred to them as Upward Bound Students. She didn't say it was only White students who helped them succeed, it was Honors Students whom she claimed helped them succeed. She hadn't marked them by race, I had done that, because that was the hidden meaning. Dr. Bradley implied it but I openly stated it. I removed the euphemism and unveiled what Moon (1999) calls "Whitespeak" which allows Whites the opportunity to distance themselves from race and their participation in white supremacy (Moon, 1999).

At this point, my anger about the situation was beginning to subside and feelings of hopelessness replaced it. Dr. Bradley, Abigail and I met in my office a few days later. It was uncomfortable to say the least. Abigail, with her bouncy blond hair juxtaposing her face, looked unpleasant and riddled with resistance. Dr. Bradley arrived with flushed cheeks and red-rimmed eyes. I don't know what I looked like, but I remember feeling tense and sad. When these efforts go awry, self-doubt creeps in and I begin to wonder if I have been too hard, too critical and overly sensitive. Our conversation was stifled, but we began to address the previous meeting's failures.

## The Beginning: Martha's View

Unlike the other writers in this book, I am a novice at this work. I don't come from a discipline where whiteness theory is taught across the curriculum and I was tremendously unprepared when I made my entry into diversity work. My lack of preparedness was emblematic of the privilege I inherited as a White woman. I didn't earn it, I didn't deserve it, and it prevented me from seeing the people around me, imagining how they experienced the university, and importantly, I was blind to the work that needed to be done. I was invited to contribute to this essay because of my difficult beginning, but also because I stayed with it.

Much of my writing has been about patriarchy and the damage done by patriarchal systems to women, but I had not read my way through whiteness theory or theories about white privilege. And, more importantly, regardless of the damage wrought by patriarchy, it is not an equivalent experience.

As a White woman I inherit privileges that others do not and that cause harm to others.

I came unprepared for the meeting. My colleague scheduled the meeting, put it on my calendar, asked me to join for introductions. I showed up, but that's about all. We sat around a large, square table in the seminar room at the Honors Center. I knew some of the faculty who had come, but not all, and none of the students.

After brief introductions, someone asked me to describe what we were doing about diversity in Honors. I described a mentoring program that we had at a local high school. Our living and learning students were mentoring under-represented students to recruit them to the university. I briefly mentioned some work two Honors students had done with students from the Upward Bound program the summer before, including a tutoring program we had just launched to help interested students refine their writing skills before enrolling in college. This targeted students who had huge potential but needed some catching up before they took Honors classes. The long and the short of it was we weren't doing much.

When I was done, the woman who proposed diversity training for Honors challenged my comments. She asked me to adjust the way I talk about diversity. She suggested I had used deficit language. Although I don't remember exactly what she said, I do remember feeling cornered, misunderstood, and upset. I became immediately defensive and thrashed about trying to figure out how I had failed.

Over time, I learned that my response in that meeting was a sort of textbook example of a White girl functioning from a position of white privilege. I had implied that students of Color needed to be fixed before they could enter Honors under the guise of mentorship or tutoring to be Honors worthy, a grossly flawed way of thinking either about them as individuals or the immense wealth of experience they bring.

What's more, during the next few days I tried to "fix" this mess. I was horrified that this meeting had been witnessed by two talented students who put themselves on the line, two respected colleagues and three other persons I barely knew.

Virtually as soon as I left the room I was hyper-aware of the disconnect between my experience of that meeting (and of the world) and the persons of Color in the room. The fact that I didn't speak the language they were using embarrassed me. More important was the "oh, my God," sense that their vantage point of the world was so profoundly different from my own and I was part of the problem they face.

I felt baffled, confused and keenly aware there was knowledge in that room—of the world and the university both—that I did not possess. Even though this woman was terrifying to me at that moment, I sensed she would play a role in bringing me closer to an understanding. This painful experience—for Kristi and me—initiates a process of self-reflection, education and becoming an ally that continues to the present. It changed my sense of my work and what I want to do in the world.

I am not normally someone who cries her way through difficult situations, but this experience shook me up tremendously. I cried for days, couldn't sleep and was deeply upset. These emotions were not merely the result of my embarrassment, that was a minor part of it. I was shaken. I don't believe this is a necessary ingredient for change, but for me it was critical. I was shaken awake.

By nightfall, I had communicated by email with one of the other faculty of Color in the room who worked with Kristi in the Center for the Empowerment of Students of Color. I also called another faculty member of Color, a friend and mentor to us both. These two men assured me that she was a woman of great integrity (it would have been easier if she was a sort of crackpot but she was not), and if I got to know her I would like her. They and others shared readings, recommended articles and books that I poured over that night and in the weeks to come.

Abigail and I met with Kristi the next afternoon to see if we could indeed do the diversity training as planned. It was clear we needed to talk. There was tension in the room so brittle it might have cracked. Bruised ego oozed across her desk in both directions.

That conversation was incredibly important for me. For one thing, I didn't feel outnumbered, not that it mattered, but it was the beginning of a dialogue. I got a sense of Kristi as a woman—she was formidable but I started to sense her deep commitment to equity and inclusiveness that was rooted in her proud heritage as a Japanese American, as a mother, as a teacher and as a fierce mentor to students. In some ways, this is the common ground where we stand. Although it was grounded in theory it was also deeply personal and tied to her identity. I got this. It was something to hang on to. What's more, I knew her access to students was critical, she was a powerful gatekeeper.

Although we batted around a bit—"you did this" and "I thought this"— eventually that seemed to matter less and less than what we were going to do next, what we could do together. I remember how offended I felt when she said, "I am so tired of taking care of White folks." My response was an uppity one that was again so much about white privilege. It is not the role or the job of the person of Color who faces discrimination or inequities to teach or take care of us. It's our work and we must confront it before we can become allies and evoke change. Instead of "hearing" what Kristi was saying or "seeing" her as a woman and importantly as an ally, I thought only about how her comment impacted me.

Historically, Honors programs and colleges are elitist. They are predominantly white or populated by wealthy foreign students. In many ways they are the embodiment of white privilege, of hierarchical ways of thinking about relationships and people. We have seen, in our Honors College, a prevailing sense of entitlement that blocks many students from hearing the stories of others whose experience of the world and indeed the university is different from their own. Like privilege, entitlement is an enemy of this work. Change in a program like Honors requires a sort of earthquake, one more dramatic than a paradigm shift. Only the most powerful commitment imaginable makes change happen.

There is so much ego in the air in academia, particularly in Honors— the performance of brilliance, of a lifetime of good grades and awards, of institutional acknowledgement and privilege. But to be effective at changing the institution we must develop humility, an empathetic awareness of others.

One of the most amazing results of engaging in this work is that you find out that you don't know anything at all. (And the reason we don't know anything is that we think the world looks the same to everyone.) We assume our own way of looking at the university, our curriculum, what students need or want, is the only valid point of view. Or we believe that because we are human beings we all see the world similarly, but we don't.

By engagement I mean really staying at the table, taking whatever is waiting to jump out at you, trip you up or discourage you. In some ways, the produced knowledge constructed in our academic disciplines fails us in conflicts like the one Kristi and I experienced. In comparison, the knowledge we gain from relationships with those who are most different from ourselves empowers us and makes us more effective agents of change.

How can we possibly get it, or even enter the work, if we don't listen to each other's stories? How can we possibly work together if we don't listen to the way we experience the world—if we don't "see" each other for who we really are?

If we're serious about this work we must dive in. If you're like me you will hit your head on the bottom of the pool. You might bleed, get a headache like never before, but the day after you do and the day after that and in the weeks ahead, you should align yourself with someone who will model what it means to swim. If you're lucky enough, you'll bump into someone like Kristi.

## Lessons Learned: Kristi

Our relationships with White women are riddled with challenges. The protection that their whiteness provides and the amnesia that accompanies their actions when it suits them are indefensible. But when they are honest and direct, I hope I can always be open to hearing them. In this situation, Dr. Bradley, Martha, had an epiphany. She told a story of her own experiences with gender discrimination when the chair of her department took credit for her success in front of her male colleagues. She recalled how angry she was and the pain his insensitivity created for her and ultimately how his words dismissed the exorbitant amount of blood, sweat and tears she put into her scholarship. She realized this is what she had done to the students of Color in her program. She had taken credit from these students of Color and given it to her White students—their effort was unimportant, unrecognized. Martha told this story unable to hold back her tears. While I would like to say that I was generous, forgiving and compassionate, I am sure I was not. I was likely hard, uncompromising and probably mean. While I know I believed her, I wasn't going to let her get off that easily. As for Abigail, she slowly disappeared as Martha and I began to work together and developed a training program for the Honors faculty.

When I read Derrick Bell's (1980) work on interest convergence, I thought only White folks could "choose" to participate while the participation of people of Color was compulsory—required because it was a situation of life or death. In this situation, I could have walked away. I didn't "need" the Honors program. My students had successfully navigated the university without ever having to enter Honors and many of them had gone on to graduate school and work. But what does it mean to *choose* to work with a white organization as a person of Color representing students of Color? Now this is different—choice implies power. Whether I really had any power or not, I felt that the academic success of my students and the amazing leadership roles they had assumed had given us currency in the university. Obviously it was not real or sustainable power, but in that moment when I began working with Honors I believed we had currency and cultural capital. Maybe someone should have informed Honors.

Is this the reason our story didn't end several pages earlier? Martha, too, could have walked away from this relationship. Honors had been seen as "successful" for a long time without diversity and while the program would have been stronger with my students, their participation wasn't mandatory. Her students had gone on to graduate studies and assumed leadership positions within the university just like my students. We could have both moved on and this would have been just a blip on the screen. But we didn't. For whatever reasons, Martha and I chose to work together, carefully.

I am not sure at what point I stopped punishing Martha. This is something I must admit to doing. I watched her like a hawk. She was vulnerable, a novice and because she had hurt me, I was set on returning the favor. But at some point, after a lot of work, Martha and I came to be partners. I introduced her to faculty of Color and brought students of Color into her program. We talked a lot and shared research. Martha was consistent in her efforts and responsive to ideas. She made policy changes that ensured *all* students could enter Honors through the front door and continued to find resources that would help her make the structural changes necessary to be successful.

Martha is for me an enigma, a White woman professor in a powerful university position who is sensitive, moral, committed to diversity, loves students and still thinks she has something to learn. She has made mistakes along the way, struggling to listen and not be defensive when students of Color are critical and believing that White faculty will move along because it is the right thing to do, but that has been nothing in comparison to the achievements she has made to improve her understanding of diversity and the program's commitment to our students. Martha has done a lot of changing and made choices that have taken her out of the status of "good White girl." She might be seen as a race traitor or have lost some credibility with her advisory board and other White elites for making the decisions she has to be inclusive. Soon after our initial meeting when a senior academic affairs official learned about our "scuffle," Martha did something unusual, unpredictable, some might say unheard of. She apologized and formally retracted her early comments about my behaving unprofessionally in written form. She has, in some ways, moved away from the powerful protection of whiteness and gained a new sisterhood and brothers. To do this work there is always a trade-off. I hope Martha thinks it was worth it.

> One can say that one is a friend of the oppressed, but one can only mean it by doing something about it, by tearing down and by building up. In the end, friendship for the oppressed can only be proven in an extreme situation where one is forced to choose—once and for all—for either the oppressor or the oppressed. In this sense friendship is an act to the end. (Bennett, 1964, p. 121)

## Lessons Learned: Martha

I said this was hard. But what I have not emphasized is that it is worth it. My world has exploded to include new friends—faculty and students to be sure, but also a wide range of community partners and allies as well.

When I said I was unprepared, I meant literally for the meeting but it was far larger than that for I had not even begun to do my homework or the work required to be an effective ally in our "home place," our community, our job and at my school. I read my way through life but had done no serious reading on white privilege. I read numerous narratives about the experience of persons of Color, but not the more hardcore, this-will-really-make-you-feel-uncomfortable types of theory or critique. I, more often than not, passed on campus lectures on diversity issues, busy with other things, also assuming I got it. I never attended diversity training. I was lazy about recruiting faculty and students of Color. I was complacent, self-congratulatory and believed what we were doing was a good start.

145

I was blind, deaf and dumb to the voices around me that suggested otherwise. It took 60 minutes of embarrassingly hardcore, profound discomfort and dis-ease to shake me awake and push me to initiate the process of change. Here is some of what I learned and would recommend to others:

1  We must start our work at home. Robert Pirsig (1974), in *Zen and the Art of Motorcycle Maintenance* reminds us, "The place to improve the world is first in one's own heart and head and hands, and then work outward from there" (p. 297). But don't stop, or get lazy or linger too long there. We have too much to do and we must get ourselves into shape to be effective allies. We have to be willing to change, to travel down the rocky, painful road it takes to evoke change. Complacency, pride and willfulness need to be peeled away, to find our better selves. We cannot expect to inspire social change in our institutions, in our communities unless first we begin the process with ourselves.

2  It is so easy in our roles in the university to think we have all the answers. I'm the dean after all, doesn't that mean something about how much I know? Actually, it doesn't, and we should never forget that. We must check our egos at the door and try on humility instead. Humility will tell you to change. It will inspire you to listen to the stories of others and try to hear what they are really saying.

3  Resist the urge to fix things. Even some of these comments will gurgle up as naturally as your breath, but don't say:
   I didn't want to hurt your feelings;
   I didn't mean it that way;
   I was trying to be polite and avoid conflict.
   None of that matters. Impact matters. Instead, listen, listen, listen, resist chiming in, fixing the moment, and listen.

4  Make a commitment to inclusiveness and think about what that might look like at your institution. Look around you and ask who is in the room. If you all look the same and think the same, you've got trouble. We miss out on the enormous resources diversity produces in terms of ideas, cultural understandings and better plans for the future. We will never have academic excellence until we have inclusive, equitable environments. Think about what needs to change in your office, at your institution, to get there.

5  Welcome more people into the mix—recruit faculty of Color, students of Color, staff members of Color. Be unrelenting in this, with each step forward you will make two steps backward. You cannot give up, but find new ways of broadening your recruitment efforts, what you value and how you work.

6  Form alliances. There will be people who are further along in the evolutionary process that can help you. Surround yourself with

individuals who have equity in the forefront of their minds. It is important to stand with people of Color in the fight for equity, but it is also important to form allies broadly—find White allies who can help you process what you are seeing and experiencing. You will be angry and discouraged at the institution and society and you need to figure out how to make that anger your strength. Make it work for you and the work for equity and accessibility. We must challenge our existing procedures, institutional practices and traditions and beat down any potential obstacles to inclusivity or access.

7 Consider your core values. What does equity and inclusiveness look like? What do you stand to gain? What will you stand for?

8 Find something to hang onto. For me, these were simple things: a comment Kristi made about doing this work for her daughter, the fierce mother love she expressed for her and the world she would inherit. The absolute devotion she had for her students, which was, if you think about it, another version of the same. Kristi gave me the chance to meet students, powerful women faculty members, all of whom have become allies and friends. I cannot imagine my life without them.

9 To administrators I say, raise money for this work. It is extremely vulnerable in tough financial times. Never miss a chance to talk about the immense value of inclusiveness, equity and diversity and embed these ideas in what your institution most values. Work for cultural change where you have influence.

Instead of being afraid of Kristi and some of the individuals around her, I feel honored by the trust she has given me. If I had run away from this, if I had stayed huffy and prideful, if I hadn't listened to her or stayed in the room as they say, if I hadn't been willing to be vulnerable, to make mistakes and to change, I would be impoverished and I would be denying something in myself.

If we value excellence, academic and community, we need to act on our conviction that a diversity of persons, ideas and experiences is at the core of the excellence it inspires. Unlike the climate change that occurs because of the selfish and sloppy way we live that destroys our natural environments, the kind of climate change we need to create through this work requires a profound change in consciousness, through which we celebrate and value the differences we bring to the table. Our diversity is the only way we can save ourselves, our families and our shared future.

## References

Bell, D. (1980). Brown v. Board of Education and the interest-convergence dilemma. *Harvard Law Review, 93* (3), 518–533.

Bennett, L. (1964). *The Negro Mood*. New York: Ballantine Books.

hooks, b. (1994). *Outlaw Culture: Resisting representations.* New York: Routledge.

Mayo, C. (2001). Civility and its discontents: Sexuality, race, and the lure of beautiful manners. *Philosophy of Education,* 78–87.

Moon, D. (1999). White enculturation and bourgeois ideology: The discursive production of "good (white) girls." In T.K. Nakayama & J. N. Martin (Eds), *Whiteness: The communication of a social identity* (pp. 177–197). Thousand Oaks, CA: Sage.

Pirsig, R. (1974). *Zen and the Art of Motorcycle Maintenance: An inquiry into values.* New York: William Morrow and Company.

# 13

# TWINS SEPARATED AT BIRTH?

## Critical Moments in Cross-Race Mentoring Relationships

*Stephanie A. Fryberg and LouAnn Gerken*

This chapter explores a cross-race relationship between a White senior faculty mentor and an American Indian junior faculty mentee in a large public university. The relationship evolved from a college requirement that junior faculty select a senior faculty mentor, but over time it developed into a successful mentoring relationship and a close friendship. In this chapter, we offer some observations, which arose from hours of in-person and email conversations, about what works in that relationship and the lessons we learned along the way.

In preparing to write this chapter, the mentor revealed to the mentee that due to the interesting content of our initial conversations, she had saved all the emails exchanged since early in the mentee's junior faculty tenure. We thought these emails presented a unique opportunity to look back at the development of the mentoring relationship and to closely examine how we negotiated particularly difficult situations, what we refer to as *critical moments*. The title, for instance, comes from a set of emails partly about race. We realized early on that we could not pretend that race was not an issue, and so we made it part of the relationship. In talking about difference in the way that we approached our personal and professional lives, LouAnn (mentor) wrote, "What? You don't think we're twins separated at birth?" In a good-humored response intended to emphasize the difficulties that race adds to life in the academy, Steph (mentee) replied, "If we were twins separated at birth, I definitely got the short end of the stick."

In the narrative that follows, we share our recollections of three critical moments: our first meeting, a meeting we attended with a high-level administrator regarding diversity efforts on campus, and a faculty meeting where diversity issues were discussed. Following a description of each moment, we spend time reflecting on them. We conclude by discussing some of the ways of "navigating" our mentor–mentee relationship that we found particularly useful. To set the stage for the dialogs, we provide a brief sketch of the mentor and mentee.

LouAnn, the senior faculty mentor, is a full professor who studies language development. She was raised in a White, blue-collar family in upstate New York and is married to an academic. Steph, the mentee, was a junior faculty member during the critical moments, but is now a tenured associate professor. She studies social and cultural psychology. Steph grew up on an Indian Reservation in Washington State and was the first person in her family to attend college and the first person from her Tribe to get a Ph.D. As a junior faculty member, she was raising her teenage nephew.

## Critical Moments in Cross-Race Mentoring

When we began the chapter, we agreed to write our responses as letters to one another to better illustrate some aspects of our interactions. We wrote these letters separately, because we did not want to influence each other's recollections.

### *The First Meeting*

**Steph:** Early in my first semester, the chair of the department asked the three new junior faculty members to select senior faculty mentors. I did not know any of the senior faculty well and I was not sure what the best strategy was for selecting such a person. I had recently seen you present at a grant workshop and I found your style of interacting engaging and entertaining. I also liked that you talked about the politics of grant writing and that you did not gloss over the political muck implicit in the review process. I found your honesty refreshing and, at times, funny, and I took your honesty as a sign that you do not readily accept the status quo and that you would not expect me to either. Given this and my lack of grant writing experience, I asked you to be my mentor.

By the time we first met, I was already experiencing some difficulties. First, the semester was nearly half over and neither my office nor my lab was ready. I was meeting with students from an old wooden cubicle in my lab. Second, the head of the department had just informed me that there was not enough money to fix my lab, so I was going to have to wait until the next academic year. While I did not doubt the lack of money, I found myself wondering whether the fact that the offices and labs of the other two new junior faculty members, both of whom were White males, were being completed that semester meant something about my status in the department. I did not want to make any trouble for myself and I did not want you to form a negative impression of me. I didn't want you to see me as a person who easily utilized the "race card." Yet, these situations did not feel right and I needed help figuring out how to navigate them.

The problem, being a new faculty member, was that I really did not know where to turn for help. During our first mentoring meeting, we spent a long time chitchatting about the department and the university, sharing ideas and beliefs about a variety of things. The whole time the commentary was running through my head … should I tell you, should I not; would you think I was a trouble maker or worse, one of those angry minorities; would you legitimate my concerns or tell me I was wrong to think or feel what I did. Even as the meeting started to wind down, I was still waxing and waning about whether to share my concerns about the department. In the end, the issues were weighing heavily on me and so I made a last-minute decision to trust my gut feeling.

When I told you that I was having a problem and asked if we could discuss it, you got up and closed the door. I tried to carefully frame the story to suggest that I was not sure about the department head's motives, but I also admitted to wondering if the fact that the research labs of the two White males were being completed, but the lab of the one woman of Color was not had meaning. You never once interrupted my story or made an unsupportive gesture. I felt you were listening and that you were concerned.

When I finished, you said you could see why I thought what I did and you asked if you could talk with the department head. I thought I should fight my own battles and I guess, deep down, I still did not trust you to frame the issues to the department head in a way that reflected positively on me. I found the situation really scary. Then you explained that it would be better if you talked with the department head because if he got upset he would be mad at you rather than me. I definitely understood your point, but as a slow to trust person, I did not agree to let you talk with him—I needed time to think about it. When I left, you assured me that you wouldn't tell anyone and you suggested that I think about it over the weekend. This made me feel better and after thinking about it for a few days, I decided you were right. In the end, the situation worked out quite well.

**LouAnn:** When you first asked me if I would be your faculty mentor, I was surprised—I had only barely met you and my research area is far from yours. When I asked you why, you pointed to an interaction we'd had when I was advising junior faculty across the college on grant writing. You said that you'd liked my response to your question about potentially political and biased grant reviewers, plus you noted that I was funny. I suppose that many people would not take being viewed as funny as a basis of a professional relationship, but your view seemed reasonable to me.

I had mentored half a dozen or so junior faculty before you, but it was clear from the first meeting that our relationship was going to be different. I think that it was in this meeting that you told me that you disliked white middle class individualism. We've laughed many times since then about my response, "Stab me through the heart." I see now that your declaration was both brave and well executed. You managed to raise the issue of feeling you did not belong in the academy early in our relationship, but I didn't feel accused of making you feel that way. My first response was humor, but I was also open to more talk. Such an exchange could easily have gone wrong, but instead it became a first point of real contact.

For me, the aspects of our first meeting that I remember most were the cautious forays into discussions of race, your research, and life in the academy. I had no idea at the time that you were sizing me up as someone with whom you could share upsetting information. When you finally told me the problem with your lab and office, I could see how easy it would be for you to attribute these problems to the fact that you are a woman of Color. I wasn't sure how much of the problem was attributable to that fact versus the shortage of money and ability to plan at the university. But what was really clear is that it would be hard for you to go in to our department head and present your case without revealing at least some of the emotion I saw in our conversation. I wasn't sure how the department head would respond, because you would be effectively accusing him of unintentional racism. Given that I not only interacted with the head as a faculty member in the department, but also as an administrator in a separate unit, I felt comfortable asking him to discuss your situation. My feeling was that the best approach to getting your problems resolved was for me to prepare the way for you by explaining the issues before you spoke with him. As you noted, this approach worked well—your meeting with the department head went smoothly and led the way to a positive long-term relationship with him, and your office and lab were completed during your first year on the faculty. You *are* very socially adept, and you might have managed these same outcomes without my help. But I like to think I contributed to the positive result.

**Steph:** This incident, in many respects, changed the direction of my career at the university. I started to feel, despite all the uncertainty the first few months yielded, that there was one person I could trust. You set the stage for a positive relationship with you and with the department head. I once read that for Native college students the best indicator of future success was being able to identify one person in their institution who was there for them (Tierney, 1992). As a first year faculty member, connecting with you helped me feel like I belonged and that I could survive. You did not become my one person after this incident, but the likelihood that you could be the one emerged as a possibility.

In fact, you may recall that shortly after this incident, I confided in you that the university was not the place I thought it was going to be or the place people told me it would be when I interviewed. I felt, however, that I had made a choice and that now I had to live with it. Your response to me, as I recall, was to remind me that I am a free agent and that I can leave anytime. Other mentors might have encouraged me to stick it out or to deal or to cope with it because this is the way in which departments and universities work. I generally find these types of responses oppressive. They suggest that the institution is broken and can't be fixed, so the only option is to persist. Your approach sidestepped these approaches entirely. By reminding me that I was/am a free agent, you freed me from this feeling of being "stuck" and you reminded me that with my skill set there were many opportunities available to me. Although I had one foot comfortably located out of the metaphorical university door, on that day, I became a happier junior faculty member.

**LouAnn:** As I told you early on, my own tenure trek was very painful, full of negative feedback, despite the fact that my own research was yielding interesting results and that I was being a great university citizen who served on many committees. I had struggled with how to continue to see myself as a smart and creative scholar, no matter whether my colleagues viewed me that way or not. It was during that time that I made an observation that I later shared with you, I think to good result—there is no reward in university loyalty, which means that your colleagues may appreciate your non-research efforts but they may well hold them against you in the tenure process. Therefore, the best approach to the tenure process is to set your own standards and to try to meet them. This observation led me to the more positive strategy of seeing yourself as a free agent. A general theme for me, stemming from our first meeting and subsequent discussions on how to survive the tenure process, has been the pleasure of translating some of my own lessons into your particular situation.

### Meeting with High-Level Administrator about Diversity Efforts on Campus

**LouAnn:** One source of strength and pleasure in our friendship is our ability to be both intellectual and emotional about social justice issues, which is reflected in our discussions of issues such as "conservative mentoring" and the "struggler phenomenon." Early on in our relationship, you told me about people of Color being viewed as strugglers in the academy. I think our discussions of "conservative mentoring" were the basis of my 2005 email to you, "… we somehow mentor women and people of color to take more conservative career paths than white men. So, the under-represented group might be more likely to get tenure when mentored that way than if they aren't mentored at all, but they are less likely to be stars in their field." (I now retract the part about the under-represented group being more likely to get tenure from conservative mentoring than from no mentoring.)

Although social justice issues are outside my main field of research, I felt that I was learning so much from you and beginning to talk more coherently about gender and race in the academy. I was soon to learn, however, that conservative mentoring and the struggler phenomenon weren't just the subjects of academic scholarship; they composed the reality of the academy for you. I'm referring to the incident when, at my urging, we met with a senior administrator who was working on making the academy more equitable, primarily with a focus on women faculty. You and I had been discussing the possible "saleable" motivations for greater equity, and we had some ideas that I thought the administrator would find new and compelling. We had barely got started talking in her office when she turned to you and said something like, "You shouldn't be thinking about these issues until you get tenure." Gulp. You looked stricken. I couldn't wait to get out of there. I had walked you right into the lion's den. I felt horrible.

**Steph:** When you convinced me that talking to this administrator was a good idea, I figured she would be *an ally* or at least *part of the choir*. You told me she was a major figure in the diversity efforts on campus, so I went with high expectations. When we arrived, however, I felt like we were immediately derailed. The comment that surprised me was not that the administrator told me that I could not get involved in diversity efforts, but rather it was her reasoning, "because women and minorities do not do well here." Being so clearly addressed and stereotyped according to my social identities, as both a woman and a person of Color, was shocking to me. I was really taken aback.

Since arriving at the university, I had consistently been surprised by the lack of dialogue about diversity issues and all I could think was that if this person is the champion for diversity, then I really do not belong here. To be honest, I was so derailed by the initial comment that my memory of the remainder of the meeting is quite hazy. Well, until the end of the meeting. As I remember it, the meeting was wrapping up. The administrator turned to you and asked if you could stay for a few minutes. She then turned to me and told me I could go. Feeling dismissed and upset, I looked at you. I wanted you to get up and leave with me—to take a stand and to walk out. What I saw, however, was a look of uncertainty. In hindsight, I can see that the administrator probably had another agenda and just did not think about how excusing me would make me feel, especially in lieu of her earlier reference to my female junior faculty of Color status. This meeting proved a critical moment in our mentoring relationship because, when I left, there were many points, level heads aside, that could have created quite a rift between us.

**LouAnn:** Until we talked about this critical moment in preparing to write our chapter, I had forgotten that the administrator asked me to stay for a few minutes. In retrospect, it seemed that she wanted to make some connection with me, to not deal with us as a team. However, at the time, I was just very surprised and confused by her comments and I was largely unable to analyze the situation. I remember coming out of the building and being relieved to see that you had waited for me. I wasn't yet saving our emails, and I particularly regret that we can't look back to see how we ultimately moved beyond this incident. I think the main lesson for me was that seemingly safe situations could so quickly become dangerous for you.

**Steph:** What helped me move beyond this situation was the sheer number of times we talked about it. One thing I have always appreciated about you is that I can tell you I am upset about something and you are always open to it. Even if you perceive that I'm being critical or that my feelings are irrational, you listen and, as best I can tell, you do not get defensive. This sense of safety, in my opinion, is rare for people of Color in the academy. Many of my junior faculty of Color friends around the country talk about having to take care of the feelings of their White colleagues—to shield them from their own biases. I never feel this way around you. I always want to reciprocate the gesture.

### *Faculty Meetings: A Team United, Individuals Divided*

**Steph:** During a faculty meeting the spring before I went up for tenure, we were discussing faculty diversity. As had become typical of faculty responses to diversity issues, I was very unhappy with how the conversation was transpiring. Normally, I would say something, but given my upcoming tenure review, the risk felt great. Nonetheless, I desperately needed someone to do or say something, so I looked at you. I was surprised when you looked at me and then looked away. Then, after the meeting, when I went to your office you told me that sometimes it was hard being my friend.

**LouAnn:** Reconstructing this incident also made me recall some other discussions that we have had about faculty diversity. For example, I remember vividly a hike we took not long before this faculty meeting. On the hike, I discussed my desire to have a colleague who does computational modeling and being frustrated by the fact that my desire is likely to be in conflict with our shared desire to hire more faculty of Color. What I have enjoyed so much about most of our conversations over the years is how we try to develop principles for approaching social justice issues in the academy and beyond. Developing such principles helps us to better understand each other's perspectives, gives us a better chance of acting as a team when an opportunity to make change arises, and allows us to be more convincing by having constructed a set of arguments that we can present to others. I feel that we've made serious progress on many issues.

Nevertheless, developing principles surrounding the issue of faculty diversity is ongoing for us. When this faculty meeting occurred, I feel that we were absolutely not ready to "go public" by arguing for a particular strategy that the department should take. In addition, I had during the same spring put myself on the line to argue against a particular senior hire that would have further tipped the balance in favor of White males. Several people who said they would back me in this argument failed to do so. You had volunteered to back me then, but we both agreed that, given your untenured status, that wasn't a good strategy. As I reconstruct my memory of the faculty meeting where I didn't jump in to support you, I think that I was already feeling very visible for having taken such a vocal and relatively solitary stand in the last battle.

Regardless of why I didn't support you, I understand at least some of your motivation to have one or more colleagues who are people of Color, and I want to support you. I also understand that it was horribly frustrating and depressing to hear the discussion at the faculty meeting and not feel that you had a single ally. The conflicting forces at the meeting to support you, to not voice an opinion that I was not fully sure of, and to avoid becoming stereotyped as the department contrarian, made me feel trapped. I reacted afterward by being angry.

**Steph:** In terms or supporting me in the faculty meeting, it did not take me very long to realize that I was being unfair. I was a junior faculty member and I did not want to stand out too much given my pre-tenure status, but I also held high expectations that you, as my friend, should jump in and "do the right thing." The issues seemed so clear to me. You had proven over the years that you were committed to social justice issues, yet, in that moment, I turned to you to carry the banner of social equity and you decided not to carry it. I was surprised and I guess, if I'm being totally honest, disappointed.

Honestly, I didn't even consider the last battle. It's true that you and one other colleague single-handedly fought that battle. As I recall, due to some prior interactions I had with a very powerful person in our department, we decided that I should not get involved in that discussion. I always appreciated how you kept my long-term survival in the department front and center in our battles. Nonetheless, it was hard to sit by and watch you fight. I too was disappointed at our colleagues who said they were going to fight and didn't.

What I learned from this situation brings me back to one of my dad's commonly used proverbs, "two wrongs don't make a right." The added burden I feel to fight every diversity battle, at that moment, was the same burden I placed on you. I expected you to fight my battles even when, in the interest of self-survival, I was not willing to do so. I didn't even consider your perspective. In that moment, when you said I was a hard friend to have,

I realized that while I may be an expert on issues of race, culture and social class, I am not an expert on interracial relationships.

This situation also brought into high relief the fact that in the department and in the university, we are still struggling over basic issues of power and that members of under-represented groups are still trying to undermine age-old hierarchies with two hands tied behind our backs. As a Native woman, I know that I cannot fight the battles all by myself. The issue is not about my persuasive abilities, but rather because my social identities (woman, Native) and what I study make it easy for non-believers to dismiss me. I want the university to be a place I can inhabit as a career, not just as a place I am visiting, but I need you and others like you if this change is going to happen. This reality is very difficult for me.

While I want you to be there anytime I pass you the banner of social equity, the reality is that it's unfair to do so without first considering your situation and without finding our common ground (the places where our motives and objectives match). We have proven that we are an effective team—we are change agents—when we have the opportunity to discuss and strategize ahead of time. Yet, as these moments of uncertainty and disagreement reveal, we are not *twins separated at birth*.

**LouAnn:** Reconstructing this critical moment is helping me to see so many facets that I didn't perceive when it happened. For example, I think that in my anger, I didn't fully appreciate your ability to see my perspective as well as you did at the time. I think that being a White person who has entered into a serious cross-racial relationship has caused me to expand and change my self-view. I definitely value this aspect of the relationship. This critical moment also illustrates to me that our relationship sometimes seems to require two kinds of commitment. The first commitment is one with which I have prior experience and that I feel that I understand. I am committed to supporting you as an individual, and I have made this commitment explicitly and without hesitation. The second commitment is new to me, and it seems less explicit than the first. This commitment requires me to support a social cause, in this case, faculty diversity. In this critical moment, I think that I was reacting against being held to this implied commitment and to the fact that, by not honoring it, I was letting you down as an individual.

## General Discussion

The preceding dialogue illustrates several themes and offers several lessons. The first theme is that we experienced the critical moments differently at the time, and we remember them differently now. Our advice is to acknowledge differences in perspective at the beginning of the relationship and to use them as learning tools. We'll say more about how we've done this below.

A second theme is that all three critical moments involve the mentor and mentee trying to determine how to interact with other members of the academy to support the mentee's career—the department head, the senior administrator and the department as a whole. By construing ourselves as a team with a goal, we were able to bond and to generate trust.

The third theme is the dialogue itself. We would like to focus the remainder of the chapter on the nature of our dialogues that have led to a successful relationship. Most important is that the dialogues reveal how careful we are to take the other person's perspective and thereby to find a common ground for discussion. We did not begin the relationship with an expectation of trust or even respect, but rather started from a place of neutrality. We are not sure how we found such a beneficial starting point. Perhaps we were both motivated to learn more about how people from different social and cultural backgrounds interact. Or perhaps we were just surprised that we liked each other and wanted to understand why. In any case, we advise going into a cross-race mentoring relationship with an open mind and to acknowledge the ways in which your own perceptions are likely to be different from the other person's.

One strategy that we frequently use to understand the other's perspective and to keep the relationship strong is to check-in with one another to see if everything is okay, usually after a face-to-face meeting that seemed to end oddly. Check-ins work if we trust that neither will say everything is fine if she does not mean it. Sometimes this leads to, at least temporarily, difficult conversations, and when it does, we typically learn something new or at least feel relieved after all is said and done. There are a number of these check-in examples in our emails. For example, in 2007, LouAnn wrote, "I felt bad leaving you feeling that you revealed too much," and in the same year, Steph wrote, "I didn't mean to imply that you did something wrong by not asking me how I was doing with respect to the death on campus" (regarding the murder of a Native American student). We think that this process of checking in is useful in any relationship and we strongly recommend it. Notably, it is uncomfortable at first, but it definitely becomes easier after a few attempts.

Another aspect of our dialogues involves humor and teasing. For us, humor and teasing denotes a sense of connection and helps us to keep tabs on the friendship. For example, in some emailed cultural banter about individualism and collectivism, Steph teased, "I would actually argue that you are more communitarian than libertarian or liberal, but I know you have a visceral need to resist your communitarian self ..." In another exchange, LouAnn advised Steph not to eat worms over some perceived failure. Steph responded by saying, "If you were Native, you would have said, 'hey, can I come over and eat worms with you?'" We recommend easing into joking or teasing about racial or cultural differences by building a base of trust and a clear sense or understanding of your partner's interaction style.

The last observation that we will make here about our several years of dialogues is that, as we noted in the introduction, our mentoring relationship soon became a friendship. The dual nature of our relationship is both satisfying and a possible source of problems, because our two respective roles (mentee and friend, mentor and friend) could easily become confused. Therefore, we tried to clearly distinguish mentor meetings from when we were just hanging out being colleagues and friends. Distinguishing between meetings helped both relationships; it denoted when we slipped into our more hierarchical positions of mentor and mentee and when we were equals and friends. We end by hoping any of our readers who enters into a cross-race mentoring relationship will enjoy the complication of mixing mentoring with friendship because the friendship will continue to nurture you long after the official mentoring ends.

## References

Tierney, W. G. (1992). *Official Encouragement, Institutional Discouragement: Minorities in Academe—the Native American experience*. Norwood: Ablex.

# 14

# PLAY ON WHITE

## The Intimate Politics of (Be)Longing

*Karen Lee Ashcraft and Lisa A. Flores*

### Introduction

Differences in race/ethnicity, class, sexuality, gender, nationality, ability, religion, and age can easily become barriers to intimacy. Women of Color, for example, detail countless instances in which they came together with White women, hopeful and expectant, but were left standing alone. Attempting to bridge such fundamental differences often induces tensions that appear insurmountable. So what accounts for friendships that develop and flourish across social location? In this chapter, we return to the roots of our 13-year friendship, born of evident difference and emergent sameness, in order to expose some of the complex dynamics that enable and constrain the relationship.

Our specific goal in the dialogue that follows is to initiate between us a kind of "intimate politics"—a candid, public account of how we maneuver dynamics of difference within the privacy afforded interpersonal relations. Central to this purpose, Lisa sees herself as a queer Latina whose class and skin privilege along with her own comfort and familiarity with performances of heterosexual white femininity open entrée into a white heterosexual world. Karen identifies as a White, heterosexual, middle class woman who simultaneously embodies and challenges notions of white femininity and masculinity, and who encounters much privilege in the process. As we turn a reflexive eye on ourselves and our relation, we confront our shared sense of entitlement, our dis/ease with white femininity, our class comfort, our commitment to anti-racism and anti-essentialism and our contested gender/sexual politics. Ultimately, we come to grips with a truth that can be taken as both ugly and fruitful: constant and contradictory play around whiteness—desire for, enchanted toying with, revulsion toward, mockery and rejection of whiteness—threads through our relation to difference. We suspect it is this

160

pivotal dynamic of play that makes a friendship, which according to much research should be tense and strained, feel anything but. Our dialogue strives to honor the gift of this playfulness and the deep friendship it nourishes while also holding us accountable for the political bargains and excesses it entails.

We are reminded of Aimee Carrillo Rowe's insights in her essay on Be Longing: "This yearning to belong is grounded in politics" (2005, p. 27). It is a yearning to belong in and to whiteness, in and to heterosexuality, in and to each other. It is a longing silenced by privilege. Reflecting on her own yearnings, Carrillo Rowe continues:

> My increasing awareness of white longings for inclusion-as-safety in an otherwise unsafe world of scarcity was accompanied by my desire for intimate belonging to and with women. The latter grew, and grows, with the help of my friends like Rebecca who showed me how my heterosexual privilege excluded and erased her. I never realized that as the popular white male academic held the door open for me, it slammed in her face as soon as I walked through. I never realized how I participated in slamming doors on other women, let alone my best friend. (p. 29)

## Our Longings

**Karen:** I pulled into the parking lot in a flustered state, a few minutes late. Little did I know I'd be waiting for an hour. Since neither of us knew the city, we had chosen to meet, of all places, at a restaurant that turned out to be attached to a seedy downtown motel (hey, the magazine promised good Mediterranean food!). So there I sat, staring at a glass case flooded in fluorescence and brimming with baklava, waiting for her to arrive. As time passed, I felt something rising from my core; weeks of frustration with Salt Lake had chosen that moment to converge in my chest. Like most major moves, it had been a slow and uncomfortable transition: the usual snags, the growing pains of first-year faculty life, a sense of loneliness despite the warm welcome from my new department, an unhappy husband who had radically altered his career to follow mine, and not one friend with whom to vent over a drink. It dawned on me: You might not come. Okay, you weren't coming. And how fitting, really, that my best prospect for a friend in this godforsaken (regardless of what the locals say) town should fall through as well. The lump in my chest rose to my throat, which surprised and embarrassed me. I was just about to leave when you made an apologetic appearance, and I brushed off the shameful meltdown. Before long, we were nestled into a booth at a cheesy (in both senses) Italian restaurant, wine on the way. Soon, talk and laughter flowed faster than the Chianti, and Lisa felt like a cherished new friend. Let the mayhem begin, I thought. And for what felt like the first time since arriving in Utah, I was right.

161

**Lisa:** Where was I going?? I thought I knew, but then I made a wrong turn and I was headed who knows where. Lost and late. So lost and late. And increasingly frantic. Out of control. Because here it was, mid-fall semester at a new job, and I was getting together with someone for the first time since moving here in June, and I was so lost. Though everyone had been very nice, it seemed as if I had somehow ended up in a department of all old White men and a city where everyone looked so white they were almost translucent. The White women in my department came to work dressed in what looked to me like hiking clothes! The friends I had made at my old job were far away, and even my home life seemed increasingly desolate, barren, almost sterile. So I was headed to meet Karen for dinner … . Karen! The image of our first meeting still strong. Raw. It was new faculty orientation. I had heard of her—that she was smart, talented and fun. When she stood up across the room to introduce herself, she waved to me and said "Hi!" in a voice that still today rings in my head as high pitched. She was young, tall, slender, fit, blond. Perky! Everything in White women that still today makes me shrink in insecurity. That perfect, beautiful, sexy white femininity that transforms me instantly and completely into fat and ugly. Lost, late, and alone, and where was I going?? When I finally found my way that night, I rushed in, apologetic. The place was awful and we immediately agreed to leave. When we finally sat down to eat at a (mediocre) place for which I still have fond memories, we laughed. And I began to relax. Not just for the night, but I began to learn how to relax into myself and my body. From that night forward, Karen grounded me, giving me something I had never really had before and that I continue to struggle to keep.

Carrillo Rowe's words capture the tension that underlies women's friendships across difference as it reveals the often-realized fears of women, that doors will be slammed on us again and again. And shouldn't it have been so with Karen? There we both stood, entitled and expectant. You, so smart, so gifted, shouldn't you have been the one I had to compete with and win against? How did we become friends? And in the words of Phil Collins, was it "against all odds?"

**Karen:** To me, the evolution of our friendship felt effortless, 99 percent joy, pleasure and relief at having discovered a kindred spirit, not only in Salt Lake but in my new workplace. We seemed to share many things—endurance and savvy for discount shopping, a weakness for the happy combination of drinks and raucous laughter, ruthless commitment to research and young careers blessed with early success, struggles to belong in our department, husbands who enjoyed one another yet seemed perfectly content with "ladies nights out," the list goes on. Beyond these rather superficial yet nonetheless significant similarities, we were enticed—magnetically and erotically, I would say—by one another's minds. We sparred beautifully, spawned edgy ideas together, and wrote seamlessly and energetically, as if we were cerebral fuel for the other, two halves of a destined pair (though, to be fair, the late nights and 80's soundtracks may have served a lubricating function).

**Lisa:** But the erotic enticement, Karen, was not just cerebral. It was also embodied. For when we played—whether in the endless dressing rooms of our many shopping trips, in the coffee shops and wine bars where we wrote, or in the dismal faculty meetings where we too often passed notes— we were there in our bodies. Me, at least, watching you in yours, envious of the seeming ease with which you controlled your space. And I think perhaps you as well, curious about if not somewhat desiring of my fierce embracement of a femininity of skirts and heels amidst the granola style of the "west." Safely playful and contained, a simmering eroticized desire was always there. It had its roots, I think, in that racial desire that has threatened and undermined the possibilities for trust between and among White women and women of Color. Typically racist, what developed between us was playful, invigorating, and dare I say, shared, almost equitable. Is that possible? Would critical race and critical feminist scholars scoff at my seeming innocence. In no way did I *not* see your color. You were never just "woman." No indeed. Always white, blond, tall, fit, sexy, smart, successful … perfect. And how I longed—to consume, to embrace, to embody—that sexy smart white perfection. Racial longing, it is part of the "problem," and yet was it not, for us, part of the power. I longed for your whiteness and you for my brownness. Often openly, (almost) always playfully and lovingly, and there, in that space of racial longing, we flourished. The academy demands such objectivity and (masculine) professionalism of women, and luckily (sadly?) for us, you and I did (and do) that fairly well. But at the same time, together, we had spaces and places where body and mind came together.

**Karen:** Perfection, eh? You've said it a few times here already, and it's not the first time you've leveled the charge. You must know that it's a profound misrecognition, this funny way you airbrush me with a glossy sheen. Let's take that confident bodily bearing you admire. Do you *still* forget that it's the result of a fused spine that eased a lifelong struggle with a disfiguring disability that still scars and limits my body? How easily (and hilariously, to be sure!) you've long dismissed these "little imperfections." Frankly, I'm relieved that you think I wear (hide) them so well. So all these years, I continue to participate in the endless touching-up required from both of us to make me over as your race-gender-sexuality target: Smart Sassy Sexy Barbie, in the flesh. When I think about it, you and I enact far more explicitly—and, here, you've helped me see the undeniable racial underpinnings of—a latent exchange common to many (though not all) of my friendships with women of varied racial and sexual identities, including several White women. It's a contract wherein I eagerly consent to bend over backwards like a circus performer—usually, of potent white masculinity (e.g. sarcastic banter, brainy sparring) cloaked in white heterosexual femininity (e.g., knowingly "naïve" flirtation, that naughty-yet-ever-above-reproach seduction reserved for a certain kind of White girl)—for the pleasures of being the desired object on display. Even when I know that object is a collaborative deception, even when I'm thoroughly exhausted of feeling "always on." A confession which, I hasten to underscore, is *not* meant to deny or diminish the considerable privilege entailed in the performance, in being the one on stage. That is my investment in the contract, and it is incumbent on me to own it, though I never feel I do so enough. I try to parody the performance—*over*do it—as a means of making it transparent, exposing it to light and thereby arresting its power.

You say I long for your brownness. Well, the parody falls flat without it. You are a vital partner in this crime. Without you as co-conspirator (or do I mean, without your approval?), I'm forever at risk of being one more White girl who left the Brown girl standing alone, that same old trickster "sister" crouching behind clever. Believe me, I don't like what this implies: that my desire for your brownness is in some part an antidote to chronic white guilt? As if you'd care to be enlisted in *that* narcissistic project yet one more time! But when you and I pull off an innovative performance of difference together—and, sometimes, we do it so well—I think we share a genuinely intimate high in the improvisation (would you agree?) … *and* it quells my racial anxiety. Other times, when the intended irony gets lost and the privilege persists, you've seen me surrender. Oh hell, you've seen me relish it. Maybe you have too? All I know is: this is my stake in whiteness, my shame in whiteness.

**Lisa:** Oh, I did (do) so enjoy that play. Talk about wicked fun, particularly when we could pull it off in some sort of work environment. We defined it as theoretically-sophisticated performance even as we also mostly knew we expected certain things to happen for us. We grounded our academic and professional success in what we knew were problematic arguments of merit and hard work. But wasn't that partly true, too. We *did* work hard, we *were* smart, we *deserved* the successes we got, and because we were both rewarded, we could share our secrets and enjoy our own and each other's success. Right??? Ok, I know, *I know*. Notions of meritocracy—just another manifestation of whiteness. Still, to be able to share with you my successes and hear yours without fears of insecurities, jealousies or competition crowding in has been such a treasure. Perhaps my stake in whiteness is my need to believe that I *am* smart(er).

**Karen:** It feels equally true that we find not only invigoration but a sense of equitability, as you say, in these ongoing plays on difference. Now bear (bare?) with me here, any readers out there, but our earliest bonds formed over a mutual taste for mock sexual harassment and other forms of "off-color" (pun intended) jabs at political correctness. Rarely had I encountered another scholar so thoroughly committed to feminism, anti-racism, and radical sexual politics who simultaneously savored the pleasures of exploring forbidden humor with like-minded intimates (e.g., "I'm sorry, what were you saying? I was too busy staring at your tits" or "[I'm/you're] not *that* kind of Mexican—*White* Mexican's more like it!"). Adding to this sense of clandestine camaraderie was a flourishing economy of secrets. I say "economy" because, to a significant extent, I think this is how we established unflinching trust between us. At a glance, this observation echoes a truism of the gendered communication literature: namely, women (that dangerously homogenized category that generally universalizes some *White* women) tend to establish connection through mutual self-disclosure. But for me, that glosses the point. Or at least, it misses the masculinized, or perhaps gender-ambidextrous, contract we developed: a transactional view of self-disclosure—not devoid of emotional content (far from it!) but, rather, merged with a kind of instrumental pragmatism—wherein we loved *and* had so much "dirt" on each other that it was impossible to conceive of transgressing against such a deep and mutual investment.

Among the many things we shared in those early years, a profound sense of entitlement figured prominently. Both of us had long received the message—from family, friends, colleagues, strangers—that we were somehow different, special, apart, an exception; we both enjoyed a lifetime at the top of our classes and a healthy helping of socioeconomic class advantage to boot. Enacting many forms of privilege, we recognized and openly discussed them to the (limited) extent that we can ever grasp them, alternating among critique, embrace, resignation, gratification and gratitude. We were lucky—wavering in more and less comfort with our fortune—and we knew it. We were smarter together, more radical and uncompromising together. We were wicked together, drawn together. And at that vulnerable moment in our lives, we needed each other.

**Lisa:** Need. That may be what made it ok for me because in all your perfection, Karen, and in all the insecurity that perfection generated in me (I will still always be reminded that you "don't need to rehearse because [you] have *perfect* pitch"), you still needed me as much as I needed you. That intersection of need and trust, of the need to trust, born both out of the various lonelinesses of our pasts and our presents and of that dangerous economy of secrets that you reference, created a foundation that was both defined by its racialized and gendered foundations even as it almost transcended it. As I write, I feel such the fool. There is no transcendence of race or gender. The theoretical premises of critical whiteness, feminism, and queer theory drive my politics, my teaching, my research. There is no transcendence. But in the intersections of need and trust, grounded in the personal and the political, there is love, care, compassion, faith and oh so much wicked fun. And for me, too, our friendship was effortless and easy, except when it wasn't.

**Karen:** You're right that I needed—I need—you. Thankfully, the vulnerability never ceases. And I couldn't agree more that we never transcend difference. We mark it, interrogate it, integrate it and *recreate* with it. I suspect many friends who span social locations, especially those who do so while studying difference, practice at least the first two or three. But the latter feels like a distinctive part of our contract, wherein difference is almost like a kind of "play-doh"—a consequential material to be handled with care, yet also playfully refashioned in creative ways that grow our sense of possibility. (Um, yeah, that metaphor quickly breaks down, but you get the point …) Within our racial-ethnic difference, we also played with many other differences that emerged. I was highly extroverted; you were on the shy side. You worried about "imposing" on our friendship; I invited you whenever I felt the whim (ever the White girl socialite, or "Hair Flip Susie" as you once called me, to my chagrin). You came from Mexican Catholic origins; mine was a white fundamentalist Christian heritage (we still snort in laughter over the observation that "my people say your people make Jesus sad"). You had a gentle southern tinge born of Texas and Georgia; I was a California Bay Area girl to a near tee. I grew up in a family loaded with dysfunctions born of odd fusions: relative wealth, extremist conservatism, old-school (even by the standards of my youth) male dominance, conflict avoidance and mental illness—to name a few. You claimed a comparatively loving and idyllic family experience. As that suggests, we may have shared an upper middle-class sensibility, but with differing regional, familial, economic and emotional influences. While these may at first glance seem like individual idiosyncrasies, they too were shot through with race, gender and sexuality. We both identified with hybrids of masculinities and femininities, but we did so in different ways. Among your countless gifts, you brought hyper-feminine shoes and "handy-man" skills to my life; I sense I may have brought certain modes of embodied play (or is it confidence?) to yours. These differences required navigation, but they brought much stimulation—stimulation *in* the navigation, I would say. You know that 1 percent I left open earlier? That's about the ratio of joy to difficulty I experienced: 99 to 1.

**Lisa:** When you say that—99 to 1—you make me smile. Mostly it was so easy. When it wasn't, it required reflexivity. I recall quite vividly the first time we went to the Ethnic Studies/Gender and Women's Studies gathering. It was packed, barely room to move. I had met lots of these folks before, and so I moved with what was for me relative ease. I think I actually even had fun. But for you, it was very different. In that fairly politicized space of gender and race, you were immediately positioned as … what? … blond? Mostly dismissed by the crowd as irrelevant. Maybe I'm completely misremembering the experience, but I know that then and there I had to reflect upon what it meant for you as a smart, successful, critical gender and race scholar to walk in your body. The identity politics that still pervades the academy didn't provide you with much space to exist in that moment except as blond. (Hey, so is it the 13 years of built-up hurt from that which explains your rebirth as a red-head?) Though I was familiar with the academic literature on privilege as complex and I could spout endlessly about the problems with ranking oppression, I don't know that I really understood it before then. Because for me, so often ravaged by my bodily insecurities, there you always stood, perfect. Until that very perfection was what undermined your academic legitimacy and your "authenticity" as a critical feminist and race scholar. Just as the whiteness of my body made me suspect in ethnic studies and the "brown-ness" of my body so often situated me as a diversity hire, so too did the white light of your body become a threat. I think we talked about it afterwards, but I'm not sure if I gave your experience much credence. I can tell you today that it remains one of my most vivid memories. You allowed me to bear witness to your hurt. And I hope that I did so in a caring, thoughtful and reflexive way. Difference made meaningful and relevant. You, vulnerable, just like me.

**Karen:** I remember that evening well, and you may not be far off on the change in hair color, ha! It's a vulnerability of a kind, to be sure, but I would never say it's "just like you." Just as I chide my White male students about claims to know the experience of Otherness from a single evening spent in a bar with predominantly Black patrons, so I can hardly pretend that ours is a comparable experience. And really, the reaction makes sense to me. My body and self-presentation trigger suspicion of a white heterosexual femininity that remains in wide circulation and *is* wily, however un/deserved her full projection onto me. Frankly, I'd say the response is "paid for" many times over. In our early years as colleagues, I looked on fairly quietly as I became a kind of Golden Child in the department, you a Golden Brown Child. We were both respected "feminists," but I sensed that I enjoyed the status of a "regular" colleague, whereas your contributions were often couched in a diversity shadow. Even earlier, I remember a beloved (to me) colleague walking into the department Halloween party at my house, clad in a stereotypic Mexican *serape* and *sombrero*. The instant he laid eyes on you, I watched him become gripped with alarm, as he rushed to ask me for a room in which he might change. I'll be honest: it took me a second to raise an eyebrow at the costume, another to grasp the fuller nature of his freak-out, even longer to understand that most costumes in the room reflected the presumption of a White audience who could be counted upon to miss or only mildly scold a racially dubious costume (such that only *your* presence marked the outfit unacceptable), and one more minute to process that I participated in white bonding by ushering him to an empty room while nodding that of course he meant no ill. In the moments it took me to wrap my dense White self around the situation and feel the shame of it seep beneath my skin, I earned the reaction of the Ethnic/Gender Studies crowd. Why *you* showed me such generosity and faith in these moments is another question. Did you trust that I would eventually get it on my own, or know that I could hear it if I didn't? Did I somehow keep these moments from you? Are these the times when our play with whiteness inhibits a deeper dismantling? I guess I'm asking: are we really playing with fire? Or do our less subversive moments arise when we *drop* the play?

**Lisa:** You wrote above that we existed together in a kind of shared Golden sisterhood, you the Golden Child and I the Golden Brown Child. Even now, several years away from that time, it is difficult to hear that characterization. My failed longings for whiteness were exposed. Being Golden was often so easy, but Golden Brown ... living in that Golden Brown space was so difficult. Sometimes our colleagues (God love them!) were so racist. I was fortunate to have a senior colleague whose own racialized body seemed to offer her much less access to whiteness, who helped to buffer some of that racism. When she was there, I didn't have to speak the voice of race. When she wasn't, I felt alone in that space, and often in those moments I felt the differences between you and me more keenly. Mostly you knew when you needed to speak and you spoke, but I think sometimes you didn't. Did you not know? Or did you not want to go there? Most of my memories are vague. Intentionally forgotten?? I think there were moments of hurt, and my trust in you was sometimes shaken. Those were the moments in which we couldn't parody, couldn't playfully perform.

**Karen:** I'm so sorry, Lisa Marie. I can't quite grasp specific memories either, but my earlier confession that I know I was sometimes too quiet suggests that we're on the same page. Remember that other big moment when we dropped the play? We still—though now more gently—refer to it as the "Will Smith incident." Basically, one late and intoxicated night, we started talking about two recent blockbusters from that time: *Men in Black* and *Pelican Brief*. The issue was what to make of Black men cast in roles typically reserved for White men—that is, not only leading roles opposite White women, but roles that were ostensibly not about race *per se*. As I recall, I said this was an interesting turn—not necessarily progressive, possibly a mere blip, but a potentially productive shake-up nonetheless. You balked at this read, insisting that it was more of the same, the latest face on the exploitation of Black men. Couldn't it be both exploitative *and* usefully exploited toward meaningful change, I wondered? You said no, emphatically. As the volume increased, I remember little except that we got careless with each other. Spirited argument turned into thinly veiled expressions of disgust. It's funny, we never returned to the debate, but it's clearly part of our archive, incorporated now as the "Will Smith incident"—the loudest struggle we've had, the *only* time we fought instead of played, the container in our friendship where racial hope and cynicism can butt heads, where our conflicting truths and uncertainties— born of our respective experiences living racial embodiment—come spilling out.

Lisa: I was angry that night. I don't remember much about what we said, but I can picture us in the booth at dinner and later, I must have parked at your house, as we awkwardly ended the evening. And I remember that I was angry. How could you actually think those films constituted racial progress? I doubted you then. Was it the content of what we said? Or, as you note above, that we were careless? I think that I went into a racial essentialism, immediately positioning you as White, privileged.

Could or would these moments have been meaningful, to us individually and to the strength of our friendship, had we not both come to them with considerable theoretical and political grounding in an anti-racist feminist queer politic? Might we have been more blind to the micro-aggressions that each other encountered? Who knows? I hope that women's friendships across "difference" don't *require* such theoretical and political commitments. I want to believe that they don't. I suspect, however, that such moments do necessitate our willingness to bear witness to *and* accept the truths of the hurts, and not just in the kinds of moments that we have recalled here, but in the many, many hurts of our lives.

At the same time, those were rare moments between us. You wrote above of our shared "special-ness." I have wanted to ignore that. Must we confess here, publicly, the centrality of privilege?? I'm somewhat (screamingly) afraid that I'll learn that the key to our friendship lies in my (your? our?) comfort with and desire for whiteness. But even as I say that, I think I know better. We both come from considerable privilege. True. We have both regularly leveraged that privilege—at work, at play, maybe even at home? Two mostly "good (white) girls" (Moon, 1999). We have called each other out, usually in good-natured play (remember that night at Green Street, with the sexually-ambiguous server?). Was it our shared dirty secret that we, self-identified feminist scholars, would play into expected gender norms if we thought it might help? Which takes me back to my fear—that my (your?

our?) complicity with whiteness is relevant here. But how so? Do you know? Maybe I know, but I can't yet speak it? The (in)visibility of my whiteness is sometimes so very visible. I think it's no accident that our friend and colleague has nicknamed me "Porcelana." Much of the time I can accept the insistence among close friends that I am (sometimes) so very white. Sometimes the relative ease with which I navigate an academic environment that so many women of Color, queer and straight, struggle in means that I can *almost* forget. I can almost achieve whiteness, or so I think. You know, people tell me that I'm smart, but I wonder ... If I were, wouldn't I know better?

Is our friendship special? To me it is *so very special*. Does it work because of our shared anti-racist, feminist, queer politic? Because of our mutual complicity in a masculinist whiteness? Because of our racialized longings and desires? Women's friendships can and do enact a politics of intimacy grounded in complicated histories of race, gender and sexuality. We carry those histories with us, re-enacting, re-visiting, re-creating and sometimes even re-visioning what it means to long and to belong. The spaces of intimacy we are gifted in our friendships demand care and cultivation, for the scripts and contracts of gender, race and sexuality are too easily played out in ways that damage and demean with the result that Carrillo Rowe identified above—women slam the doors on each other. The longings persist. And whiteness plays on.

# References

Carrillo Rowe, A. (2005). Be Longing: Toward a feminist politic of relation. *NWSA Journal*, 17, 15–46.

Moon, D. G. (1999). White enculturation and bourgeois ideology: The discursive production of "good (white) girls." In T. K. Nakayama and J. N. Martin (Eds.), *Whiteness: The social communication of identity* (pp. 177–197). Newbury Park, CA: Sage.

# 15

# WHAT'S LOVE GOT
# TO DO WITH IT?

*Pamela Huang Chao and Elizabeth Cassanos*

Pam Chao is an Asian American professor of sociology and director of a community and diversity center. She has studied and taught diversity issues and race relations for nearly 20 years. Liz Cassanos is a European American doctoral candidate in psychology and has moved between the academic and business worlds through her career. We approached this chapter as a discussion, and our focus goes beyond being allies to the idea of friendship— the quality that underlies and sustains a lasting and mutually satisfying alliance. Our individual contributions are indicated by name.

## Anais Nin (1974): "What I cannot love, I overlook. Is that real friendship?"

What is real friendship? At its core, our experience of friendship is rooted in love and trust. This is not a static experience but a dynamic field, which allows each of us to feel, think, express and grow. The key to honoring the dynamic is to be present in the moment to what is unfolding in each of us. In this way, our definition of friendship begins to resemble a practice. It is a practice of patience, empathy, curiosity, and perhaps most important, good humor. The capacity to laugh at ourselves, to poke fun at each other, lightens the burden of ongoing self-inquiry. These qualities have allowed us to venture into difficult terrain, addressing issues of race and class in our friendship and to accommodate our different styles of addressing conflict.

In this way, the love that sustains our friendship is a choice and an act of will.[1] It requires that at times we put the other person's growth first. It includes taking responsibility for what we each bring into the relationship; and that's the rub, for the real material that we bring into relationship is often unconscious. When it surfaces, it appears in the murky fibers of projection, unvoiced fears, assumptions and biases. The love required to untangle these webs is a courageous, persistent love. It creates a trusting container in which we can play with our assumptions and identifications; where we can try on alternative, if uncomfortable ideas and step into the shoes of the other. At its core, this is the love of learning, deep learning about self and other and ultimately the recognition of the other inside our selves.

How does one introduce this type of practice in hierarchical institutions that are steeped in the myth of individualism? According to this myth, we stand alone. We are judged by our individual achievement. Our rank and privilege are reflections of our value. Rather than fostering love and trust, this worldview fosters competition based on a Darwinian belief in the survival of the fittest. The myth itself stands in a broader ethos that values the masculine over the feminine. This worldview has been under assault from various disciplines and movements, each challenging the predominant power structures and the enforced injustices they represent. And while as a culture we struggle with developing a new myth, a new way of valuing the individual while fostering interconnectedness, we hope our friendship illuminates how the practice of love sustains an inquiry into meaning, empowerment and spiritual growth.

## Friendship as a Container

**Pam:** My friend Liz was the first person I thought of when it came to co-authoring this chapter. She and I have a 30-plus year friendship that began in the hallway of our freshman dormitory during orientation week at the University of Chicago. Our friendship has grown through different stages of our lives and remains a daily force. When we began this friendship, I would not have known the difference between friend and ally. Liz is both.

**Liz:** I have to admit when Pam invited me to co-author this chapter I had mixed feelings. My own awareness of the role of race in all relationships has grown slowly over time, often with real growth coming through a struggle to see past the blinders of privilege. Acknowledging privilege, openly, without defenses is challenging. It forces me to confront my deep fear that engaging in the dialogue is to admit to a level of privilege that makes me "other," the oppressor, and perhaps most honestly, challenges my own identification as the victim. As women moving through a still male dominated culture, it is easy to find and commiserate with the wounds we share; to yearn for and imagine common ground for us to share. Maintaining the illusion of that common ground without acknowledging the complexity of difference does each of us a disservice. It denies us our full, unique experience and that small patch of ground that we might call our own.

When Pam and I first met we were co-conspirators. In an institution devoted to the mind, we sought soul, joy and laughter. Without knowing it, we formed a good enough container in our friendship. A place where we could air our doubts and shame and begin to unearth parts of ourselves lost in our family and cultural histories. The trust came out of sharing our whole selves—our fun and adventurous sides, as well as our dark, mysterious and potentially shameful parts.

**Pam:** Liz and I began our friendship because we heard each other laughing. For me, laughter is one of the important ways our friendship opens to embrace dialogue. We share a love of laughter. I think when we met in the academy the humor and expression of emotion let us be young women in a heady male environment that devalued any sense of the "feminine." Our laughter filled rooms, took up space, attracted people. It was not a mean laughter or one based in self-importance. It bubbled out of the friendship, affection and love we have for each other and a sense of the absurd.

Our friendship hasn't been easy at all times. I was 16 when I started college. My parents were immigrants from China, my father a college professor, my mother a housewife. I grew up in blue-collar Dayton, Ohio. I wasn't sure how to survive this strange world at the University of Chicago. How could anyone live a life of the mind? My heart and gut felt sadly ignored and I didn't know how to navigate the terrain. Liz quickly became my informant. She translated for me. I recognize that this was in many ways an "evenly uneven relationship" that reflected and contained all the elements of racism and oppression inherent in any interracial friendship. Liz was the one with more racial power and cultural knowledge in this setting. I actively sought that out. At that time, I believed that in a "race neutral" setting that values the intellect, race is never supposed to be a factor. I know today nothing is race neutral and race is always a factor. Fortunately for our friendship, we have not shied away from explorations of race, as well as ways that we are both complicit in dominance and oppression.

**Liz:** I was older, all of 18 when we met, and I came from a background that made me think I fit at a highly-competitive university. My father was first generation Greek American and my mother of mixed English, Irish and German ancestry. They both came from poor families and rode the wave of prosperity that followed World War II into a comfortable middle-class lifestyle carefully constructed to erase all evidence of ethnic and class origins. While our last name clearly marked us as "other," we studiously adapted the dress and mannerisms that allowed us to blend into the establishment power structures we aspired to join.

At that time, I felt more at ease with the life of the mind and less comfortable in the realm of the heart. In this sense Pam and I complemented each other. Her enthusiasm, openness and sense of play gave my competitive and reckless sides a safe harbor, a relationship in which I could express, even if I could not yet name, my deepest fears. At this point in our friendship

I got to play the "big sister," a role I yearned for, being both the younger child and the designated caregiver in my family of origin. I felt protective of Pam in a sisterly way. Looking back at this through more mature eyes, I recognize a piece of me that might have felt this protectiveness as a kind of noblesse oblige; that my white, middle-class background gave me something of value to pass on. In this early phase of friendship, our racial differences were points of interest, curiosity and a way to discuss the forces that molded us. I heard in Pam's family story the tale of immigrants, not dissimilar to my own family's history. I was still naively blind to how our racial backgrounds shaped different experiences for us in the same classrooms.

**Pam***:* When Liz talked about my enthusiasm, openness and sense of play I had an emotional reaction in that racial minorities and women often do emotion work in institutions under rules that are different than rules for dominant group members (Wingfield, 2010). One of the ways I make a place for myself is that I try to make others comfortable. I attribute this characteristic to multiple influences, among them the fact that I am a middle child, the second daughter in a Chinese family, a woman in a patriarchal society and a Chinese American who is finding her way in a white context. I do emotion work willingly. These traits usually help me build bridges and create a bigger world. But the flip side is a deep hurt and a feeling that I have not been seen or appreciated when my emotion work is taken for granted or assumed to be the only way I can interact. I also believe it is a way that my internalized oppression manifests itself and I participate in the ongoing oppressive dynamics in our society in who I make comfortable and how I do that.

**Liz***:* I feel some shame and guilt here. I have not always seen Pam's capacity to build emotional bridges and maintain interconnectedness. I am guilty of valuing her academic intelligence rather than acknowledging her emotional intelligence. Responding to Pam's insight, I am aware that I relegate feelings and physicality to my shadow. I had a number of reasons to do so, many rooted in my personal history of childhood abuse and chronic illness. And there is the cultural dimension to my experience. I relate to the cultural ideal of the "masculine," with its emphasis on rational linear thought, rather than to the "feminine" associated with the body, emotions and intuition. In that way, I let Pam carry that part of the cultural shadow. I would like to think of this as a dynamic part of our friendship, where in some way I am seeking wholeness by reclaiming shadow aspects Pam processes. This hasn't been conscious, but rather some instinctive yearning for something missing in my experience. It would be naïve to assert that my longing for wholeness somehow excuses my complicity in maintaining the split. Additionally, I have to point out the irony of this, given that I went on to study depth psychology which focuses on emotions and the unconscious.

So, I'll add a depth psychology perspective to this wrinkle in our friendship. In this exchange, Pam and I engage in what can be called shadow work: we explored how those parts of ourselves which operate unconsciously impact how we feel about, conceptualize and respond to experience, allowing us to bring greater consciousness to how race and class operate in our friendship. Here it is perhaps important to note that the shadow is neutral, although it is often thought of as lesser or negative. Pam makes the point that racial minorities and women often do the emotional work of institutions, and one way to understand this is in terms of projection and projective identification. Simply put, in projection we unconsciously split experience, assigning threatening or destructive aspects to an outer object, which may take the form of a person or group, while internalizing the useful and loving aspects of experience. The psychological concept of object is that of a liminal symbol that connects inner experience with outer experience, the subjective with the objective. In this example, I denied myself access to the embodied experience of emotion, and instead projected that onto Pam. Projective identification is the phenomenon whereby a projection is internalized by the recipient of the projection as a part of their identity. This creates a polarized dynamic, in which shadow elements are unconsciously split off and projected onto another, and the "other" seemingly responds by internalizing these elements and acting them out. In the exchange above, we see Pam take on the role of feeling and expressing emotions that are repressed by others, in this case me. All the "-isms" operate through projection. In this way we demean and demonize whole groups of people by casting those attributes we fear or hate in ourselves onto others. And when the projection is experienced consistently, in many aspects of life, it becomes internalized in the individual carrying the projection, as Pam described. A projection is a self-referential view of another. It distorts and constricts experience. The same is true of projective identification, in that one becomes identified with one aspect of the self, limiting expression of whole self. When we split off parts of ourselves we become less as individuals. We lose access to the full range of human experience and creativity.

Maintaining such a split comes at a tremendous price. It negates the completeness that includes the whole human: the instinctive, sensual, feeling and direct intuitive nature of human perception along with the abstract, analytic, rational capacities of thought. The challenge in mending such a split is that it is deeply entrenched in how we perceive and experience reality so that it operates automatically, without thought, and requires conscious and conscientious effort to bring it to the foreground.

**Pam:** I feel compelled to add a piece about our older sister / younger sister roles. On an interpersonal level, our friendship contained an older sister / younger sister dynamic. Part of this was just the reality of the situation. Liz was older and I was very young to be in that environment. And at a cultural level, there is racism in the "big sister / little sister" metaphor of interracial friendship. And so we have an "and" statement: on the personal level this dynamic was real and mutually beneficial; *and* on a cultural level and at the level of metaphor, this construction is inherently racist as it perpetuates a pre-existing power structure. The key to our friendship is the *"and"*— that both realities can simultaneously exist, be acknowledged and worked through. Thus the presence of racism and our participation in racist dynamics is an *"and"* statement; it is only one element in the organic whole of the friendship. It can be read as part of the complexity of who we are rather than as a condemnation. This complexity allows for the recognition of the oppressions and "isms" in each of us. Our friendship becomes a vehicle for action and acceptance.

## The Invisible Wall

Skip forward about 10 years in our friendship. We're both moving forward in our careers, Pam at a university in California and Liz in the business world of Chicago.

**Pam:** I became immersed in diversity training and teaching race relations. I was enthusiastic about the insight I experienced and would eagerly and frequently talk about racism. I felt like for the first time in my life real choices, authentic words and explanations about these complex issues were available to me. I was finding my voice. And I was using this voice to say things, in public and frequently, that made other people uncomfortable and angry—even when I used humor. Even with this exhilaration of new-found knowledge and emotion, I was also often uncomfortable and angry. Liz listened, witnessed and participated in daily conversations as I processed. At times our words became stuck and weren't sufficient to communicate in these long interstate phone calls, but I trusted Liz's friendship and love to hold those pauses. I knew Liz moved in interracial social settings and in those awkward times, her actions outside of our friendship spoke volumes.

Liz and I had many exchanges where we openly talked about racism and elitism. Liz would push back but each time she owned hers. I remember a particularly painful exchange where we were fighting but we didn't turn away from the conversation or each other. I recall feeling frustrated and angry and thought I heard something similar in Liz's voice. If I had given in on my position it would have been a negation of our friendship—but Liz came back with questions that didn't depend on me to explain my experiences in her terms. I knew she heard me. Without friendship, I would not have spent the emotional energy. Had it been a colleague, I would have walked away before trust was re-established. Liz and I can each be very difficult in our own way—we are probably freer to be difficult with each other than with others. Liz has challenged me to look at my own privileges and push my awareness of internalized oppression. She can sit with her part in these explicit issues of race and racism. Our friendship's trust and love are deeply resilient and support our recognition that we are each always more than any given moment.

**Liz:** I remember these conversations—they were difficult. I felt fear and a healthy dose of guilt and shame. At that time, I was struggling and I didn't feel privileged. The fear I felt in these early conversations was that somehow I was in the wrong; that I'd have to give something up or make amends for a situation beyond my making; that somehow, I had to make it right. Feeling threatened, I became literal and defensive at times.

Flowing beneath the surface of these conversations was another dynamic. Pam argued with an urgency and conviction I had never heard in her voice before. I have always trusted in Pam's intelligence. Her intensity provided the focus and courage I needed to abandon my defensive position. The leap took me to the place I know best with Pam—trust and love. From that vantage point, I was able to engage in a conversation about race and privilege from a place of curiosity. In many ways this marked a turning point in our relationship. If I had been Pam's informant in college, she was now mine.

In college the presumed norm was the rational analytic self, the "masculine." In conversations about race, class and social justice, we had to go deeper to understand how our unconscious views shaped our experience and our reactions. We had to tap into the feeling symbiotic sense, the "feminine." Pam drew me into conversations in which we had to explore our shadows, our projections and where we remained stuck in identification with a cultural norm, rather than an authentic expression of self. And I was able to follow because I trusted that my guide, ally and friend always had my back, even while I had to own shameful and painful realities around privilege.

## Friends and Allies

**Pam:** We have all heard people of Color say (or have said ourselves) that we don't want or need any more friends, that we want and need more White allies committed to the cause of racial justice. But would we be better served in our ultimate goals if we did want and need more interracial friendships?

As an ally, one is challenged to find the space and motivation to do a great deal of painful and uncomfortable work—to excavate personal reasons to persevere in dismantling systemic privileges from which one benefits. This is usually done with a single-issue focus. While one does need to parse out a place to start, it is the interlocking nature of oppressions that make them so entrenched within ourselves and in society. In cultivating allies, we can easily create an "us versus them" psychology and often are guilty of contributing to the oppression of other groups to gain leverage for ours. Our issues and battles remain fragmented—isolated kingdoms of concerns. We become politicized to the point that there is no sense of a whole. Would the energy expended to develop allies be better spent in cultivating friendship?

My friends are my allies. I believe that the relationships and social justice we seek may be found through the container of loving friendship. The historical stories of friendship across race are not typically ones where women of Color have fared well or were considered peers to White women. Yet despite the social inequalities, I believe friendships have occurred. I am not under any illusion that our institutions will suddenly become just and loving places because Liz and I are friends. I am not under any illusion that people in friendships will always carry the burden equally. But I am certain that if I am loved and in relationship with other committed people—often outside of the day-to-day institution—I have more energy, strength, courage and support to speak my truths and continue to push for change. In that space, I risk and challenge myself to unearth my own unspeakable truths.

Friendship offers the possibility of the wholeness that we need. In friendship, we are held and witnessed in the places where we are stuck; we can rage or cry as we come to terms with our past; and together we can make sense of and create our present and move towards a future where we are in connection. It is in the sustained container of friendship that trust and love needed to do this work develops. This trust and love builds bridges between the complicated kingdoms of each issue so we truly are one of many. This is the "more" I aspire to internalize. And it is only when I am familiar with this space that I can offer the possibility of "more" to others.

**Liz:** Does friendship occur between two people? Or does it start within the individual? While the way we understand and experience our friendship is in an interpersonal dynamic, much of that experience occurs in an invisible realm that shapes how we perceive experience itself. Our personal history, patterned within the larger culture, informs our ability to sustain trusting relationships. Between Pam and I, some leap of faith allowed us to form a loving bond that has lasted all these years. At the same time, the biographical and cultural lenses we each brought to the friendship often gave us different perspectives on the same events. Elitism and oppression exist within us as much as outside of us. To untangle this complex web takes patience, trust, vulnerability and a willingness to get messy. It requires us to be willing to own our internalized forms of elitism and oppression. To do that, we have to be willing to engage the shadow. Looking back on our most challenging conversations, I realize that when I am at my most defensive I cling to the myth of the rugged individualist: that we are self-created independent individuals, rewarded for our personal effort and accomplishment. This defensive pose gives me cover when it's too much work, or too threatening to my identity to tease apart the complex web of privilege. When I am open and feeling more expansive, I recognize that we are all connected and that whatever I love or hate in myself is what I love or hate in the other. In this way I see myself in the other, and my capacity to feel into the experience of someone else deepens and enriches my experience of being human. Then it is easier to get some distance from my small "I" identity, and participate in a more expansive sense of self. Through love and compassion my experience of being human grows. That only happens through relationship.

## On the Path: Some Advice

Unlikely alliances need to follow an unlikely path. We're suggesting that alliances based in real friendship stand a better chance at that. Friendship in this case is based in respect, honesty and a willingness to look openly at one self and to hold space for the other. It allows each of us to be "more." It is based in a love that transcends the concept of the individual; a type of agape, an intentional, unconditional, reflective, thoughtful act of will directed toward the betterment of all involved. The modern academy or institution does not hold a place for this type of force. It is not the language of the dominant culture that so recently ridiculed the President's use of the word compassion as a desirable quality in a Supreme Court Justice. Yet, compassion is the core feeling sense that gives rise to justice. And one hurdle to achieving this sense of social agape is the very fact that we deride the notion that feelings, connection and compassion are core values of a just society.

To bring our whole selves into the conversation, we have to be willing to work with those disowned parts of ourselves—our internalized oppressor and victim. We need to explore our personal and cultural shadows to bring consciousness to our own fears, shortcomings and repressed genius. To do this we need a place that is safe enough for us to risk exposure, make amends, experience forgiveness, celebrate our successes and laugh. We need alliances based in a sustained and committed relationship. We need friendship.

Conversations at the individual level are essential to the process and will at the institutional level is essential for change. This is where our unlikely alliances have the potential to make a difference. As women we have some common ground to unite around. Can we look past our wounds and our pride to expand that territory, making room for each other, for our differences and our similarities, for our whole selves?

In the beginning of this chapter we spoke of the need for a new myth. This is a myth that embraces the "feminine" equally with the "masculine"; that values the deep feeling intuitive side of human nature along with our capacity for reason and abstraction. It seeks wholeness where once there was separateness. This heroine's journey takes her into the depths of the shadow. Unlike the classic hero however, our heroine does not seek to destroy what she finds there, but rather to understand it. Stringing her bow with arrows of patient compassionate love, her demon transforms into a fierce ally. Together they return, bringing new life into their community, weaving new connections and understandings. Our heroine's boon is the gift of sight—her capacity to see herself in the other, and the other in herself.

## Notes

1  Ideas reflected in our conception of friendship are similar to those expressed by M. Scott Peck, M.D. (2003) in his works, particularly *The Road Less Traveled, 25th Anniversary Edition, A New Psychology of Love, Traditional Values and Spiritual Growth*. New York: Simon & Schuster.

## References

Nin, A. (1974). *Diary of Anais Nin 1947–1955 (Volume 5)*. Orlando, FL: Harcourt Brace Jovanovich.

Peck, M. S. (2003). *The Road Less Traveled, 25th anniversary edition, a new psychology of love, traditional values and spiritual growth*. New York: Simon & Schuster.

Wingfield, A. H. (2010). Are emotions marked "whites only"? Racialized feeling rules in professional workplaces. *Social Problems, 57*, 251–268. doi 10.1525/sp.2010.57.2.251.

# 16

# RACE AT FIRST SIGHT

## The Funding of Racial Scripts
## Between Black and White Women

*Lori D. Patton and Rachelle Winkle-Wagner*

Racial scripts are entrenched in the social fabric of society. They exist before, during and as the result of interactions between Black and White women. Racial scripts not only define, but in many ways dictate how we live our lives (Williams, 2007). They are comprised of "detailed instructions" that shape our perspectives of individuals who we perceive as having a racial background different from our own, how we interact with them, and how we subsequently make meaning of such interactions. These scripts can be activated at any time (Williams, 2007).

In this chapter we explore how interactions between Black and White women scholars "fund" racial scripts alongside one's racial identity, racialized experiences and racial privileges. We also discuss how seemingly simple interactions activate racialized histories and experiences of race in the lives of Black and White women. These interactions contribute to a larger, complex web of racialized social memory—to be deposited in one's memory bank in one instance and transacted in the next. We consider how race and racism permeate the interactions of Black and White women scholars before these women enter the same physical space, requiring them to contend with the resurrection of old scripts and the establishment of new scripts. Finally, we share strategies for how Black and White women contend with racial scripts through disrupting them in some situations and ignoring them in others.

This chapter offers a genuine and candid dialogue between a Black woman and a White woman who study racial issues in higher education. We discussed personal experiences where racial scripts were *funded* in an interaction and how race and racism affected the capacity to foster relationships across racial lines. For this chapter, we focus specifically on the research process and address issues such as trust-building between White and Black women and the enactment of stereotypical thinking and behavior. We

181

conclude with potential strategies for acknowledging and challenging racial scripts and offer implications for higher education research.

## What are Racial Scripts and How Do They Work?

According to Williams (2007), "a racial script is a series of programmed messages (e.g. stereotypes and myths) about a particular ethnic group and transmitted to children by parents, relatives, teachers, media, religious groups and significant others" (p. 43). Racial scripts stem from sources within the environment and are learned and transferred generationally. Individuals are *taught* to *see* race, ascribe particular characteristics to individuals from various racial groups and judge these individuals based upon these observations.

Enacted racial scripts are based solely on "salient attributes" or the aspect of one's identity that are most visible (e.g., skin color). These attributes are used to view racial groups homogeneously, despite very real intra-racial differences. Racial scripts are ingrained into the psyche and difficult to change. While some racial scripts can carry positive, negative or neutral messages, those that promote negative imagery and distortions are the most detrimental; particularly because they are adopted from external influences that afford individuals little space to generate their own unbiased understandings of racial groups. Racial scripts are not only dependent upon what individuals see and perceive, they are equally grounded in one's lack of consciousness or their purposeful choice to ignore what is visible. Regardless of racial standing, all are complicit in the racial scripting process.

Bailey (2000) maintained that race can be a "performance" based on "preestablished scripts" that are based on a person's location in the existing stratified social structure (p. 289). In order for racial scripts to exist and be recognized, there must be some acknowledgement that society shapes and is shaped by dominant, hegemonic structures that dictate people's lived realities. Racial scripts persist due to the complicit nature in which race is performed and embedded within historical and current contexts. Racial scripts are heavily based on how our respective identities are performed, or how we might think they should be performed (Bailey, 2000). Thus, they are related to the actual performance of our identities (e.g., how we act in an interaction) and to the anticipated performance of others (e.g., how we think another person might act in the interaction). Racial scripts represent what we think of one another and how we behave toward one another as a result of these thoughts.

One example of the activation of racial scripts between Black and White women is interracial dating. The context of interracial dating is made more complicated by the media where White women are represented as the epitome of beauty in magazines, the dutiful mother and wife on television sitcoms, or the object of affection and attraction for men (of any race) in feature films.

The racial script that extends from this attention toward White women is that they are *valued and desired above all other women*, and in this case Black women, who in many instances have neither been deemed as beautiful nor desirable. As a result, three separate but interrelated discourses emerge: 1) White women as desirable, particularly for Black men; 2) interracial dating and marriage, particularly between Black men and White women is taboo; and 3) there are too few Black men from which to choose (Chito Childs, 2005). These discourses complicate the idea and possibility of interracial, heterosexual relationships that exist among Black and White people and position White and Black women as opposites in an awkward, competitive racial script that gets funded in their interactions with one another. The resulting script suggests that Black women are *angry* because White women are *taking their men*. Conversely, a parallel discourse commoditizes White women as a prized possession in demand by Black men and that must be protected by White men.

For example, in her essay, *Witnessing Whiteness*, Fine (2004) shares an interaction she had with Hulond Humphries, a former Alabama high school principal who threatened to cancel the prom if students chose to engage in interracial dating (Jamieson, 1997). Humphries was quoted as saying, "It's not that I have anything against interracial dating … It's just that those black boys really want our white girls … Now with that feminism, black girls are wanting our black boys" (p. 248). Fine reveals two dominant racial scripts, "*Blacks as sexual predators. Whites as prey*" [emphasis added] (p. 248). These scripts maintain white privilege by excluding Black people; and not only do Black people get relegated to the margins, but also their White counterparts erroneously embrace the belief that they possess some form of *superiority over Blacks*, preventing any challenges to the racist status quo. Our point is that these kinds of racial scripts exist *before* the interaction between Black and White women, even if these particular scripts are not explicitly referenced in the interaction. The universal thread that closely links all racial scripts together is that they uphold white privilege (Bailey, 2000).

## A Candid Dialogue about Racial Scripts

After discussing the concept of racial scripts and exploring our experiences with them, we conducted a candid conversation about the ways racial scripts had been activated in our lives as tenure-line or tenured professors, one African American (Lori) and the other White (Rachelle). We each hold positions as faculty in Higher Education programs and have known one another for several years. While we have not been close friends during this time, we have become increasingly friendly colleagues. Due to geographic separation, we opted to have a Skype conversation about racial scripts in the research process. We present examples of our conversation on racial scripts in the research process without analysis or interpretation to allow the dialogue to stand on its own, followed by our reflections on emergent trends.

**Rachelle:** Since most of my work is with primarily African American women, there is this moment where we can either build trust or not. It only is a moment and it is either used or it disappears. One example of a time when trust didn't go the way it probably could have … I am doing this life story project with African American women who have graduated from college, trying to understand strategies that they used to try to get through college and hear their history of college experiences. One African American woman was probably in her early 40s, maybe late 30s. I didn't ask her age, but that would be my guess given her life experiences. I didn't tell her coming into the interview that I was White. I made the assumption that she might know that I was White because she was recruited by another participant. When she came to meet with me, it was clear to me that she did not expect that I was a White woman. And that was also the moment where trust could have been built and it wasn't. It was like this wasted moment where it went in the opposite direction where she maybe distrusted me because she may have made the assumption that I was a Black woman and I made the assumption that she knew I was a White woman. So, there were assumptions going both ways. But I knew who she was and she didn't know who I was. It didn't spoil the interview, but it definitely changed the trust. We probably met for 90 minutes and it was a good 45 minutes into the interview before it felt like we had any kind of a rapport. And it all started with this moment of not knowing that she didn't know I was a White woman. I have played this over a million times in my head and wondered what I could have done better.

**Lori:** I don't know if you could have done anything better. One of her assumptions might have been that as African American women, the only people who are genuinely interested in those experiences are other African American women. She may have thought that you were Black. Especially since the person who referred her apparently didn't mention that to her. Did you meet with the other person face-to-face as well?

**Rachelle:** Yes, and the other person was someone I had known as an acquaintance. I asked her if she wanted to be in the study, but we had known each other a little bit for a couple of months. The first woman came in knowing I was a White woman because she knew me. She recruited this other woman. I really thought the first person would have prepped the second one, but she didn't. Maybe I should have even said, "Hey did you expect that I might not be a White woman?" It was this big elephant in the room.

**Lori:** Do you think you didn't address it because you didn't want to put her on the spot? What would have been the impact had you asked?

**Rachelle:** Honestly, I think I felt a little vulnerable because I was surprised that she didn't know what she was walking into. I felt really bad about it. In reflection, I wish I would have made myself vulnerable and just said, "I bet you didn't expect that I was a White woman, how are you feeling about this?" But I don't know exactly why I didn't say anything. I wonder if it was a failure on my part of not wanting to be vulnerable.

**Lori:** I think that is a good point. When I think of the research process and the topic of this project on racial scripts and if you think about these historical relationships between Black and White women, one thing is clear: neither group wants to be vulnerable to the other. When we think about being vulnerable, though the historical racial scripts are there, we don't necessarily think consciously about them, they are just there. And we respond to them unconsciously. Otherwise, there would be no reason for either group to be apprehensive about being vulnerable to the other.

**Rachelle:** It is like the lack of trust is already there before we are even engaging.

**Lori:** Right, and neither group is really thinking about where that lack of trust stems from. And you, prior to meeting her, I'm sure you would not know about any of the interactions she has had with other White women or, what her experiences have been to make her react in that particular way.

**Rachelle:** Instead of actually calling it out, "What racial scripts just got invoked?" in some ways, the failure to actually approach it in that interaction just created another script for both of us. We had this awkward moment and instead of talking about it, it created this further history for us. I am hoping I can learn from it for the future and next time actually say something.

**Lori:** I was trying to think about my own research experiences and where this emerged for me was not actually with White women. It was with White men. I had decided to do this study looking at White male allies in higher education. And in asking them questions on the interview protocol, I knew they were all White men and they knew I was a Black woman. But I couldn't help but wonder, not about the genuineness of their comments, but to what degree did my race and gender enter into their thinking about how to respond to the questions I was asking. There was this part of me that wondered if they answered questions in a particular way to not be perceived as racist or sexist. I didn't get the sense that they did. But when I got to the point of getting ready to do member checking and wanting to send them some of the analysis, I was apprehensive ...

**Rachelle:** Was it not always positive?

**Lori:** In their minds, I'm sure they would not have perceived it as positive. It was not overtly negative as if these men are racist. But I identified things that they said where, for me, as a person of Color interpreting that, it means something very different. I was trying to think of ways ... as a researcher there is the piece where you are supposed to allow people to change things and revise things; and I didn't want them to change things to make it sound more positive. This is what you put out and that is okay. But this is what it means when it is being interpreted through critical race theory. I kept wondering, how do I work around this? One of the things I did was to ask a White graduate student who was interested in this to collaborate and help me with the interpretation. I kept thinking maybe I am missing something or maybe there are other things I need to see in this interpretation. She was very helpful in that regard. But the analysis still ended up the same way. I didn't want these men to think that they couldn't participate in another study where there might be a person of Color asking them about this topic.

**Rachelle:** Did you end up sharing the interpretation with the participants?

**Lori:** I shared it with some of the participants. They were honest. They recognized how they were co-implicated in these systems of oppression. They also talked about ways where they tried to engage in ally work. Some of the other men in that study would have maybe really had a problem. This raises the question for me as to whether they really are allies. That is the struggle I felt ... because the whole goal was to look at men who perceive themselves to be privileged in these different identity groups. I wonder how that study might have been different had I been asking White women.

**Rachelle:** I think that even the participants in the study may have monitored what they said. There are not very many people who want to appear racist or sexist. So there is this monitoring that happens ... it also speaks to the idea of racial scripts, "I know that I shouldn't say this word or this thing," but it is easy to get caught. Even if the participants were trying to be careful, eventually, they kind of "outted" their true feelings.
     Peer debriefing was a really great way to approach this issue. I do think that sometimes participants want to change things when they see it in print. You might have had participants wanting to change everything ... for me the group that has given me the most questions about my work has been White

women ... it is a lot of, "Why would you study that? It doesn't seem like that kind of work would matter that much." They are being careful but there is this underlying assumption that we couldn't possibly be interested in a group that we aren't a part of. I believe there is a race issue there.

**Lori:** The other thing I wanted to ask you about when you are engaging in this kind of research where you are interviewing Black women: how do you deal with the potential of being perceived as a White woman who is commodifying this experience? Or benefitting from the experience? There are some White scholars who get accused of that ... a radio show host or a newspaper journalist might look to someone who is White to be the expert while there are others who have done this work who are African American. Or being perceived as exploiting the experience ... or how to handle the tension that may arise if you are perceived in that way.

**Rachelle:** One of the things that I have started to think about and do more is to offer authorship, especially now that I am working with some women who have advanced degrees. I think maybe that has helped in some ways. I would have to ask them to see if it really has. But that is something I am trying to do so it does not always have to be me speaking on behalf of them and that is not really my intent. My intent is to give voice to people's stories. But there is this line there. I think you are right. As a White woman attempting to give voice to Black women's stories, at what point do I begin to be seen as the expert on that? Does that deny women who have actually experienced those stories from speaking on their own? I think it is a constant tension, honestly. Part of it, when I worked with undergraduate women, I asked them to be involved in all kinds of ways. If you want to help write, that is cool. If you want to draw cover art for a book, that is cool. Part of it is being upfront with people, letting people determine their own involvement. Instead of, I am this researcher-expert person, because I don't really see myself that way. I always see myself as a researcher-as-learner. I always see myself as trying to learn from people's experiences. Honestly, I think it is a constant tension in research done across racial lines.

**Lori:** Something I have done, because I don't typically get a lot of students who are interested in the writing part, is ask graduate students to challenge my interpretations on things, I ask them to be involved. Graduate students often jump at that.

**Rachelle:** For undergraduate women, I try to give back in other ways, like developing a mentoring program that continued past the research. They helped to develop it, but I helped to make it institutionalized because I was in the position to do so.

I am going to have to think more about this, Lori. I would love to hear more of your ideas on this too. I would be really devastated if people felt that I was commodifying their experience, especially if it was a bad experience.

**Lori:** Again, I have the same hang-ups, not necessarily with research on White women because that is not what I have been doing. I certainly don't want to be perceived as this voice for Black LGBT populations in college, and right now I don't think that I am but my research might be the only one out there.

**Rachelle:** Right, but somebody has to do it. I don't think it would be fair to say that you have to be a lesbian woman to do research on gay and lesbian students, for example.

**Lori:** Right, absolutely not. That is probably the biggest way that I have tried to challenge it is to find someone who more closely identifies with these experiences and who will challenge the assumptions and assertions, or interpretations that I am making. That is the thing that scares me the most because I am interpreting things through a heterosexual lens. I know there are things that I will miss. But what makes that work only slightly different from what you are doing is that there is a certain sense of trust there when they know that I am Black or that I am in a Black sorority. Some of those things give me a little credibility with these students. I guess the racial script with them is very different. It is not necessarily about race, it is about sexual identity. It certainly is a script that plays out very differently.

## Thematic Reflections

As a result of our conversation, we have clarifying observations and additional questions about racial scripts. We engaged this dialogue with honesty and authenticity, which required us to establish trust and vulnerability with one another and share our true thoughts regarding our cross-racial interactions. The issue of trust emerged often in our discussion. One of the factors that makes trust-building a challenge may be previous interactions. When a woman enters an interaction, she brings with her the positive and negative interactions she has had with Black/White women. As Rachelle noted, instead of building trust, not only are racial scripts funded, but new racial scripts might be created (see also Williams, 2007).

We also thought more about what racial scripts exist before interactions between Black and White women occur. Through this reflection another theme emerged in our dialogue related to assumptions that Black and White women were making about one another. For example, given her first name, Rachelle, the research participant may have assumed that she was a Black woman. Thus she would not have necessarily sought verbal confirmation of Rachelle's racial identity based upon the first name. Also this first name might have prompted the participant to believe that since Rachelle was Black she could speak freely and be more vulnerable with her about her experiences as a Black woman. As a result, finally meeting Rachelle in person was likely surprising to the participant, particularly if she entered the interview with the two aforementioned racial scripts; one being that Rachelle is a "Black name" and two that a Black woman has the capacity to better understand another Black woman's experiences. The participant might have also thought, upon finally meeting Rachelle, "why is a White woman doing research that focuses on Black women?" Indeed, this is not an uncommon question for Rachelle who is often approached by White women with a similar inquiry. However, the racial scripts that undergird this question are quite different for Black and White women. This question funds two racial scripts, one focusing on the worthiness of Black women (e.g., "it doesn't seem like that kind of work would matter that much"), the other highlighting the centrality of White women's experiences (e.g., "we couldn't possibly be interested in a group that we aren't a part of").

For Black women, the racial script diverges and this is what led Lori to ask Rachelle about exploitation and commoditization in the research process. Given Lori's own understandings about research and how people of Color have been used by White researchers, she wanted to know more about Rachelle's meaning-making process and how she might accrue certain benefits as a result. This issue of exploitation and commoditization is yet another revealing racial script, not simply between Black women and White women, but also between people of Color and White people, broadly speaking. This type of tension in the research process led to a rich conversation as we discussed strategies to alleviate such tension.

The discussion regarding commodification and exploitation linked to racial scripts in that it centered on the history of privilege and domination afforded to White people in the United States (Bailey, 2000). This history of oppression in the United States may lead individuals to have very different reactions to an interaction because of one's own position. Research where the researcher is a White woman and participants are Black women may fund a historical racial script of White people exploiting the experiences and skills of Black people. Lori related to this concern in her own research with Black lesbian women because she does not self-identify as a lesbian, although she recognized that the script might be different because it would be more about sexual orientation than race. Lori suggested that one way to potentially remedy this situation was to invite participants to join in the writing process or identify scholars with those identities to collaborate to ensure accurate representations of experiences. This is a topic that certainly requires further reflection and dialogue for all researchers.

## Reflections and Strategies

Honest conversations about race are often difficult to have, particularly among Black and White women. There were important factors that helped this conversation to be successful. We approached the dialogue as equals. It would be more difficult to have a truly candid dialogue if one person were in a position of direct authority over the other (e.g., between a supervisor and an employee). Additionally, we sought to uncover racial issues between Black and White women and established goals beforehand to frame our conversation. Finally, while we have different experiences with race, we are knowledgeable about the literature, use similar perspectives in our academic work, use similar language and have a common understanding of each person's perspective. Doing a common reading or discussing a common idea might be one way to assist others in their approach to dialogues on race.

While our conversation was generally successful, our dialogue must continue and expand. The challenges we raised would benefit from further dialogue and reflection, while building our levels of trust and vulnerability, and the capacity for deeper and more meaningful reflections and observations.

## Implications for Research and Practice

Two of the major factors that help to fund racial scripts are lack of trust and hesitancy to be vulnerable. One suggestion that we have for both research and practice in higher education is to provide more opportunities for trust-building between Black and White women. These could occur at a practical level in programs geared to cross-racial interactions, or in the classroom if well-trained professors are able to facilitate honest conversations.

In the research process, the potential for distrust between Black and White women could be at least partially remedied in an open approach on the part of the researcher. For example, Rachelle reflected that she hoped to be more open to talking about race with her participants. Lori discussed ways to get feedback on participants' quotes such as having someone from another racial group review them, or having peer debriefers who can review the researcher's interpretations and offer critiques or alternative perspectives.

We believe that, at minimum, engagement in cross-racial dialogues between Black and White women is not only helpful, but also extremely critical toward breaking down barriers and establishing more genuine interactions. We acknowledge that the existence of racial scripts makes such efforts very difficult and in some cases less likely to happen because of the complicated histories between Black and White women. Despite these difficulties, we believe that engaging the conversation is important and can certainly begin to open up the pathway toward more genuine and open dialogue. Willingness to be open to such dialogue is a first and valuable step that can possibly lead to more trust and openness.

# References

Bailey, A. (2000). Locating traitorous identities: Toward a view of privilege-cognizant white character. In U. Narayan & S. Harding (Eds.), *Decentering the Center: Philosophy for a multicultural, postcolonial and feminist world* (pp. 283–298). Bloomington: Indiana University Press.

Chito Childs, E. (2005). Looking behind the stereotypes of the "angry black woman": An exploration of black women's responses to interracial relationships. *Gender and Society, 19*(4), 544–561.

Fine, M. (2004). Witnessing whiteness/gathering intelligence. In M. Fine, L. Weis, L. C. Powell, & L. M. Wong (Eds.), *Off White: Readings on race, power, and society* (pp. 245–256). New York: Routledge

Hill Collins, P. (2004). *Black Sexual Politics: African Americans, gender, and the new racism.* New York: Routledge.

Jamieson, R. (1997, July 2). Alabama town fears new school superintendent's alleged bigotry. Retrieved from http://www.cnn.com/US/9707/02/humphries.return/index.html?iref=allsearch.

Williams, R. L. (2007). *Racism Learned at an Early Age Through Racial Scripting.* Bloomington, IN: AuthorHouse Publishing.

# CONTRIBUTORS

**Karen Lee Ashcraft, Ph.D.** is a professor in the Department of Communication at the University of Colorado at Boulder.

**Martha Sonntag Bradley, Ph.D.** is a professor in the College of Architecture and Planning and the associate vice president for Undergraduate Studies at the University of Utah.

**Elizabeth Cassanos** is a doctoral candidate in psychology at Meridian University.

**Angelina E. Castagno, Ph.D.** is an assistant professor of Educational Foundations at Northern Arizona University.

**Marquita T. Chamblee, Ph.D.** is an educator and consultant who has spent over 28 years working in higher education.

**Pamela Huang Chao** is a professor of Sociology and director of the Community and Diversity Center Initiative at American River College.

**Karen L. Dace, Ph.D.** is deputy chancellor, Division of Diversity, Access and Equity and an associate professor in the Communication Studies Department at the University of Missouri—Kansas City.

**Lisa A. Flores, Ph.D.** is an associate professor in the Department of Communication at the University of Colorado at Boulder.

**Stephanie A. Fryberg, Ph.D.** (Tulalip) is an associate professor in the Department of Psychology and an affiliate faculty member in American Indian Studies at the University of Arizona.

**Marybeth Gasman, Ph.D.** is an associate professor in the Higher Education Division of the Graduate School of Education, University of Pennsylvania.

**LouAnn Gerken, Ph.D.** is a professor in the departments of Psychology, Linguistics, and Speech, Language and Hearing Sciences and director of Cognitive Science at the University of Arizona.

**Frances E. Kendall, Ph.D.** is a nationally known consultant who has focused for more than 30 years on organizational change, diversity and white privilege.

**Liz Leckie, Ph.D.** is assistant dean in the College of Fine Arts at the University of Utah.

**Peggy McIntosh, Ph.D.** is associate director of the Wellesley College Center for Research on Women, founder and co-director of the United States S.E.E.D. Project on Inclusive Curriculum (Seeking Educational Equity and Diversity).

**Adreanne Ormond, Ph.D.** is a programmes coordinator at the University of Auckland with Nga Pae o Te Maramatanga, New Zealand's Māori Centre of Research Excellence.

**Lori D. Patton, Ph.D.** is an associate professor in the Higher Education Program at the University of Denver.

**Kristi Ryujin** is assistant vice chancellor, Diversity Initiatives at the University of Missouri—Kansas City.

**Ronald B. Scott, Ph.D.** is an associate professor in the Department of Communication and the associate vice president for Institutional Diversity at Miami University.

**Theresa L. Torres, Ph.D.** is an assistant professor of Religious Studies and Anthropology at the University of Missouri—Kansas City.

**Malia Villegas, Ph.D.** is an Alutiiq/Sugpiaq (Alaska Native) with family from Kodiak and Afognak Islands in Alaska and O'ahu and Lana'i in Hawai'i. She recently completed a post-doctoral fellowship at Queensland University of Technology and is director of the Policy Research Center, National Congress of American Indians.

**Rachelle Winkle-Wagner, Ph.D.** is an assistant professor of higher education at the University of Nebraska.

# INDEX

academic excellence 146; freedom 72, 119
ACT score 138
admissions: decisions 128; graduate school 127; standards 138
advantage: systems 8
advocacy 39, 55, 57, 60, 62–3
advocate 39, 42, 55, 57–61, 65, 71, 77
agape 179
agenda: advocacy 39
aliens: illegal 15
alliances: building 6, 11, 20, 37, 58, 62, 104, 107–8; creating 3, 7, 10, 13, 16, 63–4, 82, 137; cross-race 3, 86; exclusionary 104; selective 104; white racial 109
allies: public 88; secret 87
American Association of University Women 69
amnesia 143
"and" statements 176
Andersen, Margaret 92
angry 73, 78, 81, 139, 143, 147, 156, 169, 176; Black woman 84; Black women 183; minorities 151; people 17–18; women of Color 17, 42, 45, 52, 71–2, 85
Anthony, Susan B. 72
anthropologists: damage done by 30–3
anti-ethnic studies bill *see* House Bill 2281
anti-racist 11, 61, 63, 112, 116, 169–70
Anzaldua, Gloria *vii–viii*, 3, 4, 72
attack(ed) 40, 47–9, 70, 87, 139
Aunt Jemima 21
Baldwin, James 27–8

baggage 7

barrier(s) *xi*, 12, 17, 34, 55, 108–9, 112, 120, 138, 160, 190
behavior: infantilizing 17
Bell, Derrick 144
Bell-Scott, Pat 91
big-girl panties 16
bonding: white 106, 108, 168
bonds of approval: white 106
bootstraps narrative 127
Bureau of Justice Statistics 16
Burpee, W. Atlee 93

capital: cultural 144; institutional 29; political 58
Carillo Rowe, Aimee 106–8, 161–2, 170
Clinton, Hillary 29
collude 16, 21
colonial gaze 28
colonialism 27, 31
colonization 28, 33, 95
*The Color of Privilege* 71
colorblind 119
commensurable differences: myth 29
commodify 31, 187–8
complicity 174; mandate 139; white 20; whiteness 170
co-optation 33
commitment 6, 13, 33, 47, 52, 59–61, 64, 67, 76, 86, 100, 107, 112, 121–2, 127–8, 137, 139–40, 140–3, 145–6, 157, 160, 162
cost(s) 13, 33, 54, 58, 60, 64, 72, 110–11, 139; emotional *x*
counter-hegemonic: scholarship 66
courage *ix*, 3, 14, 22, 47, 64, 177–8
courageous *xi*, 9, 23, 53, 88, 171
covert action 60

194

credibility 79, 145, 188
critical feminist 163, 167
critical race theory 65–6
critical whiteness 112, 166
cross-race alliances: risky 13
crucibles 16
*The Color of Fear* 92

Daly, Mary *x*
defensive *x*, 11, 18, 21, 34, 64, 138,
    140–1, 145, 155, 177–9
deficit language 141
depth psychology 174–5
discipline(d) 84–6, 108–9
discomfort 8, 13, 46–7, 51–2, 74, 76,
    95, 146
discourage(d) 128, 143, 147
discrimination 69, 71, 113, 142;
    gender 69, 143; systemic 58
disempowering 122
disempowerment 116
diversity 15, 38, 40, 47, 49–50, 55,
    66, 103–4, 106, 112–13, 120–2,
    128, 130, 132, 137–41, 144–7,
    149, 154–7, 167; biological 40;
    commission 113; conference 84,
    council 18; nuanced 18–19; officer
    18, 59–60, 105, 107–8; training 57,
    141–2, 145, 176
do-gooder syndrome 139

Elders 27–8, 36, 38
emotion(s) 87, 108, 125, 142, 152,
    173–6
empowers 143
empower(ed) 5, 71, 73, 77, 131–2
empowering *x*, 39, 64
empowerment 7, 172
enemy 18, 143
engagement 36, 66, 143, 190
equity 13, 22, 70, 74, 76, 86, 112,
    121, 126–8, 131, 142, 147, 154,
    156–7
entitlement(s) 101–2, 109, 119, 143,
    160, 165
essentialism: racial 169
Ethnic Studies 15, 113–14, 116–18,
    167–8
exclusionary: environment 126; view
    of power 70
expert 29, 31–4

fear 5, 8–9, 15–16, 23, 38, 58, 67,
    69–72, 74, 76, 78, 95, 97–8,
    116, 129, 162, 164, 169, 171–3,
    177, 179
femininity: white 85, 160, 162;
    white heterosexual 160, 164, 167
feminist: ideas 49; interests 139;
    movement 49; scholars 67–9,
    169
Flyswithhawks, Brenda 93
friend(s) 8–9, 13, 20, 28–9, 33–4,
    37, 61, 73–4, 81, 83, 93, 95,
    101–3, 105–9, 122, 124–6, 142,
    145, 147, 155–6, 161, 166, 170,
    172, 177–8
friendship(s) 5, 10, 13, 22, 28–30,
    32, 62, 91, 98, 101–2, 104,
    106–10, 145, 149, 153, 158–9,
    160–2, 164, 166, 169–70, 171–9
Friere, Paolo 69
Frieze, Deborah 23
fund: racial scripts 181, 183,
    188–90

gold medal: oppression 29
good white girl 145, 169
guilt 11, 12, 15, 33, 43, 74, 164,
    174, 177

habits: deadly 96–7; instead 96–7
Harvard 94–5
healing 11, 28
hegemonic systems 69
hegemony 27, 65
*The Help* 13, 20–1
hierarchy: imbedded 8
Historically Black Colleges and
    Universities 127
history: white 19
hooks, bell 49–50, 101, 104, 106,
    109, 139
hopelessness 77, 140
House Bill 2281: Arizona 114
Huerta, Dolores 72
Hull, Akasha 92
Hull, Gloria 92
humor 152, 158, 165, 171, 173,
    176
Hurtado, Aida 71

identity politics 28, 167

immigrants 67, 115, 174; China 173; Latina/o 74; undocumented 67
immigration 74; bill 115
Indigenous identity development 31
integrity 9, 22, 42–3, 74, 128, 131, 142
interest convergence 144
Irwin, Kathie 29
"isms" 57, 175–6; institutionalized 5
Ivy League 127

Jesus 87, 166
Johnson, Charles Spurgeon 128

Kendall, Francie/Frances *xi*
*Killing Rage: Ending Racism* 102, 109
King, Martin Luther 130
kinship 34–6, 38
Kivel, P. 62

Leckie, Liz *xi*, 3, 83–5
lens: cultural 178; heterosexual 188; of limitation 70
Lewis, Victor 92
liberal(s) 18, 22, 73–4, 112, 116, 120–1, 139
limen 72
*Lies My Teacher Told Me* 20
Loewen, James 20
Lorde, Audre *vii*, *x–xi*, 3, 4, 72
love 10, 12, 27, 171–3, 176–9
Lugones, Maria 73

McIntosh, Peggy *x–xi*, 44
MacKinnon, Catherine 76
Mandela, Nelson 130
marginalization 30
mentor(ing) 6, 22, 27–8, 34, 37–9, 50–1, 55, 72, 81, 108, 132, 141–2, 149–51, 153–4, 158–9, 187
messiness 13
messy 8, 23, 64, 178
microaggressions 17, 72, 74, 116, 169
Minutemen 66–7
Mitchell, Margaret 20
Molina, Popusa *xxi*
Moon, Dreama 140, 169
Moreton-Robinson, Aileen 29–30, 32
Mukhopadhyay, Carol, C. 110

National Conference on Race and Ethnicity *xi*

National SEED Project 93, 97–100
Nin, Anais 171
non-tenure track 54–6, 68, 71, 77

Obama, Barack 29, 131
objectify 31, 33
offended 49, 52, 66, 92, 140, 142
old boy network 57
ontology 11; White female 29, 33
oppression 10, 29, 33–4, 59, 70, 72, 74, 96, 98, 173, 176–8; attitudes and behaviors 50; history of 189; internalized 10, 69, 174, 177; olympics 29; patterns 58; perpetuation 129; ranking 167; sweepstakes 29; systems 4, 8, 59, 65, 186
oppressor(s) 58, 69, 145, 172, 179; White male 58
otherness 167

pain(ful) *vii*, *ix–x*, 6–9, 12, 16, 18, 77–9, 81–2, 84–7, 96, 108, 139, 141, 144, 146, 153, 176–7
Parks, Rosa 72
paternalism 139
patriarchy 27, 140
permission: white 97
Pirsig, Robert 146
power 9, 12, 17, 22–3, 33, 43, 49–54, 57–9, 63–4, 69–71, 79, 86–7, 91–4, 97–9, 106, 108–9, 119, 125, 128, 131, 137, 144, 157, 163–4, 172–3, 176
prejudice(s) 20–1, 113, 126–7
privilege 7–9, 12, 22, 44, 47–9, 52–3, 55, 57–61, 63–5, 70–3, 93, 97–8, 118–20, 128, 139–43, 145, 161, 164–5, 169, 172, 177, 179, 181, 183, 186, 189
progressive 116, 120, 169; liberal 73–4; political analysis 62; project 97; white *x–xi*, 87

race card 85, 87, 150
race talk 140
race traitor 145
racial distancing 109
racism 8–9, 12–13, 15, 27, 30, 45–6, 51, 60–3, 65, 74, 79, 82, 84, 45–6, 51, 60–3, 65, 74, 79, 82, 84, 86,

93, 109, 112–13, 117, 119, 121, 168, 173, 176–7, 181; covert 74; institutional 29; overt 74; systemic 30; unintentional 152
recruiting: diverse students 137–8; faculty of Color 132, 145; race-based 133
Radcliffe College 94
relationships 3–4, 6–13, 15, 19–20, 22–3, 27–33, 35–9, 42, 52–6, 61–4, 68, 97, 101–4, 106–10, 119, 143, 157, 159, 172, 178, 183; authentic 63–4; cross-race 3, 55, 181; healing 28, 40; historical 185; mentoring 22, 36, 149; reciprocal 33, 40
retaliation: fear 69–70
Rich, Adrienne 23
risk(y) 7–9, 13, 28, 37, 50, 54, 68, 70, 87–8, 93, 118, 129, 155, 164, 178–9

safety 155, 161; femaleness 131; whiteness 131
scripts 170; racial 181–6, 188–90
Senate Bill 1070: Arizona 114
serial testimony 98–100
Setlock, Leslie 16, 20
silence 22, 29, 38, 46, 49–51, 55, 59–60, 67, 70–3, 87, 95, 116, 118–19, 121, 138, 161
sisterhood 10, 35–8, 145, 168
sister-scholars 34–5, 37, 39
skinship 38, 40
slavery 20–1, 95, 126
social identities 154, 157
social justice 5–6, 13, 59–62, 65–6, 97, 100, 103, 113, 132, 153–6, 177–8
solidarity: white 104, 106–11
Solorzano, Daniel G. 65–6
Southern Poverty Law Center 67
Stanton, Elizabeth Cady 72
status quo 13, 22, 30, 55, 71, 107, 128, 133, 150, 183
stereotype 18, 21–2, 31
Stockett, Kathryn 13
struggler phenomenon 153–4
Style, Emily 99–100
subordination 9, 65; gender 139
superiority 4, 32, 35, 183

supremacy: white 9, 11–12, 19, 22, 61, 64, 77–9, 82, 86, 101, 104, 108, 139–40; white male 10, 55, 59; whiteness 11, 16, 20, 22, 61
suspension: moments of 112–13, 115, 118, 120–2

Teaching to Transgress: Education as the Practice of Freedom 101
tears: private 77, 80–2; public 77, 81–3, 86; raced 82, 84
tenure 4–6, 18, 21–2, 39, 54, 56, 68, 91, 121, 124, 132–3, 153–4; power of 131
three-fifths compromise 20
trust(ed) 37, 42–3, 45, 63–4, 73, 81, 91–3, 98–100, 109, 137–8, 147, 151–2, 158, 163, 165–6, 168, 171–3, 176–8, 181, 184–5, 188, 190
Truth, Sojourner 72
truth 16, 23, 32, 36–7, 67, 69, 125, 160, 169, 178; conflicting 169; painful 64; unpleasant 8; unspeakable 178; whiteness 42–5, 48–50, 52, 79, 119

University of Chicago 172–3
University of Pennsylvania 127
unveiled 140
unveiling: motivations 110
Uprooting Racism 62
Upward Bound 138, 140–1

veiled 35, 55, 169; racial reality 102; white realities 106
victim(s) 29–33, 46, 50, 52, 72, 172, 179
victimized 61
vignette(s) 31–3, 35–6, 65–7, 71, 73
voyeur 29–33
vulnerable 8, 46, 48, 52, 110, 144, 147, 165, 167, 185, 189–90

Walk Out Walk On 23
Wellesley College Center for Research on Women 91
Wheatley, Margaret 23
White: men 5, 7, 11, 15, 17, 22, 31, 53, 55, 57–9, 71, 80, 131, 139, 153, 162, 168, 185

white bonds: insecure 108

whiteness 7–8, 29, 44–5, 49, 52, 58, 61, 91–2, 94, 113–18, 120–1, 125, 129, 131, 139, 160–1, 164, 168–70; consequences 49; course 112–20; enactment 119, 121; innocence 42, 45, 52; possessive investment 120; property 119; protection 143, 145

Whitespeak 140

Whitestream institutions 28

*Witnessing Whiteness* 183

Women and Gender Studies 167–8

*Zen and the Art of Motorcycle Maintenance* 146